28 May done

30 pieces wool
3 barrels ...W...

6 hds ... from ... Bolling ...

6 from ... Lee   1 from ...

2 ...   1 from Mrs Whitlord

8th May   3 hams, have been boiled
           2 hams have been boiled   ... 23
19th   2 more sent from Mr Harris
12 June   1 ...   2 pieces ...
4 from ...

Received from Mrs Bacon
barrels flour
sugar
rice
molasses

Always

&

Forever

[signature]

31 October 2001

A beginning
that knows no
end ——

The Robert E. Lee Family Cooking & Housekeeping Book

ANNE CARTER ZIMMER

The University of North Carolina Press

Chapel Hill and London

This book was set in Monotype Bell by Eric M. Brooks.

Book design by April Leidig-Higgins.

The paper in this book meets the guidelines for permanence and
durability of the Committee on Production Guidelines for Book
Longevity of the Council on Library Resources.

Library of Congress Cataloging-in-Publication Data

Zimmer, Anne Carter.   The Robert E. Lee family cooking and
housekeeping book / by Anne Carter Zimmer.

p. cm.   Includes bibliographical references and index.

ISBN 0-8078-2369-4 (cloth: alk. paper)

1. Cookery, American   2. Lee, Robert E. (Robert Edward),
1807–1870—Family.   I. Title.

TX15.Z6   1998   641.5973'09034—dc21   97-14383   CIP

03 02 01 00 99   6 5 4 3 2

Page i: Cover of the Lee family notebook.
(Courtesy of Virginia Historical Society)

Frontispiece: Mary Anna Randolph Custis Lee, circa 1868.
(Photograph by Michael Miley, courtesy of the Lee family)

Endleaves: The opening pages of the notebook contain a drawing by
the Lees' eight-year-old niece "Little Mildred," daughter of Robert's
brother Charles, and a list of food supplies for a church supper.
(Courtesy of Virginia Historical Society)

THE PUBLICATION OF THIS VOLUME WAS AIDED BY THE GENEROUS
SUPPORT OF WASHINGTON AND LEE UNIVERSITY IN HONOR OF
ITS 250TH ANNIVERSARY OBSERVANCE.

To my aunt

I hope she approves

CONTENTS

ACKNOWLEDGMENTS

This book had its beginning when Agnes Mullins, curator at Arlington House in Arlington, Virginia, sent me a photocopy of a faded little notebook, part of the George Bolling Lee Papers (1813–1924) donated to the Virginia Historical Society by my cousins Mary Lee Bowman and Robert E. Lee IV. It would never have been finished if Agnes had not also provided plentiful encouragement, detailed knowledge of my family, and sources for information and pictures.

The Virginia Historical Society's director, Charles Bryan, allowed me to work with the original notebook as well as copies and to reproduce some of that document here. Patiently the Society's Howson Cole, now emeritus, taught me to identify Lee and other handwriting in the book, and a suitably anonymous Federal Bureau of Investigation expert grouped the writing according to writer.

No request was too much for many generous people in Lexington, Virginia. Mary Coulling shared masses of research gathered for her book *The Lee Girls* and other works about the family. At Washington and Lee University, Barbara Brown, librarian at the university's Leyburn Library, along with C. Vaughan Stanley and Lisa McCown in Special Collections, Evan Atkins and Julie Cline at the university's News Office, and photographer Patrick Hinley also contributed, as did Professor Emeritus Charles Turner. I am grateful, too, to Nell Paxton, who shared her firsthand memories of my great-aunt "Miss

Mary" (Custis) Lee, and to Director Michael Jackson and Wendy Fulwider at the Stonewall Jackson House in Lexington.

In Alexandria, Virginia, Michael Miller, director of the Alexandria Library's Lloyd House, and Director Juanita Miller, Virginia Bruch, and Ruth Fuller at The Boyhood Home of Robert E. Lee all have my thanks, and at Historic Williamsburg, Katherine Arnold, Dennis Cotman, and Patricia Gibbs. I am indebted at Stratford Hall to Director Junius Fishburne, Joyce Wellford, Bea Smith, and Walker Allard. Particularly helpful at Mount Vernon were Curator (now emeritus) Christine Meadows and Karen Peters.

In and around Upperville, Virginia, I thank in particular Tom di Zerega, the late Jack Howry, and my "chosen cousin," who chooses anonymity, as well as Louise and Harry Sinclaire, Charlotte Miller, and Bunny Nesbit, and the many other friends who offered cheer and encouragement.

I appreciate being able to use Lee family photographs from various members who do not wish to be identified. Carter L. Refo allowed me to use the portrait of Light-Horse Harry Lee, and Norvell Caskie Sharp Loughborough, the likeness of her great-grandmother Norvell Caskie, a good friend of the Lee daughters. Several private collectors were equally generous.

The eight fellow Gourmet Group members at Ohio State who tested receipts with me for over a year are Wendy Edwards, Ginny Gauthier, Wauneta Kerr, Susan Lohse, Georgia Naylor, Manel Tuovinen, Buena Valentine, and Jeannette Wallschlaeger; I also thank Colin Bull, who offered to try the wine. In Lexington, Virginia, Adelaide Simpson recruited another group of volunteer receipt testers, too numerous to name. And Martha Parthemos worked out the adaptation of the Robert E. Lee cake included here.

Archer Jones, Calvin and Elizabeth Kytle, Joan Symmes, Muriel Townes, and my daughter Susan Vogel read parts of the manuscript, although I alone am responsible for the use put to their perspectives.

Acknowledgments

At the University of North Carolina Press, David Perry, Pamela Upton, Rich Hendel, April Leidig-Higgins, and especially Katherine Malin shepherded the idea into reality.

Last and most of all I thank my husband Fred, who did so much, including the cooking, so I could write about it.

The
Robert E. Lee
Family Cooking &
Housekeeping
Book

Introduction

The Lees & Me

We didn't make much of ancestors when I was growing up. Maybe that was considered bragging, or maybe the grownups were somehow protecting us. Or, as I learned only recently, my aunt once said: "I tried to raise my children not to be bitter, but sometimes I find it hard to forget." That feeling probably accounts for at least some of the family's reticence. At any rate, I didn't always know who all the people on the walls were, but I liked the stories. Many were funny and fond, and they made me feel part of a comfortable continuum. "Don't forget who you are and what you represent," said lightly as we went off to birthday parties, was about as serious a burden as being a Lee was then. But as we grew and the phrase began to mean more than "Don't put pepper on your host's ice cream," it became an unspoken duty to live up to those who had gone before us. At least it did to me.

Note: The author is the great-granddaughter of Robert Edward and Mary Custis Lee; her maternal grandfather was Robert E. Lee Jr.

We descendants of Robert E. Lee did unveil a few portraits, which I rather liked doing. When I was about eight, I went to the White House, scrubbed and knobby-kneed, my hair in tight braids, to give a smoked turkey to President Roosevelt. He was busy, though, so his son James took the bird.

It was during my hypersensitive early teens that being on display began to feel unpleasant. On one occasion I crawled over the floor with a radio personality, dodging wires and furniture and reading stilted dialogue. For this initiation into show business, I had bought a new girdle, maybe my first, and when after lunch the constriction became unbearable, I had stuffed it into my equally new purse. As I stood up in front of an audience after the program, the purse fell open and the girdle fell out, while people clapped politely. I wanted to die, of course.

Forebears came to the forefront only once in college that I can remember, in an anthropology class. Kinship expert Dorothy Lee (Greek and no known kin) had assigned students to write down as much of our family trees as we could remember, to demonstrate, pre-*Roots*, how comparatively unimportant lineage was to Americans. Mostly for devilment, a Bostonian, a Charlestonian, and I stayed up all night filling strips of shelf paper with ancestors, many of mine wildly misplaced. Without batting an eye, Mrs. Lee acknowledged that ancestors were of consequence in a few pockets of the United States.

Working in New York after college, I began to realize that, at least in some circles, white southerners were considered second-class citizens or worse. When a Jewish artist informed me that there was no difference between southerners and Nazis, he left me speechless. That was just as well. I didn't know enough about the prewar South, or about how my family treated slaves, to argue. I wish I had known then about Robert Carter of Nomini Hall, who freed 500 people in 1791—though I might not have mentioned his father, also Robert Carter, the richest man in Virginia, who lacked such compunctions.

Introduction

Introduction

The author and her escort Ralston Brooke at a Confederate Ball about 1952; her dress, from the family dress-up trunk, may have belonged to a Lee daughter. (Courtesy of the Lee family)

Slavery in America, even in one family, I have learned, can be a complex subject.

I had left New York and been living in Ohio, where Lees were not exactly a frequent topic of conversation, for over twenty years when Agnes Mullins, curator at Arlington House, sent me a copy of a little notebook that belonged to my great-grandmother Mary Lee. Typical of the times, the receipts ran heavily to eggs, butter, and cream. Having spent most of my adult life dieting, I stuck the notebook and its temptations in a drawer. It stayed there for years, until I realized I might not have to cope with all those calories alone: at a meeting of the Ohio State University Gourmet Group, I asked if anyone wanted to help try out the receipts of Mrs. Robert E. Lee, and was surprised at how many did.

Culinary Archaeology 101

My aim was to find out as closely as possible what the Lee family actually ate, not just to unearth a few forgotten treasures and gussy them up to appeal to people today. The Gourmet Group volunteers and I set out to try every receipt in the notebook. At that time I had no idea of the tangled path ahead or the detours I would take in attempting to understand this unpretentious little book.

After some predictable early attrition, nine of us stuck with the project for over a year, cooking at home and meeting twice a month to taste, critique, and then—often—try again. We were a diverse bunch. Our baking expert came from Iowa, and when the conversation turned one day to ancestors, the Sri Lankan with a Ph.D. in nutrition owned softly that hers had been kings from the ninth century until just recently. A Tennessean's first bite at the first meeting took her back, like Proust with his madeleine, to her grandfather's

Introduction

Sunday-night suppers of cornbread and milk. A gourmet cook from the South owned a whole wall of cookbooks, but even so she could not always answer the questions of an astute but less experienced member.

Sometimes what we did was more treasure hunt than testing, and occasionally serendipity served us well. "Butter the size of a goose egg" was an easy measurement to track down, because somebody's sister-in-law raised geese. But the size of a "bottle of oil" remained questionable and a "dripping box of flour," impossible to determine. Two receipts for caromels [*sic*] made a primitive chocolate fudge that either crumbled or relaxed into puddles; only later would I puzzle out why. And eventually I learned (from an eighteenth-century source) to make boiled puddings, but only after producing ugly, gluey concoctions that looked, as one helpful tester remarked, "like a brain."

Some errors seemed to stem from the kinds of mistakes common in passing on receipts. The cup of ground ginger that made one gingerbread receipt's outcome inedible may have been fine if the cup was in fact meant to be a tablespoon instead. Those delicious little chocolate volcanoes probably erupted because someone forgot to put any flour in the list of ingredients. And surely more liquid would have kept Mrs. Lee's Muffin Bread from falling apart like damp sand.

A bigger problem was vagueness. Sometimes it rose to great heights in the notebook, probably because the contributors, family members and close friends, could explain in person what was not written down. Such vagueness was common in early cookbooks, particularly before Fannie Farmer published a system of measurements in her 1896 watershed *Boston Cooking School Cookbook*, and it reflects the depth of knowledge and repertoire of techniques possessed by centuries of cooks. Black and white, slave and free, earlier cooks, working with equipment far from precise and with ingredients as yet unstandardized, achieved often superb results with little more to go by than a list of ingredients. In addition to dishes for the table,

Introduction

they also made products such as yeast at home, and gelatin, which was just beginning to be manufactured at the time of the notebook. No wonder the Lee daughters had to struggle to master the arduous art of cooking.

The Ohio testers found that most of the receipts can be made easily with present-day ingredients, techniques, and equipment. Most of our attempts, we judged, were good to excellent and reasonably close to the originals. But was a higher degree of historical accuracy possible? And how to understand those curious disasters? What did the collection of receipts represent, anyway—with so many different kinds of bread, so many sweets, and only three vegetables? Why were they in dozens of different people's handwriting, and who wrote them?

And then there were the notebook's other contents, the lists—of General Lee's godchildren, of groceries bought and wagonloads of food received, of hundreds of socks and gloves knitted from bales of cotton and pounds of wool, the myriad household uses for common ingredients like salt and ammonia. As I puzzled over the brittle pages, the shabby little notebook grew in fascination. Might it, if understood, illuminate the intimate domestic life of the people in those dim portraits, at least in part?

So in 1989, when my husband Fred and I moved back to Virginia where I grew up, I began to read about saleratus and syllabub churns and many other facets of the times they belonged in, as well as the people who used them. And just in time, as it turned out, I began to find my family.

Linking Generations

My aunt, the last descendent of the Robert Edward Lees of her generation, was then in her nineties. She asked not to be named, but she matched handwriting in the notebook to letters from her aunts

Mary and Mildred and generously shared her many memories: stories about both of those aunts, her father and mother, her Uncle Custis, all of whom she had known, and others she had grown up hearing about. From her I went to her father's book about his father and to other sources of information about the family. When accounts differed, she told the family's version as she knew it. When she died peacefully several years ago, a comforting connection to the past was severed, but in a very real sense, she is still with me.

Today, when many children know their great-grandparents, it amazes me that mine lived before and through the Civil War; that my great-grandmother's father George Washington Parke Custis was raised from infancy by George and Martha Washington; and that her husband's father, Light-Horse Harry Lee, was also a hero of the Revolution.

The Washingtons even have some indirect connections to this little notebook. A Mount Vernon servant, George Clark, worked side by side with George Washington Parke Custis to build Arlington and was the head cook while Mary Lee was growing up and forming her taste. Mrs. Lee probably knew a family cookbook owned by her grandmother, Martha Washington, too. And since her father spent his life memorializing his adoptive father and turned the house into a shrine to the father of his country, it is not unlikely that there was a culinary carryover as well.

As I explored the stories and photographs connected to the little notebook, I became fond of these forebears, except for formidable Great-aunt Mary, who was nevertheless the most adventurous, outrageous, and fun to learn about. (She and Mr. Custis deserve books of their own.) I felt jolts of recognition, too, over what I had considered mine that turned out to have been "pre-owned." There was my nose—on two Mrs. Robert E. Lees, the one the mother-in-law of the other. "Precious Life," my nickname as a small child, had belonged to Great-aunt Mildred first (happily, I outgrew it early). Chairs and a sofa that were just always at our house showed up in an historic pho-

Introduction

tograph of the Lees' parlor in Lexington. I began to play "takes after," that comforting form of folk genetics that lets you blame your flaws on those who came before you. (Scientific gene research may yet bear us out.) Am I messy, unpunctual, and feeble in arithmetic? Well, so was Mrs. Lee. I'd have preferred her talent for exquisite sewing (inherited from her mother), but at least a trunkful of botched garments shows I share their persistence. Whenever this book threatened to finish me before I finished it, I thought of Mr. Custis, plunging in beyond his competence to glorify his adoptive father George Washington in paintings, plays, and even agriculture — by starting a breed of sheep from a Mount Vernon ram.

Both Robert and Mary Lee were frugal; I am cheap, a useful trait for those not attracted to endeavors with much money in them: a great-grandfather who chose a salary of $1,500 a year over riches can be a comfort. Other qualities I share with him, though not the ones I'd choose, include the way our hair flips up above our ears and our propensity for getting in trouble when people take our jokes too seriously. I rather like knowing that we share the habit of keeping our accumulated mail in wash baskets, though mine is mostly catalogues, not correspondence about healing a nation.

Having safely reached the age when sad, melodramatic romance is unlikely, I do not regret my lack of Great-aunt Agnes's beauty, if it was a cause of her blighted love. I would have liked the tidiness gene that her father passed on to Great-aunt Mildred, but no. As for Great-aunt Mary's insatiable appetite for travel, sometimes I wonder if my husband Fred could have inherited that by marriage.

I do not wish depression on anyone, but it helps to realize that others before me fought the black demon — without, alas, the remedies available today. And I hope some day to find in my own life the thread of integrity that ran through theirs.

A Whirlwind Finish

I had been steeping myself in the lore of wood stoves, rose water, cornmeal, and flour mills as well as my nineteenth-century forebears when Adelaide Simpson, kitchen guru of Lexington, Virginia, offered help with the loose ends still dangling. To test the thirty-five receipts that still needed more work, she gathered twenty-five more volunteers, ranging from a professional caterer to a bride who feared she'd flunked lemonade. Then what seemed like half the population of Lexington descended to the basement of the R. E. Lee Memorial Church for a final free-for-all tasting of their efforts.

For one reason or another, a handful of receipts still escaped. The winemaker's currant crop failed, so the Currant Wine has yet to be tried. We failed to find tough mutton (a blessing, judging from an earlier trip to Greece) and did not boil lamb because a nineteenth-century cookbook claims that it tastes terrible. And the arthritis cures seemed far too dangerous to swallow.

Although I have tried to follow at least partway the many paths the notebook led down, I have not made an exhaustive search of the thousands of Lee family letters or read anywhere near all the books, especially those written about the general and his military career. Nice as it is to have a family so thoroughly researched by others, there is a downside: I could never have finished all the reading.

At first I decided that more than enough had been written already about Robert E. Lee and that I would simply leave him out. But he was too deeply woven into the fabric of his family to exclude. The person who emerges here is a private family man, who in my mind rose to greatness in defeat, coincidentally about the time most of these receipts were collected. He has helped me immeasurably in my research, too. "Anything for Marse Robert," said Adelaide Simpson cheerfully, and many others who went so much farther than the extra mile to help must have felt the same way.

Introduction

I have tried to represent the family's point of view, but I have not shown this manuscript to any of them; they are all free to deny responsibility.

About Terminology

I grew up saying "receipt" and use that spelling here because it is the older form. But both "receipt" and "recipe" appear in the notebook and family letters. Having studied the War Between the States and the Civil War in three different schools in three different states as a child, I was an adult before I realized that both, as well as the War of the Rebellion, were the same cataclysmic conflict. I was writing this book before I began to appreciate how emotionally charged the terms—and the event—remain. I chose "Civil War" as the most neutral name and ask anyone it offends to forgive me.

I ask the same of African Americans and Native Americans. Words are powerful but not all-powerful. I believe it is the perceptions behind the words that need to change. While that is happening (and it is), new terms will continue to be coined in the effort to change those perceptions and will in their turn be dropped if and when they do not have the desired effect. The above terms came into my life too late for me to feel comfortable with them, so I have used whatever feels right in context, with no intention of disrespect.

Victorians were far more flexible about spelling and far more exuberant with punctuation than we are today, particularly when, as here, they did not write for outside eyes. I have reproduced the text of the notebook as written, hoping to convey its flavor and trusting that readers will not mistake casualness for ignorance.

Now may I introduce the Lees, their household notebook, about seventy of the dishes that appeared on their table, and some of their housekeeping hints.

Introduction

Mrs. Lee & Her Family

When diminutive Mary Anna Randolph Custis married Lieutenant Robert Edward Lee, she became the link between two icons of American history. Her adoptive grandfather, George Washington, had led the United States through its birth and greatest triumph, the Revolution; her husband would lead the Confederacy through our greatest tragedy so far, the Civil War.

America idealized both men, and Martha Washington became a household name, but history hardly noticed Mary Lee. Earlier writers seem to have made up for finding so few flaws in her husband by emphasizing hers. When later historians revisit the general, they tend to leave Mrs. Lee much the same—a vague and rather incompetent nonentity. To the people who knew her, though, she was far from that. She was, in the opinion of historian Charles Flood, "a law unto herself, and always had been."

Sometimes Mary Lee spoke and wrote before she thought. Her firm opinions were not always those of her circumspect husband. But the two agreed on essentials, and she backed his decisions wholeheartedly even when she knew they would bring her hardship.

Though severely crippled with rheumatoid arthritis and in pain most of her adult life, she was the emotional core of a family of seven children, leaving her husband, who set great store by them all, to attain that mythic stature he never sought. Without her, I wonder whether he would have.

War and destruction seemed unlikely when as children "Molly" Custis and Robert Lee played together at their relatives' plantations and planted trees at her family's, Arlington. Later he proposed to her—either at Arlington while she cut him a slice of cake, as Mrs. Lee told a young neighbor in Richmond years later, or at Chatham, as her playmate, cousin, and bridesmaid Marietta Turner Powell remembered. At Chatham, once the home of Mary's uncle William Fitzhugh, wrote Powell, "under the trees of the terraced garden which sloped down to the Rappahannock River, Mary consented to be the wife of Robert Lee." He himself recalled courting her there but did not say where they became engaged. This detail, like so many others, has been obscured in the mist of history.

Young Molly was not pretty, although a stranger commented on her "winning face" at age sixteen, but tradition gives her many suitors. At the advanced age of twenty-five she had accepted none, even though popular wisdom held that such an heiress needed a husband to look after her affairs. Perhaps she said to them all what she reputedly told Sam Houston—that she would have no one but Robert Lee. According to their nephew Fitzhugh, she was smitten the first time she saw Robert in his West Point uniform, "handsomer than ever," and "he was in love since boyhood."

Some say her father, George Washington Parke Custis, took three weeks to agree to the engagement because the young officer had no fortune beyond what he could earn. Earlier historians felt he simply did not want to give his beloved only child to anyone, let alone a military man who would take her away. This assessment seems likely given the remarkable, impractical nature of Custis.

Mrs. Lee & Her Family

Left: Mary Anna Randolph Custis in 1831, shortly before her marriage. Family tradition says the artist, Auguste Hervieu, put in the parrot because he couldn't do hands; further research strongly suggests the family was right. (Portrait by Auguste Hervieu, courtesy of the Lee family)

Below: The George and Martha Washington family, with George Washington Parke Custis at left, his sister Nelly Custis behind the table. Including a servant in a family portrait (far right) was highly unusual. (Engraving after a painting by Edward Savage, courtesy of the Mount Vernon Ladies' Association)

Mrs. Lee & Her Family

Mr. Custis had been raised by George and Martha Washington, a circumstance that shaped his life. He was an infant when his father, Martha's son by her first marriage, died. "I adopt the younger children as my own," declared Washington, and so for all practical purposes the father of his country was also the father of "Washy" (also called "Tub"; he was chubby) and his older sister, Nelly. Years later Custis would tell visitors that he and Nelly "stood in awe of [Washington]. . . . Altho' he was kind . . . we felt [we] were in the presence of someone who was not to be trifled with." For his part, the first president found the boy mischievous, lazy, and disappointingly indifferent to education. But when Custis found his true calling—which was to emulate, memorialize, and advance the ideals of his adoptive father—he pursued it in an astounding number of fields, sometimes with more enthusiasm than talent.

Tub was eight at Washington's inauguration, and indelibly impressed by the attendant pomp and adoration. He went to the theater often with the man he looked upon as father, and later wrote ten plays, with and without his own music. They are mostly of historical interest now, but at the time all but one were acclaimed. Not so his grandiose paintings of Washington, which some critics found accurate in detail but artistically incompetent. When one canvas was rejected from the Capitol rotunda, where artists showed their works, Custis directed his agent to throw the picture in the Potomac, "that it may offend no more." Later a visitor saw it being hauled out, the "dim figures of men, & horses . . . to be boiled off & the canvas used for aprons," for Mr. Custis was also chronically strapped for cash. "I have not had a saddle horse to ride for six years," he wrote once to an overseer.

But lack of funds did not keep him from establishing an amusement ground at Arlington Spring, where Washington City residents could hold free picnics and outings. There he celebrated Washington's birthday in the general's war tent, with Charles Willson Peale's portrait looking on, gave prizes for the best sheep in his efforts to improve agriculture, and occasionally played the fiddle to entertain his guests.

Custis excelled at the florid declamatory style of his day. Daniel Webster, among others, praised his speeches, and when Mrs. Lee edited his memoirs, she noted, "had due attention been paid to its [his oratory's] cultivation, [he] would doubtless have ranked among the first in the land." But those speeches, along with songs, poems, plays, and essays, were to him only a means of exalting Washington and espousing freedom everywhere, from Greece to Poland to South America. Society despised the Irish immigrants then, but Custis gave the main St. Patrick's Day address for years. A large slaveholder himself, he also denounced the institution of slavery as "the mightiest serpent that ever infested the world." To him the only worse evil was the breakup of the union founded by his father—as a consequence of differences over that institution. Ironically, tragically, his daughter and son-in-law concurred.

The young "Washy" Custis, portrayed by Charles St. Memin circa 1807, was a fop and a disappointment to the first president. (Courtesy of the Lee family)

For a time Custis saw the American Colonization Society, established to buy land in Liberia and provide passage for freed slaves, as a reasonable way to end "the unhappy error of our forefathers" without wrecking a social system that rested on their labor. He had inherited from his grandmother over two-thirds of Mount Vernon's "servants"—a term preferred by those who considered themselves enlightened slaveholders. When Washington freed his "people"— another such term—in his will, Custis also let go everyone who had married a Washington servant, even though slave marriage was illegal. The rest he intended to provide with education (also illegal)

and a trade before they had to fend for themselves in hostile sur-
roundings.

Many of the sixty-three Arlington slaves listed at Custis's death
were too old or too young to work. Northern visitors criticized him
for the idleness of the others, but although Custis maintained he did
not have enough work to earn their keep, he refused to sell anyone
south, where slaves brought a good sum. (He did, however, discipline
several by sending them to another of his plantations.) One young
man, Charles Syphax, refused his freedom altogether. Later he became Mary Lee's mainstay during the unrest before the war, when
Robert was away.

Spritely and witty, Mr. Custis, like Washington, dressed plainly
and worked with his hands. He helped to found what became the De-
partment of Agriculture, reclaimed exhausted fields with then-new-
fangled fertilizer made with oyster shells, and developed a breed of
sheep from a Mount Vernon ram. He promoted woolen mills to fos-
ter American economic independence, and as early as 1829 proposed
universal military service, also in the cause of political freedom.

His daughter Mary, the only child of four to survive infancy, grew
up steeped in stories of the founding fathers and surrounded by furniture, silver, dishes, and pictures from Mount Vernon; the family
even used the bed Washington died in. Her father had gone into debt
to buy even more Washington relics than he had inherited and then,
when dampness and rats threatened them, built Arlington to house
them—first the wings and later, when he could afford it, the impos-
ing center section. Until Molly was six, the family lived in two small,
unconnected buildings housing the Washington treasures—which
her father also gave away with impulsive generosity. In 1830 a visitor remarked, "they are now dispersed in almost every country in
Christendom."

Of the house, whose huge pillars were theatrically visible from
across the Potomac, Lee observed cryptically, "anyone might see [it]
with half an eye." Perhaps because it was meant to resemble a Brit-

Mrs. Lee & Her Family

ish country house, Mrs. Trollope, the usually caustic English traveler, admired it. But on the inside, the house never quite achieved the requisite country-house polish. The Lee children rode stick horses in the front parlor, which was filled with dusty furniture and portraits from Mount Vernon. And when a northern schoolteacher visited in 1856, she found "the upper rooms . . . large, but we would think them terribly *unfurnished.*"

The servants provided a living connection to the Washingtons. Martha's maid, Caroline Branham, had been with the first First Lady when she died. Lawrence Parks and George Clark worked beside Custis to build Arlington. Later Parks sold the estate's produce at Washington City's Center Market, and Clark became head cook, which was often a man's job in great houses, with their huge cooking fireplaces and heavy cast-iron pots. He must have overseen and prepared at least some of the receipts Mrs. Lee entered in her housekeeping book. Another servant, referred to as "Old Nurse," had been an "outdoor girl" at Mount Vernon and opened gates for Washington, and she told first Mrs. Lee and then her children about what the Lees' daughter Agnes called in her diary "those good old days."

Young Mary Custis had her father's lively mind. Like him, she loved politics and current events. She painted better (and much smaller) than Custis, and she and her children shared his abiding love of cats. This affection was more restrained in her husband, according to youngest son, Rob. In his book of his father's letters, he called the general "very fond of them . . . in their place, and . . . considerate of their feelings." Nevertheless, Robert reported, on a stormy night when the elder Lee heard distressed meowing, he opened a window, and when the cat could not jump in, he "took one of my mother's crutches, and held it so far out . . . that he became wet . . . [and] persuaded the cat to climb up along the crutch."

Custis's four-by-five-foot painting of Washington at Yorktown has been lost; this 1853 engraving by Benson J. Lossing, which was based on the painting, appeared in Harper's New Monthly Magazine *(vol. 7, no. 40, p. 451). (From the copy in the Rare Book Collection, University of North Carolina at Chapel Hill)*

Mrs. Lee & Her Family

Top: Later in life, Custis became Washington's foremost worshipper. (Sketch by J. Kayler, 1852, courtesy of the Mount Vernon Ladies' Association; print courtesy of the National Park Service, Arlington House Collection)

Bottom left: Artist Auguste Hervieu captured the gentle calm of Mary Lee Fitzhugh Custis, mother of Mary Lee, in this watercolor. (Courtesy of the Lee family)

Bottom right: A daguerreotype of Mrs. Custis, made later in her life, captured her firmness. (Photographic copy by Michael Miley, courtesy of Virginia Historical Society)

Mrs. Lee & Her Family

Mary had a much better education than what Mrs. Trollope observed of most men "of the higher classes" in America in the early 1800s. They, she claimed, knew "very little beyond reading, writing, and bookkeeping." Chatting in a letter to her mother about her first baby, the young Mrs. Lee asked for "a Latin dictionary, as I brought a Greek one by mistake."

The only thinkable future for a girl of her station was marriage and managing a household, a career roughly comparable to running a small town. It embraced, wrote novelist Thomas Nelson Page, everything from doctoring the servants to supervising the setting of turkeys (settling them on nests to hatch eggs). Mary's mother, Mary Lee Fitzhugh Custis, taught her and the women servants to sew expertly. All the servants' clothing, family's shirts, and children's clothes were made on the place, and after the Emancipation several women servants earned their living as seamstresses. Unlike her mother, who had taken firm hold of the Arlington establishment at age sixteen, Mary was a haphazard housekeeper, but like her mother she loved gardening and flowers. She also possessed the same sweet, stable disposition and profound religious feeling, and time would show that young Molly also had more of her mother's strength and resolve than her husband—or she—knew.

Mr. Custis lost interest in the Colonization Society when he realized it could not really solve the problem of slavery, but his wife and daughter persevered. Mrs. Custis herself prepared several servants for life in Liberia and then, with money from the sale of her flowers at Washington City's market (familiarly known as Wash Market), paid to send them there. Her daughter gave generously too and may have financed at least one couple's trip. As children, Mary's daughters made wreaths and bouquets to sell for the Society.

Three generations of the Custis-Lee family also taught slave children to read, in defiance of the law that rendered 90 percent of slaves illiterate. Mr. Custis had tried to set up a school but failed to find a schoolmaster, so Mrs. Custis, later her daughter and then her daughter's daughters, taught the little ones.

Mary never wanted to be anywhere but Arlington. As a newlywed, she wrote to a cousin melodramatically, "I am a wanderer on the face of the earth"; later that would prove all too true. Her husband was in favor of establishing independence from his parents-in-law, but he lost that battle early. When bad weather in winter suspended his engineering assignments or he was stationed in Washington, back they went to Arlington. In time, Robert, whose own mother had died, came to think of the house as home and called the Custises, with whom he shared the house for thirty years, Father and Mother. All but one of the seven Lee children were born there, and the increasingly far-flung family always tried to meet there for Christmas.

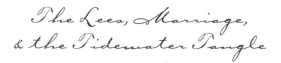

The Lees, Marriage, & the Tidewater Tangle

It was not Lee's lineage that caused Mr. Custis to hesitate over his daughter's engagement. In the words of historian Paul Nagel, "No other family produced more members of merit during the American Revolution" than the Lees. Michael Miller, a specialist in Virginia history, has found that of the fifty-four known descendants of Richard Lee, the English immigrant, and his wife, "thirty-seven held public office, ten were members of the House of Burgesses, sixteen were members of the Council [respectively the lower and higher governing bodies of Virginia] and two were signers of the Declaration of Independence." And that, of course, accounts only for the men.

But for illness, Thomas Lee, Robert's step-grandfather (and cousin), "the most powerful person in the Old Dominion," would have become the colony's first native-born governor, says Nagel. (Royal Governors had always come out from Britain.) Robert's father, Light-

Horse Harry Lee, a Revolutionary hero in his twenties, had been an intimate of Custis's idol, Washington, and the two families intermarried repeatedly.

Mary and Robert were themselves distantly but intricately related. Both came from the small number of families that dominated Tidewater Virginia economically, politically, and socially for over two hundred years. "Of course they married each other," my mother used to say. "There was no one else to marry." Given the small population and bad roads, she had a point, but marriage was also a powerful glue that held these families together. Historian William Cabell Bruce likened them genealogically to "a tangle of fishhooks, so closely interlocking that it is impossible to pick up one without drawing three or four after it." Social historian Sidney Fischer calls them a "single cousinage," a term that encompasses a large number of the people whose names appear in the notebook.

Robert and Mary both descended from Robert "King" Carter, he by the first wife and she by the second. This mutual ancestor had been the richest man in Virginia, owning over 300,000 acres, a thousand slaves, and a fleet of ships that carried his tobacco ("brown gold") to England. Royal Governor Francis Nicholson decried Carter's "Pride & Ambition" and "haughtiness and insolence," which also account for this nickname.

Edmund Jennings Lee, a close relative, confessed in his authoritative *Lee of Virginia* that completely untangling Tidewater Virginia families was close to impossible, citing some people who were related four ways. Certainly doing so is beyond this book, but the many names that I recognize in the Lee family notebook suggest that vestiges of the cousinage web have outlasted the bad roads, the isolation, and the dynastic power that were responsible for it in the beginning.

Mrs. Lee & Her Family

Family connections, however, did not keep Robert's flamboyant father Light-Horse Harry Lee from going broke. Twice court-martialed and twice exonerated, he received a special congressional medal for bravery in battle. He gave Washington's funeral oration, in which he coined the title "Father of His Country" and the often-quoted phrase "first in war, first in peace, and first in the hearts of

Mrs. Lee & Her Family

his countrymen." He was elected twice to Congress and three times governor of Virginia, the largest and most populous of the states. But he also became embroiled in politics and land speculation.

Two Supreme Court justices and financier Robert Morris, a major backer of the Revolution, owed Harry money when he was taken off to debtor's prison in 1809. Behind bars, he wrote a classic history of the Revolution in the South (later edited, with a biography, by Robert). Once freed, the fiery soldier defended a publisher and freedom of the press against the attack of an angry mob. After dripping candle wax on his eyes to see if he moved, the mob left him for dead. Not long afterward, in 1813, he left for the Caribbean to regain his shattered health, escape his creditors, or both. When he died on the way home, his son Robert inherited his military talent, his gift for words, and little else.

When Ann Hill Carter Lee, Robert's invalid mother, raised five children, both funds and furniture were scarce, but her husband's dear friend Lafayette came to dinner twice. She was determined that Robert would not repeat the excesses of his father. "Self-denial, self-control, and the strictest economy . . . were part of the code of honor she taught him from infancy," wrote Lee biographer Douglas Freeman. And it took. As a boy, he loved foxhunting but could not afford a riding horse, so he followed the hounds on foot.

Robert learned responsibility early too. His older brothers and sister had left home when at age twelve he "kept the keys" of the household and did the marketing. Taking care of his mother, he developed a tender, nurturing nature rare if not unique among military commanders. He used to carry her downstairs for drives in their drafty old coach, which he had stuffed with newspapers, and would entertain her with stories as they rode. "How can I live without Robert?" Ann asked when this son left for West Point. "He is both a son and a daughter to me."

Four years later as a newly graduated lieutenant, Lee nursed his mother in her final illness and then left for his first post. With him

Mrs. Lee & Her Family

went Nat, the old family coachman, ill and with no one else to care for him. Robert rented a room, found a doctor, and took care of the old man until he died.

Housekeeping & Potatoes by Starlight

Mrs. Lee has been called spoiled, and at first maybe she was. Certainly she was raised with more indulgence than her husband and in more comfort than Fort Monroe, Virginia, offered the newlyweds. There, at their first post, the young couple lived in one room. Later, looking for more privacy, they may have moved into two, but those rooms had dirt floors.

Like her husband, Mary disapproved of the soldiers' drinking and gambling. She read, took walks, bathed in the sea, and painted. Their friends' indifference to her beloved Colonization Society distressed her, but she taught a class of "little black scholars" after church. After their first son, George Washington Custis, was born, she filled letters home with happy doting about "Boo," "Bouse," "Bun," and "Dunket," as she called him variously.

The child was eighteen months old when Robert wrote a letter that has been quoted to show Mary as a hopeless housekeeper. "Tell the ladies that Mrs. Lee is somewhat addicted to laziness and forgetfulness in her housekeeping," it says. "In her Mother's words, 'The Spirit is willing but the flesh is weak.'" The young mother's husband and mother would seem unsympathetic at best if either one had been serious, but chances are they were not.

The letter was addressed to Andrew Talcott, to whom Lee had often joked even before he and Mary were married. Harriet Talcott was Mary's cousin and friend, and the couples were so close that Robert, congratulating the Talcotts on their new baby boy, had of-

Mrs. Lee & Her Family

fered to produce a girl next, so the two could marry. (She was, but they didn't.) Furthermore, the Lees had been stationed in the Talcotts' house previously; "the ladies" undoubtedly knew about Mary's housekeeping already.

The rest of the letter shows that its purpose was to urge the Talcotts to stay with them rather than go to a hotel, the Hygeia. And while his wife's housekeeping was no doubt casual, Lee was probably indulging in the playful banter that runs throughout his personal and family correspondence, which has often been misunderstood. For example, Lee's mock-heroic account of killing a rattlesnake appalled Douglas Freeman, who seems to have suspected him of murder. During the death throes of the Confederacy, Lee teased his wife about miscounting the numbers of socks she had sent to his troops (listed in her notebook).

Mary understood his banter, just as she did his light-hearted gallantry, which also has been taken too seriously by some. Mary Lee was neither well nor pretty, and her husband was known as "the handsomest man in the army." But she realized, as she wrote later, that his attention to the ladies was "the greatest recreation in his toilsome life."

Writing to his wife from Texas before the Civil War, Robert shared with her his amusement when, after dinner, a widow "took me out in her garden to see her corn and potatoes by moonlight." During the war, gossipy Civil War diarist Mary Chesnut commented shrewdly, "Constance Cary says, if it would please God to take poor Cousin Mary Lee—she suffers so—wouldn't these Richmond women *campaign* for Cousin Robert? In the meantime Cousin Robert holds all admiring females at arm's length." Much later, in Lexington, a male friend observing from the other side of the street watched Lee, astride his horse Traveller, conversing gallantly with ladies as he masterfully quieted the fretting, rearing horse—which was responding to its master's spur.

"Of course he liked the ladies," my aunt would say dismissively.

Mrs. Lee & Her Family

Mrs. Lee's favorite photograph of her husband was taken in 1850 by Mathew Brady; she had a uniform painted over the civilian clothes in the original and was still giving out this carte de visite during the war. (Courtesy of National Park Service, Arlington House Collection)

Mrs. Lee & Her Family

"Why shouldn't he?" And I learned myself when I moved from Richmond to New York that the fine southern art of harmless flirting can be mightily misunderstood.

But Lee's upbringing, reinforced by the lessons of a scandal that drove his half-brother "Black-Horse Harry" from the country, leads me to think he was totally sincere in another letter that he wrote to Mary from Petersburg, on their anniversary, "Do you recollect what a happy day thirty-three years ago this was? How many hopes and pleasures it gave birth to! God has been very merciful and kind to us."

To return to housekeeping, apparently Mrs. Lee never did care about surface tidiness. The wife of President Franklin Pierce diplomatically described the parlor at Arlington as "a preeminently Social Room," and another visitor enjoyed the fact that "it is not the least bit in order." But clutter aside, Mary Lee matured into a knowledgeable housekeeper.

In a letter she wrote to her daughter Annie in 1860 from a spa in Canada, where she had gone for her arthritis, she directed the servants Billy and Ephraim to wash the wool and Nurse to dry it and put it away. Then, she wrote, "when Sally and Patsey have done knitting[,] they can pick it," adding that George should harvest the tomatoes and someone should help Nurse to can them. Mrs. Lee also asked for a paper pattern for jar rings so that she could have some made in Canada, "for there are none in the [Arlington] district." After giving detailed directions for making tomato catsup, she said if more bottles were needed, they were to "buy half a dozen champagnes . . . not to be more than 4 cts a piece." Son Rob was to "keep some eye upon the apples in the orchard or they will be borne away as usual," and she warned Annie, "Do not throw the keys of the cellar about, or I fear the scuppernong wine will be absent."

Early in the Lees' marriage, conflict arose. Mary tended to be disorganized, late, and impulsive. Robert was organized, impeccable, punctual, and circumspect. Both were strong-willed, and Mary wrote plaintively to her mother from Fort Monroe to complain: "Robert . . .

Mrs. Lee & Her Family

does scold me early and late." She also wrote contritely: "It requires so much firmness & consistency to train up a child in the right way & I know that I am so remiss in the government of my servants & so often neglect to correct them when they do wrong," Mary confessed to her after Boo was born. "I must endeavor with God's assistance to be more faithful [in disciplining him]."

Although Lee found his wife "too lax, too inconstant, and too yielding" he did not maintain his own high standards as grimly as later portraits and statues suggest. Their young children had to earn stories, for example, by tickling his hands and feet; if the tickling stopped, the story stopped. As their son Rob reflected on the two in their roles as parents, he concluded, "My mother I could sometimes circumvent, and at times took liberties with her orders, construing them to suit myself; but exact obedience to every mandate of my father was a part of my life and being." "I couldn't tell you his exact words," added my aunt, "but Father [Rob] gave the impression that she was the one who kept the family together. He was doing other things."

Those other things kept him away for long periods. Rob had no memories of his father until he was five years old, when Lee returned from the Mexican War in 1848. He recalled with amusement how he ran excitedly to meet his father: "clothed in my very best with my hair freshly curled in long golden ringlets. . . . [Lee] "pushed through the crowd, exclaiming, 'Where is my little boy?' He then took up in his arms and kissed—not me . . . but my little playmate, Armistead."

Lee was surveying the Ohio-Michigan border when their first daughter, Mary Custis, was born. After suffering painful and frightening complications for months, the new mother pleaded with Robert to take early leave and come to her. He wrote back sternly not to interfere with his "duty imposed on me by my profession," but to "cheer up . . . & . . . meet with a smiling face and cheerful heart the vicissitudes of life." (Robert had some growing up to do, too.) When

Mrs. Lee & Her Family

Above: Robert E. Lee's father, Henry "Light-Horse Harry" Lee, by Gilbert Stuart (owned by Carter L. Refo, print courtesy of Time-Life); Robert's mother, Ann Hill Carter Lee (artist unknown, courtesy of Washington/Custis/Lee collection, Washington and Lee University, Lexington, Va.).

Left: Robert Edward Lee Jr. as a young boy. (Courtesy of the Lee family)

Mrs. Lee & Her Family

he did return and saw how sick she was, he took sympathetic charge. After that he never again questioned her judgment about her health — and she never again mentioned in a letter to him how ill she was.

It was months before Mary could sit up. Then, horrified at the loss of most of her hair, she took scissors and chopped off the rest. She did not fully recover until spring almost two years later, and then, on May 30, William Fitzhugh — "Rooney" — was born.

Barely fourteen months afterward, she, Robert, the baby, and six-year-old Boo set out for St. Louis. (Daughter Mary Custis, not yet three, was ill and stayed behind at Arlington with her grandparents.) In blustery March they took three trains and a canal boat to Pittsburgh, where the family waited a week for a steamboat. There the young Lees bought furniture, but the boat carrying it and most of their other possessions blew up and sank. On the steamer, Lee wrote the Talcotts, Mary "defied the crowding, squeezing, and scrambling" by taking naps, and for months afterward the little boys "converted themselves . . . into steamboats, rang their bells . . . and kept on so heavy a pressure of steam, that I am constantly fearing that they will burst their boilers."

From St. Louis, Mary sent messages to little Mary: "her Mama sends her a thousand kisses & has been looking for a pair of garters for her," and "Mee [a nickname] must . . . think of me . . . almost devoured alive by moschetas . . . thick as a swarm of bees every evening." That spring they spent eleven days returning by steamer and stagecoach, and less than a month later daughter Annie was born.

After all that, it would be hard to consider Mary Lee still spoiled, but her husband wrote a letter that has been quoted to show that she was. He was away again when this fourth child arrived, and supposedly he wrote to Mrs. Custis, "It requires much earnestness to induce her to conform to what she is not herself impressed with the necessity of. *Make* her do what is right." Once again he wrote playfully, and this time he was misquoted to boot.

Like many people before the days of telephones, the Lees chatted

Mrs. Lee & Her Family

long-distance by mail, touching on many subjects as they kept in touch. Lee began this letter by welcoming "little Raspberry" into the world (Annie had a birthmark). Then after expressing tender concern for his wife and new child and agreeing with Mary about some plans, he turned to his own news. He was gossiping about another new mother who had disobeyed her doctor and made herself ill when he added: "young women you know Mother will not be advised; so it will be useless for you to waste your time advising that *Mama* [his wife]. *Make* her do what is right." In my opinion, this passage is nothing more than a passing comment on his wife's determination and a hope that Mrs. Custis could persuade her to follow doctor's orders, but it has been used to paint Mary as truculent and spoiled.

In countering such unsympathetic misinterpretations, however, I do not want to exaggerate Mary Lee's endurance or industry. Like any Victorian woman North or South who could afford help with the housekeeping, she did have a maid.

The Lees' next child, Agnes, was twenty months old when the family left for Fort Hamilton, New York. There Mrs. Lee looked up Cassy, Old Nurse's daughter, who had been her maid at Fort Monroe. She and her husband, Louis, were among several ex-Custis people there, free in a state that did not recognize slavery. When Mary learned that Louis was too ill to work and that the two were desperate, she offered to send them back to Arlington to stay—and remain free—until Louis recovered. But, she wrote to her mother, "it seems there is a good deal of pride in the matter." Louis "did not want to go home unless 'he could do as he ought to do.'" So she gave Cassy some money and "a few things" and promised more help.

Although Mary felt she had a moral duty toward her family's former slaves, she was far from a model mistress. At least once she more than justified her early rueful admission of being an ineffective disciplinarian. After visiting Arlington in 1859, a northern schoolteacher decided, "I would not like to *live* in the South. . . . [because of] the responsibility and *bother* of those servants. . . . Just fancy waiting tea

Mrs. Lee & Her Family

until eight o'clock [she may be referring to the light evening meal taken about six] *because they could not find anything to milk the cow in. . . .* Such shiftlessness is incredible to Northern housekeepers."

Mary also had little patience with people who championed freedom in principle but lacked humaneness in practice. She ended her housekeeping letter from Canada, "tell Nurse there is a great many runaways here but I have not met with any acquaintances. . . . I am told they suffer a great deal here in the long cold winters. After enticing them over here the White people will not let their children go to the same schools or treat them as equals in any way & amalgamation is out of the question."

War & a Decision

Mrs. Lee read four newspapers a day and followed political events closely. When Lincoln was elected, she felt that "nothing he can do now will meet with any favour from the South," and when war was declared, she wrote to her daughter Mildred, "as I think both parties are wrong in this fratricidal war, there is nothing comforting even in the hope that God may prosper the right, for I see no *right* in the matter."

Nevertheless she left to her husband the decision as to whether he would oppose the Union that he had served for thirty years, reportedly telling him, "whichever way you go will be in the path of duty. You will think it right, and I shall be satisfied." When he determined that he could not invade his homeland, her life changed painfully and forever. But "if she had any regrets," wrote Rose MacDonald, who knew her well in Lexington, "neither then nor later did she ever utter them." Nor did she cease longing for Arlington. "I feel a stranger & exile," she wrote to Mrs. Jefferson Davis after the war.

Even when she left Arlington two weeks ahead of Federal troops, Mrs. Lee was concerned for her servants. She sent a letter back all

Mrs. Lee & Her Family

but ordering the officer in charge to allow her coachman to collect his clothes and to let her "market man go & return from Washington . . . where his family resides," adding, "my gardener Ephraim also has a wife in Washington & is accustomed to go over every Saturday and return on Monday."

Although some of the staff left, the housekeeper Selina Gray and others stayed on. For a while they managed to keep some of the family's possessions safe. Later Markie Williams, a cousin who had stayed with the Union (as had Lee's own sister, Anne) stopped by. When she wrote Mrs. Lee, she included Ephraim's request to "please give my best love to her & all the family, & tell her we miss her very much indeed—the people does the best they can for us, but it aint like those we all been raised with."

Mary Lee did not see her home again until the year she died, 1873. By then she was too crippled to leave her carriage and enter the house, but some of the old servants came out to greet her and gave her water from the Arlington well. Elizabeth Calvert described what she no doubt saw: "Dessolation, & sadness have taken the place of happiness, & brightness. The lilies of the valley have disappeared, the countless dead sleep, with the sunshine on them, where the numberless old trees stood in shade too dense for it to penetrate [illegible] glimpses." For her lawns and gardens were covered with graves; Arlington National Cemetery had begun.

Even five years before she left Arlington, Mary Lee's rheumatoid arthritis had sometimes confined her to bed, often in too much pain to sleep. When Robert was on his way home from Texas in 1848, she had confided to a friend, "I almost dread him seeing my crippled state." Now, leaving her home forever, she jounced for nearly a year over rough roads to reach Richmond, staying with relatives and friends. A fellow refugee confided to her diary, "I never saw her so cheerful, and [she] seems to have no doubt of our success."

More Americans died in the Civil War than in all other U.S. wars combined. It has been called the first modern war of attrition, for

Mrs. Lee & Her Family

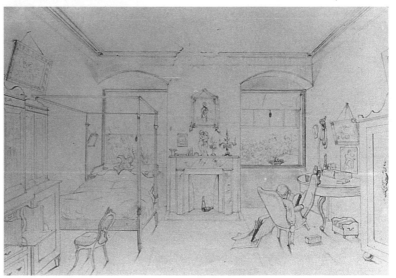

Above: Arlington housekeeper Selina Gray. (Courtesy of National Park Service, Arlington House Collection)

Top right: Union soldiers occupying Arlington, June 1864. (Original in National Archives, print courtesy of National Park Service, Arlington House Collection)

Bottom right: The Lee daughters' bedroom at Arlington, sketched by Union soldier Charly Morgan, circa 1861. (Courtesy of National Park Service, Arlington House Collection)

Mrs. Lee & Her Family

southern lands, crops, houses, animals, cities, and society were destroyed as a matter of policy. But if it had not also been a last gasp of romantic war, Mary Lee might never have reached Richmond. Twice she was caught behind rapidly shifting enemy lines, treated with courtesy, and escorted back to Confederate territory. General McClellan even allowed her to decide when she, Annie, and Mildred would meet Lee and go to Richmond. And this courteous, considerate treatment made Mrs. Lee furious.

War has become such indiscriminate, wholesale slaughter now that it is hard to comprehend why the protection of her husband's ex-fellow officers made her angry. But Mary Lee thought of herself as not just the wife of a Confederate general but as the granddaughter of George and Martha Washington as well, and to her that should have been safeguard enough. Union troops were closing in when she left her son Rooney's home, the White House along the Pamunkey River, where the Washingtons had been married, with this note pinned to a door: "Northern soldiers who profess to reverence Washington forbear to desecrate the house of his first married life, the property of his wife, now owned by his descendants," signed, "A Granddaughter of Mrs. Washington."

Later this reply appeared: "Lady—A Northern officer has protected your property in sight of the enemy, and at the request of your overseer." Some accounts say McClellan's troops burned the house, but the note from the Northern officer exists. Williams family tradition says that Lawrence, brother of Markie and Orton Williams, was dismissed from the Union army for refusing to burn the White House, claiming that General McClellan had ordered civilian property spared, and that subsequently the house burned accidentally.

When Lee met his wife, Mildred, and Agnes on Confederate territory outside Richmond on June 10, 1862, Mary Lee's increased, unexpected, and unreported infirmity dismayed him. The city's population had swollen to four times its peacetime size, and accommodations were impossible to find. Generous family friends, the

Mrs. Lee & Her Family

The other White House, where George Washington courted the Widow Custis; this estate, on the Pamunkey River, was later owned by the Lees' son Rooney (William Henry Fitzhugh Lee). (From Congressional War Record 2 (1882), p. 42; negative courtesy of National Park Service, Arlington House Collection)

Caskies, took in Mrs. Lee and her daughters. Within weeks, cannon boomed and muskets flashed outside the city. As the wounded poured in, a young friend of Mrs. Lee's, Sally Nelson Robins, described Richmond as "one immense hospital," where people "breathed the vapors of the charnel house." Sickness and death spread rapidly in the summer heat, and Custis, the eldest Lee son, who was a staff officer stationed there, fell ill.

Eighteen sixty-two was a time of great stress and sadness for the family. Charlotte, Rooney's first wife, had already taken their baby Rob to Jones Springs in North Carolina to recuperate from an illness, but he died there in July of pneumonia. Frail, despondent, and pregnant, the mother returned to Richmond to bury him. After nursing Custis and caring for her seriously ill hostess, Mrs. Caskie, Mary Lee learned that Annie, who had gone to North Carolina with Charlotte and remained there, had contracted typhoid fever. Though barely able to leave her "rolling chair," Mrs. Lee rushed to her daughter, but weeks after she arrived, Annie died. In early Decem-

Mrs. Lee & Her Family

ber, Charlotte's second child, a girl born prematurely, also died. Their grief was still fresh when Mrs. Lee, Agnes, and Charlotte went to spend Christmas at Hickory Hill, home of their cousins the Wickhams. When Orton Williams, a Confederate captain, arrived there, a bizarre sequence of events began to unfold.

Markie, Lawrence, and Orton Williams, the orphaned children of Mary's first cousin, had grown up close to the Lees, and Orton had been Agnes's sweetheart since childhood. In the army he had become reckless and erratic, though, and the elder Lees did not approve of him. No one ever said what happened in the parlor on December 26. The Wickham's young son Henry remembered years later that "we children had been warned to keep away." But to him and his sister, the affair "was the first romance of our lives. . . . He was the Prince Charming and she the Sleeping Beauty . . . and [we] believed . . . they would ride away and live happily ever after. We could not understand it at all when . . . he came out, bade the family good-bye and rode away alone. We could not understand it."

What happened afterward must have mystified the adults, too. First, Orton married a woman who was, Markie wrote Agnes, reputedly already married and probably "deranged." Then he was captured in a Union camp wearing a Union uniform. Less than six months after leaving Hickory Hill, Orton Williams was hanged as a spy, a charge he denied absolutely in a letter to Markie.

In her thoroughly researched account, *The Lee Girls*, Mary Coulling concludes that "to this day, the purpose of Orton Williams's strange escapade remains a mystery." When I asked my aunt about it, she answered matter-of-factly, "Why, he was on a mission to France." And he could have been. The South was seeking French support then, and Orton's cousin Walter Peter was with him, which suggests something beyond a lovelorn twenty-four-year-old's madness. It might even account for their speedy execution.

In the diary that Agnes had kept seven years before, she had been a charming, spontaneous child verging on womanhood. After Or-

The young Agnes Lee. (Courtesy of the Lee family)

ton's death, "she became very quiet and pensive," Henry Wickham remembered. "I do not recall hearing her laugh, and when she smiled it seemed to me that she was looking beyond."

The city of Richmond had offered to buy a house for the Lees, but the general had declined, saying the money should be used for the war. Not until 1863 could Mrs. Lee rent a place to live, and that was so small it could not accommodate the still despondent Charlotte. Then months before the city fell in 1865, Mary moved into "the Mess" at 707 East Franklin Street, with Custis and some of his fellow bachelor officers. There she and her daughters had more room, but even so, when his father came to town, Custis slept on the floor. The family, cousins, and friends all camped there on straw mattresses on the floor after Appomattox.

Life in Richmond became increasingly grim. A fortunate few received supplies from plantations farther south, but for most people "finding enough to eat was a full-time occupation," according to historian Joe Gray Turner. Food was so scarce that working-class women rioted in 1863, and in 1864 Robert wrote Mary, "how Custis, yourself, 3 girls, Billy and Sally [servants] can live long on ¼ lb. bacon and ½ pt. of meal [presumably a day] I cannot see."

Inflation soared. While profiteers drank $3 cups of coffee, Mrs. Chesnut noted the joke going around: "You take your money to market in the market basket and bring home what you buy in your pocketbook." Toward the end of the war, when $45 in the South's currency was worth only one gold dollar, the Union's currency seems already to have been replacing it. Wrote Mrs. Chesnut: "When they ask for Confederate money, I never stop to chaffer. I give them twenty or fifty dollars for anything." During this dire time, women flocked to Mrs. Lee, to help her and her daughters knit for Confederate soldiers (some records of the enterprise are in the notebook).

Mrs. Lee & Her Family

Asked during the last days of the Confederacy where his wife would go, Lee answered, "she . . . says they will have to take her. *She will move no more.*" And she and her remaining daughters did not. Confederate soldiers retreating from Richmond unlocked the penitentiary and emptied warehouses of whiskey. The streets filled with drunken, looting mobs, and the city caught fire. People rushed to the Lee ladies' rescue, and the church across the street was in full blaze, but Mrs. Lee continued knitting in her rolling chair while her daughter Mary Custis stood on the front porch with a bucket of water. Only a shift of the wind saved them and the house.

Orton Williams, Agnes's sweetheart and cousin. (Courtesy of the Lee family)

Peace & Another Decision

After the war so many people came to see the defeated general and he, ever courteous, saw so many of them, that Rob, his first cousin Dan Lee, and other young men guarded the front door to keep them out. At night Lee took long walks with Mildred, and once he slipped away on Traveller to Pampetike, the home of some Carter cousins, where he played with the children and did not mention the war. Clearly, to find privacy, the family had to leave Richmond.

Elizabeth Cocke, a widow related to both of the Lees, offered them the use of a cottage, Derwent, fifty miles west of Richmond near the James River, so that Mrs. Lee could travel most of the way by canal boat. Mrs. Lee described its four small rooms and another small building in the yard as "a retired little place. . . . the outbuildings . . . dilapidated & the garden a mass of weeds." But Lee, according to Mildred, "was enthusiastic about a *home* life, however humble, after those five years in a tent."

At Derwent, Agnes came down with typhoid fever, and Mildred

Mrs. Lee & Her Family

"The Mess" at 707 East Franklin Street, Lee's headquarters in Richmond, where Custis, Mrs. Lee, and her daughters lived for a time. (From Brock, General Robert E. Lee, *p. 325; print courtesy of National Park Service, Arlington House Collection)*

and her father nursed her as he waited to hear whether a grand jury would indict him for treason. (It did not, thanks at least in part to General Grant.) And in "a quiet so profound that I could even number the acorns falling from the splendid oak trees that overshadowed the cottage," recalled Mrs. Lee, the family considered the future.

After Appomattox, offers had poured in to the defeated general as if he had won the war. The family could have owned an English manor house complete with lands and income. Lee could have earned his living abroad, as many Confederate officers did; the Mexican Emperor Maximilian had offered him command of his army. But he would not leave his country, and when an American corporation offered him $50,000 a year for the use of his name, Lee answered, "my name is not for sale."

Outspoken daughter Mary Custis, who was never at home if she could help it, set in motion the events that led to her father's future. At a party in Staunton she announced, "the people of the South are offering my father everything but work; and work is the only thing he will accept at their hands." Word spread quickly to the trustees of tiny Washington College, who immediately voted him president.

The school was down to forty students; the campus, all but destroyed. The board had to borrow fifty dollars to send the rector, Judge John Brockenbrough, to make their offer, and he had to borrow a suit to make the trip. The salary was only $1,500 a year plus the use of a house and garden, but Lee did not hesitate, except over his qualifications and legal status. Without amnesty, with an indictment for treason hanging over him, his application for citizenship had gone unanswered. (The papers were "mislaid" for a hundred years; he received his citizenship posthumously.)

Again Mary Lee backed her husband, although they had very little other income and, as she wrote to a cousin, "I do not think he is

Mrs. Lee & Her Family

The city of Richmond before, during, and after the battle in which it fell to Union troops, April 2, 1865. (Courtesy of Virginia Historical Society)

Mrs. Lee & Her Family

· 41 ·

very fond of teaching." She knew he felt strongly, she explained to a fellow officer, that Southerners "must all set to work and if they cannot do what they prefer, do what they can." And while the general spent the last five years of his life transforming the college into a growing institution responsive to the pressing needs of the South, he also became the unofficial leader of the defeated region. Answering washbaskets of mail, he urged ex-Confederates to turn from bitterness and rebellion toward constructive work and cooperation. As admiration for him spread, the editor of the influential *New York Herald* proposed Lee—unpardoned, under possible indictment, and without citizenship—as a presidential candidate against General Grant.

The Lexington Years

When time came to move the family to the college, son Rob was recovering from a bout of the recurring malaria that had earned him the nickname "Robertus Sickus" from his father. Nevertheless, he rode the nearly 200 miles up from Romancoke, the Tidewater farm he had inherited from his grandfather, to escort his mother and sisters Agnes and Mildred to Lexington; sister Mary, as usual, was away visiting. They traveled in a canal barge fitted to accommodate Mrs. Lee's infirmities, and Rob recorded their arrival and first days in Lexington, where most of the entries in the notebook were collected.

By then, wrote Rob, his mother "had to be lifted whenever she moved. When put in her wheel-chair, she could propel herself on a level floor or could move about her room very slowly and with great difficulty on her crutches, but she was always bright, sunny-tempered and uncomplaining, constantly occupied with her books, letters, knitting, and painting for the last of which, she had great talent." Much this same description occurs in the letters and memoirs of other people who knew her.

The general had gone ahead of the family to the college and found the house, once Stonewall Jackson's, "in wretched condition." By the time the family arrived, reported Rob, the Lexington ladies had already hung Martha Washington's curtains and put down rugs rescued earlier from Arlington, the latter "much too large and folded under to suit the reduced size of the rooms." Derwent's owner Mrs. Cocke "had completely furnished" his mother's room, while "Mrs. Margaret J. Preston, the talented and well-known poetess had drawn the designs for the furniture, and a one-armed Confederate soldier had made it all."

Otherwise, furnishings were sparse. An elaborately carved grand piano inset with mother-of-pearl, the gift of its manufacturer, "stood alone in the parlor," where it stands to this day. The family ate with Lee's camp kit until Rob could dig up the blackened Washington silver, buried earlier at nearby Virginia Military Institute (VMI). Mildew had ruined the trunkful of Washington papers hidden with it, and Mrs. Lee cried as they burned. Nevertheless, wrote Rob, "we were all very grateful and happy—glad to get a home—the only one we had had for four years."

Rob also recorded the generosity of their new neighbors: Gleefully, he reported, the general showed off a "goodly array of pickles, preserves and brandy-peaches which our kind neighbors had placed in the store-room. . . . Supplies came pouring in . . . even the poor mountaineers . . . anxious to do something to help General Lee, brought in hand-bags of walnuts, potatoes and game. Such kindness—delicate and considerate always—. . . has never been surpassed in any community." Mrs. Lee recorded many of these gifts in her housekeeping book.

At the end of January 1866, a wagon loaded with more food arrived from a town nearby: hams, a barrel of flour, bushels of corn,

Top: Derwent, where the Lees lived from June to November of 1865. (Sketch by Fred Zimmer)

Bottom: Washington College colonnade, 1867. (Photograph by Michael Miley, courtesy of Special Collections, Leyburn Library, Washington and Lee University)

George Washington Custis Lee, one of four Confederate generals from the Lee family; the others were his father, brother Rooney, and first cousin Fitzhugh Lee. (Courtesy of the Lee family)

crocks of apple and quince butter, along with other provisions. According to the accompanying letter, the bounty had been intended as a New Year's gift, but "this delay is perhaps for the better, in view of the late burglary committed on your premises."

The theft referred to was one of many committed in that time of widespread hunger. Sheridan had kept his promise; a crow flying over the Shenandoah Valley, the breadbasket of the Confederacy, would indeed have had to carry its own rations, and Lexington had suffered much the same destruction as Sherman had inflicted further south. "Even in this little place," wrote Mrs. Lee, "every House has been robbed & even the spring plants pulled up out of our garden." Lexington's explosive mix of bitter, armed, defeated Confederate soldiers; a Union garrison; and freed slaves threatened to erupt. Faced with such unrest, once more Lee did the family shopping while at the same time he worked to maintain peace.

The Lees' young relative Henry Wickham had been one of the college's few wartime students. After Appomattox, he had walked home to find "desolation." His family's reaction, he said, was "like many, many other parents. [They] denied themselves the bare necessities of life that I might go back to Lexington to be under him." With Lee as the magnet, little Washington College drew students rapidly.

In the family's first house at the college, Mrs. Lee had to be carried downstairs and outside. Visitors and young relatives boarding while they went to school crammed the four bedrooms. One of the three living Lee daughters always stayed to keep house and take care of their mother, but in turns the other two went off on frequent visits elsewhere, from necessity as well as inclination.

As the enrollment expanded, Lee helped to plan more buildings, among them a larger president's house. It resembled their beloved Arlington in layout, though not, of course, in size. With his engi-

Mrs. Lee & Her Family

neering background, he may have conceived the ingenious ventilating system that carried away hot air in the summer; it now accommodates air conditioning in what is still the president's house. His wife's downstairs bedroom with bath—surely a rarity then—opened onto a wide verandah, where Lee claimed the privilege of pushing her and Mrs. Ruffner, "one of a long succession [of cats] stretching back to Mr. Custis's Tom Titta," according to Rob.

Even in the new house, space was tight. Son Custis, professor of engineering at nearby VMI, came home to live. People kept visiting the general, and he, ever hospitable, invited more, writing home from one trip that the family should give his room to friends he had met and "put me anywhere." At the first graduation under his tenure, he wrote Rob, "Mildred is full of housekeeping and dresses, and the house is full of young ladies"—there were six more besides the Lees.

General William Henry Fitzhugh ("Rooney") Lee. (Courtesy of the Lee family)

The family lived modestly, and "Mrs. Lee . . . never complained of the plain way of living and lack of money," according to Rose MacDonald, whose mother became an intimate friend of Mrs. Lee. Students came to tea in batches of four or five; "I had imagined it would be rather stiff but was very agreeably disappointed," one commented afterward. In that warm atmosphere, Henry Wickham recalled that he "ran in and out and went many times to Sunday supper," and a young friend of Agnes reminisced, "they had a grand party for me . . . at Natural Bridge. All the nicest beaux and a few of the belles were invited. We drove there in buggies and in carriages. . . . a most beautiful and picturesque drive." The Lees held occasional receptions too, but since food was scarce, they often entertained without it, simply inviting townspeople to meet their houseguests after tea.

That was also the time for "running," when bachelors customarily called on young ladies from house to house. At the Lees', young

Mrs. Lee & Her Family

Top: Mrs. Lee's rolling chair. (Courtesy of Virginia Historical Society)

Bottom: "Robertus Sickus," the general's nickname for Robert E. Lee Jr., who suffered from recurrent malaria. (Courtesy of the Lee family)

General Lee's military camp kit, which the family used during their first days in Lexington. (Courtesy of Virginia Historical Society, print courtesy of National Park Service, Arlington House Collection)

Mrs. Lee & Her Family

people chatted and played the piano in the parlor. Meanwhile the general read newspapers aloud in the dining room to his wife, who, wrote Charles Flood, might well be "darning the underwear of the 'Hero of the South.'" Promptly at ten, Rob recalled, his father "would rise and close the shutters carefully and slowly, and, if that hint was not taken, he would simply say, 'Good night, young gentlemen.'"

Mrs. Lee had always been deeply religious. The day after her husband joked about her casual housekeeping in the early days of their marriage, she had confided in a letter to her mother, "I cannot but feel that he still wants the one thing [abiding faith in God] ... without which all the rest may prove valueless." Long before they arrived in Lexington, he too had come to believe profoundly, and there husband and wife worked to support tiny Grace Church, its congregation described by Lee as "few in number and light of purse."

The general headed the vestry and building committee, and his wife led the sewing society, which often met in her room because leaving it was so difficult for her. With stiff, crippled fingers, she made "housewives"—sewing kits—that sold well to VMI cadets and even pieced a patchwork quilt. She also tinted small photographs of her portraits of General and Mrs. Washington.

The notebook has other evidence of her fund-raising efforts. Her receipt for "caromels" ends, "I believe a great number would be sold at the fair." And a page beginning "28th May boiled 12 hams" seems to record details of a large benefit dinner. After her husband's death, Mary even sold treasured Washington papers to finance the new church he had worked to build. Later it became, and remains, a memorial to him.

The Lees had taken no servants with them to Lexington, but they soon acquired Sam. Mrs. Lee regarded him as "tolerable . . . respectable but not energetic" but saw that he was taken care of when he became ill. Other domestic help came and went, recalled by Rob as "few and unskilled." His mother, confined to her chair, could offer his sisters advice and put receipts in the notebook to help them,

Mrs. Lee & Her Family

The new president's house at Washington College, General and Mrs. Lee's last home, 1870. (Photograph by Michael Miley, courtesy of Special Collections, Leyburn Library, Washington and Lee University)

while their father, according to Rob, "teased [them] about their experiments in cookery and household arts, encouraging them to renewed efforts after lamentable failures. When they succeeded . . . he was lavish with his praise." Mildred especially appreciated his sympathy when "the tomatoe catsup . . . would explode!" But basically, cooking and housekeeping was up to the daughters.

They were not alone in having a lot to learn. Mary Coulling cites a study made twenty years after Appomattox that asked Southern "'high-born ladies'" how the war had most changed their lives: "'All said that doing their own work or adjusting to hired Negro domestics was their major postwar problem.'"

Although today Lexington seems charming and old-fashioned, in the late 1860s "the grim portals of the Presbyterian church looked cold as a dog's nose," John S. Wise recalled in 1890. "The cedar hedges in the yards . . . were as unsentimental as mathematics." And

Mrs. Lee & Her Family

The Lee family parlors in Lexington. (Courtesy of Virginia Historical Society, print courtesy of National Park Service, Arlington House Collection)

while the people welcomed them generously, to the Lee daughters the town was a social backwater.

"They don't seem to like Lexington much," Marshall McDonald wrote to his fiancée after meeting Agnes and Mary, adding that he admired Agnes's "seeming haughtiness & reserve" but suspected that her manner "offends these Lexingtonians." The young Lee women went ice skating, the McDonalds' daughter Rose remembered, when in the town's opinion "no lady skates; if she does, it is a Yankee lady." She also recalled the comment caused when Mary and Agnes did not return from a sleigh ride with VMI officers until the shocking hour of eight in the evening.

In time, the three Lee daughters started the Reading Club, where young ladies and gentlemen could meet. (To their amused father, it was "a great institution for the discussion of apples and chestnuts, but . . . quite innocent of the pleasures of literature.") And they found

Mrs. Lee & Her Family

other ways to make friends and make Lexington more to their liking. Custis arranged a dance at VMI that lasted until the musicians left at three in the morning, but only Virginia reels, the lancers, and the quadrille were allowed. "Round dancing," where partners held each other, "would have brought down 'phials of rath' . . . from Presbyterian Lexington," in Rose's opinion.

Daughters Who Did Not Marry

Marriage was a woman's identity in Southern society before the war, and outward events, even disasters, do not change deeply rooted values quickly. Yet all of the Lee daughters remained single. "I am not in the least anxious to part with them," their mother declared straightforwardly, "yet I think it quite time, if they intend to change their condition [that they marry]." Their father, "though apparently always willing to have another daughter," wrote Rob, "did not seem to long for any more sons." Lee himself acknowledged, "I know it will require a tussle for anyone to get my children [daughters] from me, and beyond that I do not wish to know."

This professed reluctance has led some historians to hold Lee accountable for his daughters' single status. But, reasoned my aunt, "Who was there to marry?" By the end of the war one-fourth of all white men between the ages of twenty and twenty-nine were dead, and even in 1870 when Mildred, the youngest, was twenty-four, Virginia had 15,000 more white women than men. It was not only the Lee daughters who remained single.

Daughter Annie had a facial deformity due to a childhood accident and died during the war at age twenty-three, with little chance to marry. Agnes, the loveliest, may never have recovered emotionally from the bizarre death of her sweetheart, Orton Williams. Mary, twenty-six when the war started, had had time to marry before, but she was an unlikely candidate at best, extremely forceful and far from pretty in a time when the ideal female was sweet, biddable, and beautiful.

In my opinion, it was sensitive, affectionate, vulnerable Mildred who should have had a husband. Only fifteen when the war started, she received at least one proposal afterward, and late in life confessed to her intimate friend Emily Hay that she not only longed for her own home and family but felt the "need of *someone* to take care of me." Yet in her journal she wrote of her father, "to me he seems a Hero—& all other men small in comparison." Yes, Lee was an impediment, but how much was he to blame?

In *Lee, the Last Years*, Charles Flood demonstrates the general's resistance to losing his daughters by quoting him: "Dr. Barton [a widower and Lee's doctor] has arrived to bid adieu and to give Mildred an opportunity of looking her best. I believe he is the last rose of summer. The others, with their fragrance and thorns, have all departed." If that is his strongest statement of opposition—and I know of no stronger—I doubt that he would have seriously opposed any of his daughters' marrying any man he considered worthy. Once

Mrs. Lee & Her Family

again, I suspect, Lee's playful way with words has led to his being misunderstood.

Agnes: A Minor Mystery

Unquestionably, Agnes took an active part in Lexington social life, reporting gaily to Mildred about a Reading Club meeting, "ours, everyone said, was a real success. . . . Mary and I worked hard [to make things go]." She gave and received many of the small gifts of food that seem to have characterized Southern women's exchanges after the war the way flower starts and seeds had before it. "A thousand thanks for the elegant jelly," she wrote once. "Won't you make Hannah [probably the cook] sensible of our appreciation . . . by giving her this handkerchief 'all the way from Baltimore.'" She did her share of housekeeping, too, commenting, "I . . . find it quite a chore with an ignorant girl for a cook & the mistress no wiser."

Yet her writing cannot be identified in the notebook. Did she go through the expected social motions without caring enough to ask anyone for receipts or collect ways to make housework easier? I do not know. Handwriting changes; I, a nonexpert, would never have guessed that several samples of daughter Mary Custis's are all from the same hand. Other entries are so carelessly scrawled they must have been written by a family member or an intimate, whom I could not identify.

Mary, the "Loose Horse"

Of her Aunt Mary, my aunt, who remembered both Mary and Mildred well, said firmly, "we [she and my mother] hated her." On visits to her brother Rob's home at Romancoke, Aunt Mary expected to be waited on, while everyone else worked hard. As an example of the family's life there, my aunt told about the time President Theodore Roosevelt came to call unexpectedly. Her mother was on hands and

Mrs. Lee & Her Family

knees cleaning out the chicken house. "I must have been very little," my aunt recalled, "Mother wouldn't let me help. But I remember she just said, 'Ask Mr. Roosevelt to wait,' and I suppose she changed her dress." Aunt Mary would have been right there to meet the president, but otherwise she wouldn't have lifted a finger.

Lexingtonians felt much the same way about "Miss Mary," although the adults described her more diplomatically, calling her "wholly devoid of fear," "strong but somewhat eccentric," and "a very masterful type." When Aunt Mary returned to the college after her family had left, the townspeople held their breath until Aunt Mary decided whose household she would descend on, sending the children on innumerable errands and rewarding them with what they considered worthless trinkets from her travels. The granddaughter of Judge Brockenbrough remembers the time she and a little friend were roller-skating on campus, and "Miss Mary leaned out a window and told us, 'Do something useful. Get off those skates and pick up that trash.'"

But Aunt Mary was competent, and she could command. On one of her long walks in the countryside, she came upon a man beating his horse, which was mired with his wagon in the mud. She ordered him to stop, showed him how to free the animal, and then told the YMCA to invite him to Sunday school. Eventually the man gave up strong drink and became a model citizen and chapelgoer.

Aunt Mary could organize, too. In 1866 or 1867 she took part (no doubt a large part) in an effort to raise money for destitute southern widows and orphans. When custom dictated that a lady's name appear in the newspaper only when she married and when she died (debuts had been added by my day), the names of many prominent southern women appeared publicly for the first time. The event raised huge sums from the sale of donated handwork, including a pillow embroidered by Mary Custis, priced at an extraordinary thirty dollars.

My aunt called Aunt Mary "a loose horse," saying "She went

Top: The girl on the right is very likely the Lees' daughter Annie, shown here with sister Agnes (center) and probably two Stuart cousins. If so, this may be the only known likeness of "Little Raspberry," who had a birthmark on her right cheek and a facial deformity, which may explain why she alone is shown in profile. (Courtesy of a private collection)

Bottom left: Juliet Carter, the second Mrs. Robert E. Lee Jr. and the author's maternal grandmother. (Courtesy of the Lee family)

Bottom right: Robert E. Lee Jr. and his elder daughter, the author's mother. (Courtesy of the Lee family)

Mrs. Lee & Her Family

· 54 ·

Mary Custis Lee signed herself "Lady Lee" on the back of this photograph taken in India, which she sent as a Christmas card. (Courtesy of Virginia Historical Society)

Mrs. Lee & Her Family

where she wanted, when she wanted to." Although all the Lee ladies found themselves behind shifting enemy lines during the war, the others crossed back as quickly as possible. Aunt Mary, however, ensconced herself at Cedar Grove, the Stuart cousins' plantation, and refused to leave. She was completely cut off from the family, for her father would not risk his scouts by sending them to her. When Jeb Stuart sent soldiers to rescue her, she refused to budge.

Aunt Mary did her share of housekeeping dutifully; she even collected receipts in the notebook. But even before her parents died she traveled abroad incessantly, covering most of Europe and spending years off and on in Paris during the glittering Belle Epoque. She took Mildred, who preferred staying home, to the Arctic Circle, went alone to Australia, and traveled to India, where she passed a Christmas at a maharajah's court. Hong Kong, Ceylon, Java, Japan, Russia, Canada, and Bermuda are among other places she visited.

And Aunt Mary was no ordinary traveler. In Istanbul she went into Hagia Sophia, then a mosque, disguised as a Muslim man, when as either a woman or an infidel she would have been killed had she been discovered. When she wanted to join a party headed for Egypt and the members declined her company, Lord Kitchener sent a ship to take her. She would have been the first white woman to canoe up the Congo River if she had been able to fit the Methodist Bishop of Africa's invitation into her schedule.

Aunt Mary took shameless advantage of her father's fame. When she was not invited to a grand social event in a German principality, she wondered out loud why the daughter of America's greatest general had been left out. The next day an invitation arrived, addressed to Miss Grant. The story was often chuckled over during my childhood, but in all fairness, noted my aunt, Aunt Mary told of her embarrassment herself, with a twinkle in her eye. (Another Lee cousin, May Minnegerode Andrews, included that episode and others equally unflattering in her *Memoirs of a Poor Relation*. But, said my aunt, "Uncle Rozier said when May was a little girl, she crawled under a piano and ate a wasp, and there's been a little wasp in May ever since." Sometimes I wonder how much history is based on such suspect accounts.)

Mildred's *"Something* To Love"

Perhaps if Aunt Mary had been a man or born later, she might have been appreciated more and been easier to get along with. As it was, when Mildred was packing to leave Lexington in 1897, she confided to her friend Emily Hay, "I try to steel myself against her sharp words . . . but now, weak and wretched as I am, [she] is doubly hard to bear."

The youngest Lee daughter could not have been more different from her oldest sister. My aunt recalled Mildred's fretting over my mother's mistakes in learning the catechism but otherwise remembered her as "very sweet," although, like Mrs. Lee, bitter over losing Arlington. Mildred put many receipts in the notebook, and probably solicited more from her friends. Her letters teem with cooking: canning peaches, making jelly, preserves, and ice cream. To raise money for a church in Peewee, Kentucky, she sent family recipes to *Famous Foods of Famous People*, she and a bishop being the only Virginians notable enough to include.

Nevertheless, Aunt Mildred disliked cooking; she wrote Emily with genuine feeling cloaked in whimsical humor not unlike her father's, *"food* is a subject beneath my genius. . . . Get me a cook!" At least later in life, she did not enjoy the constant flow of visitors, either. "Miss Mildred has a house full of company, a thing she cannot abide," observed one friend.

However, she seems to have tolerated and sometimes even enjoyed her domestic role. "Papa is always unwilling to spare me—you know I am the housekeeper & very important," she wrote lightly in one letter. Her amused father reported his own view: "she expends her energies in regulating her brother [Custis]. . . . rules her nephews

Mrs. Lee & Her Family

with an iron rod, and scatters her advice broadcast among the young men of the college. . . . The young mothers of Lexington ought to be extremely grateful to her for her suggestions."

He wrote fondly, for Mildred, said Rob, "was always my father's pet as a little girl." Later, after Appomattox, they took those long night walks together in Richmond, and when the two nursed Agnes through typhoid fever at Derwent, Lee had confided in a letter to Rooney, "Mildred is my only reliance and support." Later she too came down with typhoid and, according to Rob, "would have no one but my father nurse her, and could not sleep unless she had his hand in hers. Night after night he sat by her side, watching over her with gentleness and patience." Convalescing before Christmas, "she enumerated, just in fun, all the presents she wished—a long list. . . . when Christmas morning came she found each article . . . not one omitted"—supplied, Rob implied, by their father.

Writing of a trip the two made on horseback to the Peaks of Otter, Mildred remarked that everyone along the way recognized the general and that the children from one mountain cabin had run home to wash their faces in his honor. Father and daughter spent a night with some Burwell cousins, where, Mildred recalled, "Papa was much amused when I appeared in crinoline, my 'hoops' having been squeezed into the saddle-bags." Then they continued to Captain Buford's, to pay him for sheltering the Lee ladies on their way to Richmond. Buford, however, refused the money, and "shortly after," sent Mildred a fine Jersey cow, on condition, she reported, "that I would get up early every morning and milk her, and also send him a part of the butter I made."

This gallant, whimsical, gentle woman loved pets. At Arlington, where each child had a garden, she buried her cats in hers. "Ah, the burning tears I have dropped upon those graves," she recalled. With

Mrs. Lee & Her Family

no pets in wartime Richmond, she caught and tried to tame a squirrel that she named Custis Morgan, after her oldest brother and the celebrated raider, because the captive kept escaping. Between battles, her father proposed to no effect that the animal show his "patriotism" by becoming "squirrel soup, thickened with peanuts." Still without pets at Derwent, Mildred named chickens after her friends and found them "a great comfort."

In Lexington, she acquired Tom—"surnamed The Nipper, from the manner he slaughters our enemies, the rats and mice," explained her father—and Sidney Baxter, named for an ancient former Washington College president. The latter cat Lee described as "the fashionable color of 'moonlight on the water,' apparently a dingy hue of the kitchen."

But pets were not enough. After a visit to Romancoke, she confided to Emily, "my two precious nieces occupied my entire mind and heart. One must have *something* to love in this world."

Mildred's "something to love": the author's mother and aunt. (Courtesy of the Lee family)

The Last, Sad Years

After the general's death, Custis succeeded his father as president of the college even though the eldest Lee son, first in his class at West Point (his father had been second), was well aware that he did not enjoy academic life. He had tried to resign as professor of engineering at VMI after only eighteen months, and had recently declined another college presidency, writing that he was "not so well fitted for the important and responsible duties involved in the education of the young, as for more active pursuits."

But the college, renamed Washington and Lee after his father's death, was threatened with disintegration, and his sisters and crip-

Custis Lee, president of Washington and Lee College, 1870–1897, by Benjamin West Clinedinst. (Courtesy of Washington/ Custis/Lee Collection, Washington and Lee University, Lexington, Va.)

pled mother had nowhere else to go. The college's trustees had tried to give the general the new president's house, but again Lee had refused, as he had in Richmond. Nor did Custis himself have a home, for that matter.

Arlington had been intended for him, the eldest son, but during the war the federal government had taken over the estate for nonpayment of $92.07 in taxes. (What seems to have been a special law required the assessment to be paid in person. Ailing and possibly subject to arrest if she appeared, Mrs. Lee sent the money by a kinsman, but it was refused. Finally, after the war and several suits, the Supreme Court awarded Arlington to Custis Lee in 1882. But by then, the grounds were covered with 40,000 graves. Having no desire to live among them, he accepted $150,000 for the house and 1,100 acres.

The eldest Lee son also ailed physically, quite possibly from the same rheumatoid arthritis that tormented his mother. Lexington rumor said he drank too much, and perhaps he did, to counteract what seems to have been a deepening depression. During twenty-seven years as president of the college, he tendered his resignation six times before it was accepted, in 1897. By then, the once punctilious Custis did not leave his darkened room to greet his successor.

During all this time, Mildred had remained with him in Lexington, with frequent long visits to Rob, who was farming land left to him by George Washington Parke Custis. Mary Custis traveled abroad extensively, returning only for occasional visits until the outbreak of World War I. She was not at home for her father's funeral in 1870 or three years later, when Agnes, then Mrs. Lee, followed him.

In 1897 Mildred, the youngest of the Lee children, and Custis, the eldest, left the once overflowing house in Lexington. From then on, Mildred spent the fall and winter months with Rob at Romancoke on the Pamunkey River and the rest of the year in the Virginia

Mrs. Lee & Her Family

mountains or traveling with Mary Custis. Custis went to live with Tabb, his brother Rooney's widow, at Ravensworth. There he seems to have recovered his spirits. My aunt, who remembered him as a whimsical, gentle man, said he spent most of the time during visits playing with her and my mother. When the little girls got into mischief, he used to say, mock solemnly, "they *told* me to do it," to divert their punishment. She also recalled that he financed an addition to Romancoke, so the little girls could have a room of their own.

Mrs. Lee & Her Family

The Notebook

Mary Lee and her daughters kept receipts and other domestic jottings in a little cardboard notebook. Shabby now, it has a cover bound in rusty red tape and decorated with a delicate, diagonal design in what was perhaps once more definitely green. It measures 6 by 7¾ inches and has 152 pages, many of them blank and others pinned and pasted over. Four lists inside bear a relationship to its title, "China Glass &c." The rest of the text mixes personal and household miscellanea with 120 or so receipts, with cooking spatters that speak of much use in the kitchen. To me, its complete lack of pretense is one of its chief charms.

Clearly this was no systematic, objective household manual; plenty of those were in print already by the mid-nineteenth century. Instead it is an intimate, frustratingly fragmentary pastiche of the past. The Lees' eight-year-old niece Mildred, daughter of Robert's brother Charles, drew in it and practiced her signature. Some of the household hints it contains expose unromantic underpinnings of Victorian home life, while a page headed "Rect. for a pleasant evening" conjures up its gentle amusements. Mrs. Lee's many lists are almost bits of autobiography in the raw. And dangerous arthritis remedies reveal her desperate search for relief from that painful, crippling ailment.

In the lists she wrote herself, we confront Mrs. Lee's arthritis directly. On some days, even during the year she died, she could write a legible letter; on others, she could not write at all. In the notebook, she was unconcerned about anyone else being able to read it, and her small, cramped script varies from hard to almost impossible to decipher.

Books like this provided much of our sparse information about domestic history before it became a respectable field of study. They record female folklore, handed down from mother to daughter in the American South and probably many other areas of the literate world. Many more like it still gather dust in archives and old cupboards, their own tales left untold.

The Lee family notebook along with three other closely related, earlier housekeeping books also allow us glimpses of one family's food, a view that may be uniquely long-term, stretching from perhaps as far back as Elizabethan England up into the early twentieth century.

The Notebook's Forebears

The first of these other three books, edited with copious notes by food historian Karen Hess and published as *Martha Washington's Booke of Cookery and Booke of Sweetmeats*, actually goes back much further than the first First Lady: it was probably copied about 1650 or before from an even older manuscript. The second—also edited for reissue by Ms. Hess, who calls it "the most influential American cookbook of the nineteenth century"—is *The Virginia House-Wife*, written by Mrs. Lee's cousin and reputed godmother, Mary Randolph. First published in 1824, it went through numerous editions and reprintings and was often plagiarized. The third, *Nelly Custis*

The Notebook

Lewis's Housekeeping Book, was compiled between 1830 and 1840 by Nelly Custis Lewis, Mary Lee's aunt and Martha Washington's granddaughter (and daughter—the Washingtons adopted her). This too has been edited in modern times, by Patricia Brady Schmit. The regrettably few dates in the Lee family notebook range from 1860 to 1890, but Mildred, the youngest Lee daughter, who wrote in many receipts and whose friends entered more, lived until 1905.

What I will call the Washington manuscript probably arrived in Virginia from England in the mid-seventeenth century with the beautiful Frances Culpeper. At a time when death, not divorce, made multiple marriages common, she married three colonial governors in a row. Eventually, through complex marital alliances of powerful early Virginians, the book passed to Martha Dandridge Custis, who took it to Mount Vernon when she became the wife of George Washington.

Mrs. Randolph wrote her cookbook after she and her husband (and first cousin) David fell on hard times. A cousin of Mary Lee, as well as her probable godmother, she seems to have been close to the family; she is the only person who did not live at Arlington who was buried there before the aftermath of the Civil War, when the grounds were covered with graves of the new National Cemetery. Also a descendant of "King" Carter (and of Pocahontas too), she was a cousin of Thomas Jefferson but, with her husband, kept a glittering anti-Jefferson salon. After the election of 1800, David Randolph lost his high government post, and Mary began keeping a series of boarding houses.

Long before publishing her landmark cookbook, Mrs. Randolph was celebrated as the best cook in Virginia. In 1800, when self-styled General Gabriel planned a slave rebellion that failed, he vowed to spare only one white person, Mrs. Randolph, to cook for him and be his queen. One lodger found this remarkable lady not only charming but "possessing a masculine mind"—a high compliment in those patriarchal times. Richmond tradition claims that a "shrewd Yankee"

The Notebook

boarder copied what Mrs. Randolph called her "refrigerator," patented it, and made a fortune before electric refrigerators replaced what we now call the icebox.

Nelly Custis received the Washington manuscript from her grandmother when she married Lawrence Lewis, and she used the same curious format to compile her own housekeeping book. Both, says editor Schmit, are "divided into two parts—starting at opposite ends of the volume with sections back to back and upside down in relation to one another, separated in the middle of the book by blank pages" (curious as this arrangement seems, it was not, apparently, all that unusual). Mary Lee contributed receipts to the Custis book and may well have known the Washington book as well; she was close to her aunt Nelly and went to nurse her when she was dying.

Published housekeeping books were rare when Frances Culpeper took the comprehensive Washington manuscript to the New World in the mid-1600s, where it may well have served as her only source of domestic information. More printed information was available by the time Nelly compiled hers, perhaps for her eldest daughter. The girl faced married life in the wilds of Louisiana, which may account for the snakebite remedies and Martha Washington's cure for worms along with other Washington receipts. The directions for coating paper for painting, grinding and mixing paint, and painting on wood

The Notebook

reflect the mother's (and perhaps the daughter's) interest in painting, and those related to taxidermy, the interest of her son Lorenzo, if not her new son-in-law. Some dishes come from servants and newspapers, others from relatives, including Mrs. Lee and her mother; many are from a French cookbook and several others from that recently published cooking sensation, Mary Randolph's *The Virginia House-wife*.

Contributors to the Lee Notebook

The Washington and Custis manuscripts are both primarily in one person's handwriting, and Mrs. Randolph clearly composed her book herself. But dozens of different people wrote in the Lee notebook, a practice common when it was compiled. All but one of the receipts written in Mrs. Lee's own cramped hand seem meant to help her daughters cope with their new duties in Lexington as hands-on cooks. Single entries by the girls and various other donors probably record dishes that intrigued the Misses Lee when they dined out or paid longer visits, a favorite pastime. Several sets of pages all in the same writing suggest that friends shared their repertoires or even their cookbooks. (It is not known whether the Lees owned a published cookbook in Lexington.) One collection of entries in a conscientious copybook script brings to mind a young girl practicing her penmanship, perhaps not entirely voluntarily; I have nicknamed this writer "Superneat." Many receipts are identified by donor, but others were scribbled in so casually that they must be from intimates whose identities have been lost to time.

The Notebook

Snow Pudding

Soak one oz of gelatine in one pint of cold water for an hour. Place it over the fire, stir it and take it off as soon as it ~~stands~~ is dis-solved. When nearly cold, beat it to a stiff froth with a syllabub churn.

Beat the whites of three eggs to a stiff froth, and add this to the gelatine froth together with the juice of 3 lemons and pulverized sugar to your taste. Mix the whole well together, pour into a mould, and set aside to cool

To be eaten with cream or custard

Help from Without

Perhaps because receipt contributors could explain in person what they did not write down, some directions in the notebook are even more minimal than was usual in cookbooks published about the same time. One of these proved particularly useful in filling in blanks and explaining cooking techniques probably used by the Lee ladies. Compiled by Marion Cabell Tyree and published in 1879, *Housekeeping in Old Virginia* features receipts collected from "two hundred and fifty of Virginia's noted housewives," among them Mildred and Mrs. Lee. Not one for false modesty, Mrs. Tyree called her book *"the most admirable system of domestic art known in our country"* (emphasis hers), but it is also an unintentionally awe-inspiring picture of the rigors of Victorian kitchen life. She warns cooks, for example, to check flour for weevils and to dry it in front of the fire and gives lengthy details about how and when to kill, pluck, and clean poultry. Her directions for straining wine, making gelatin (more of both later), and innumerable other processes leave this modern cook incredulous.

Mrs. Tyree's book is invaluable for learning how dishes were made in their own time, but until recently few people cared. Too often so-called historical receipts tend to reflect contemporary tastes and conditions. For example, in one book of colonial era receipts published during the Depression, the thrifty editor and adaptor wrote: "The author was sometimes guilty of using twice as many eggs as necessary . . . of adding cream where milk would have done as well, of calling for two or more fowls instead of one lone hen. . . . Soups . . . as originally made . . . are too rich and fulsome." One wonders what was left after all the sumptuous richness of the original receipts was removed.

Today we worry about health more than costs, and I for one am not against compromise, as long as the adaptation is not passed off as the original. (See "Calories and Cholesterol," page 100, and com-

The Notebook

ments on individual receipts.) Better to adapt them than forget them entirely.

Problems Within

The Lee ladies never intended their notebook for outside eyes, and so we can hardly blame them for an organization whose sole principle seems to be, what was pasted or pinned on top of another entry must have been put in later. Their approach makes understanding many of the entries tricky. For example, Mrs. Lee's list that begins "18 hams all of them cooked" at first seems to symbolize the opulent plantation life in the prewar South. But when the people in the rest of the list are identified, it suggests a very different story: most of them lived in Lexington, and the list records supplies and their donors for a church fund-raiser held after the war, when life was far from lavish.

Thus, discovering the identity of the people in the notebook became essential, and sometimes it raised more questions than it answered. What was their relationship to the family, and what does that say about why the receipts are there—and by extension, about the times? As for the receipts, what do they reveal about cooking then? Have ingredients changed? (Yes.) Equipment? (Definitely.) Can we really reproduce them? (Only with care and labor.) Approximate them closely? (Usually easily.) If so, how did they taste, and will we like what the Lees liked? There is so much to ask about, literally, the taste of the past.

Slowly, as information accumulated, I began to see the entries in this shabby little notebook as so many windows, through which to glimpse, sometimes only dimly and ambiguously, other lives and times, answering fragments of that bigger question that can never be fully answered: What was it really like?

The Notebook

Mary Lee made lists: lists of people she wanted to thank, lists of grocery prices, lists of children named for her husband (and one for her), lists detailing her efforts to clothe ragged, barefoot Confederate troops. We cannot assume that any of them tells a complete story, but the glimpses are tantalizing.

The four earliest lists, the only ones she did not write herself, may have been entered by Selina Gray, the housekeeper at Arlington, although I have found none of her writing elsewhere to compare to them. They begin ambitiously with the date January 1, 1857. By then both of Mary's parents, the Custises, had died and the Lees were at Arlington, Mary editing her father's memoirs—all related to Washington—and writing her own recollection of Mr. Custis for inclusion in it. Her husband, the only active executor of the estate, was winding up three years spent mostly untangling the affairs of his father-in-law, whose lack of system equaled the breadth of his interests, and attending to military duties, which included command of the capture of John Brown.

True to the label on the notebook's cover, "China glass &c.," these four lists seem to be inventories, but they are puzzling. Two record the same glass and china, except that twelve custard cups on one list have dwindled to only two tops on the other, perhaps a sign of some small domestic disaster. A house the size of Arlington must have had more dinner plates and goblets than the two dozen of each listed here. We know that Washington owned seven Order of the Cincinnati soup tureens. Presumably they went to Arlington, but only one tureen, the pattern not indicated, shows up in the lists (broken in February and not replaced until March), although soup at dinner was all but inevitable.

And so it goes. No kitchen sugar nippers, which were essential for dealing with the hard loaf sugar of the time. No ice cream freezer, when we know that the Lee daughters loved ice cream. A dearth of

Broken in Jan 1860.

1	wine glass.	Jan. 10
1	glass chimney of lamp	12th
1	kitchen fork lost	11th
1	White china Tea pot.	Jan 5th

Feb 1860

1	white china Soup tureen	
1	wineglass —	
1	large iron & iron. kitchen.	
1	tea cup.	Feb 23rd

March

1	dinner plate	9th

April

1	goblet	9th
1	goblet	28th

May

1	iron poker	1st
1	goblet	7th
		23rd

June

1	finger bowl

knives, forks, spoons, and other cooking necessities. And the list of breakage by the month stops with June. Puzzling over the incompleteness of it all, I began to feel an eerie connection to Mrs. Lee. Her interest in, and perhaps talent for, organizing seems to have been as minimal as my own. Perhaps her father bequeathed us both that tendency.

Opposite:
The breakage list, one of the early inventories in the notebook, promised a systematic approach that did not last. (Courtesy of Virginia Historical Society)

Namesakes

The most startling aspect of the list headed "Children named after Genl. Lee many of them godchildren" is its brevity: only thirty-four names. The first fifteen are undated; then come four under "July 26th 1866," one more following "May 20th 1867," and the rest under "Sept. 2," presumably also in 1867. Although most of the namesakes predictably lived in Virginia and the ex-Confederacy, five were in Union states, three of them in Ohio.

Either the list was incomplete or these children were the first of many more, for Mary's husband was fast becoming a mythic figure. On November 28, 1867, after their son Rooney's second wedding, crowds in Petersburg tried to unhitch Lee's carriage and pull it through the streets. They stopped, wrote Rob, only when his father declared that "if they did so, he would have to get out and help them." Three years later when (to his dismay) Lee's visit to his daughter Annie's grave in North Carolina turned into a triumphal tour, Agnes reported that "namesakes appeared along the way, of all sizes. . . . dressed to their eyes, with . . . tiny cards in their little fat hands—with their names."

Virginia Lee Letcher, who heads the list, was the daughter of the Confederate governor of Virginia and his wife, who contributed a luscious eggnog to the notebook. After the war, the Letcher family returned home to Lexington, where the six-year-old met the general, mounted on his horse Traveller. When the little girl asked him to

The Notebook

make her baby sister go home, Lee scooped up the tiny offender. "There she sat in royal contentment, and was thus grandly escorted home," recalled Rob. As Virginia explained to her embarrassed mother, "'I couldn't make Fan go home, and I thought *he* could do anything.'"

The Knitting Factory

Mary Lee's nephew Fitzhugh Lee remembered her in Richmond as "almost unable to move, but busily engaged in knitting socks for sockless soldiers." Many women came to help her and her daughters, neighbor Sally Nelson Robins recalled, some "to work, the disheartened . . . for comfort." Mrs. Lee "listened, and strengthened, and smiled. . . . The brightness of her nature, amidst uncertainty and pain, was wonderful." By the winter of 1863, "her room was like an industrial school," Mrs. Chesnut noted. "What a rebuke to the taffy parties!"

The enterprise probably started in 1861, when General Lee asked his wife for a half dozen pairs of socks and then, characteristically, gave them away. The first, he told her, went to Perry, his servant from Arlington, "as a present from you." The next he intended for his cook, Meredith, because he "will have no one near him but me to supply him." But, Lee wrote his wife, "should any sick man require them first, he shall have them."

Mrs. Lee did not begin keeping track in the notebook until December of 1864, when she entered "received 25 lb yarn" on the left side of a page, and then in a rough column under it, the numbers of pounds, bales, and hanks of cotton and wool that arrived. Next to each she noted whether it came from the government or her "yarn scouts" all over the South; then whether it was donated, came from the Confederate government, or whether she herself had paid for it, as she did for much of the supply. She did not add the subtotals on

The Notebook

Children named after Genl. Lee — many of them
(God Children

Virginia Lee Letcher god child		Va
Ashby Lee Baker		Baltimore
Robert Lee Potestad		Washington
Robert Lee Thomas		Baltimore
Eva Lee Landis St Joseph		Missouri
Fannie Lee Smith		
Robert Lee Johnson	Bairdstown	Kentucky
Katie Lee Brooke	Baltimore	Maryland
Alice Lee Cooke	Louisville	Kentucky
Robert Lee Clinton		Louisiana
Roberta Lee Fleming		Alexandria Va
Robert Lee Cline 105 East 2d Street	Cincinatti	Ohio
Johnatta Lee Morgan	Nashville	Tennessee
Lee Crute	Huntsville	Alabama
Mary Lee Pendley Lithonia		Georgia
Maggie Lee Godwin	Petersburgh	Va
1866, Robert Lee Graham	Adairville	Georgia Bartow Cy
Robt, E Lee Howell	Marietta	Geogia
Robert E, Lee Hollinsworth	New Orleans	Louisiana
Mary C Lee Downing Ripley Brown Cy		Ohio

The horse and rider (by then in civvies) who took the Letcher toddler home. (Photograph by Michael Miley, courtesy of the Lee family)

the right, but they amount to 859 pairs of socks and 190 pairs of gloves.

As the end of the Confederacy approached, perhaps Lee, who "had always been noted for his attention to small things," according to son Rob, took comfort in counting socks and teasing his wife about her weak arithmetic. "Here are sixty-seven pairs . . . instead of sixty-four," he wrote her once. But he made no secret of how desperately the soldiers needed them. "I have sent two hundred and sixty-three pairs [in all to the Stonewall Brigade]. Still . . . about one hundred and forty . . . are without socks." Later, "four hundred men [are] barefooted and over a thousand without blankets." And a few months before Petersburg fell, he wrote, "if two or three hundred would send an equal number, we should have a sufficiency."

The Notebook

Three times that I know of during the war and its aftermath Mrs. Lee received huge gifts of food, remarkable outpourings of generosity in times of scarcity. She detailed two of these gifts with their donors, presumably to thank them. The third does not appear in the notebook. It arrived with its own list of contributors, and so she had no need to record them.

The first gift reached Richmond in January of 1865 when the knitting was going strong, Mrs. Lee was ill, and food was extremely scarce. One family could not possibly use the huge quantity that is recorded: ten barrels of flour, thirty pounds of butter, and equally large quantities of other staples. Since most donors were Mary Lee's relatives and friends, I suspect she asked them to send the supplies and distributed them.

Cousin Julia (Stuart) sent five hams and "sundries for the girls" from Cedar Grove, the plantation that willful daughter Mary Custis had refused to leave during the war. A barrel of apples came from T. J. (Thomas Jefferson) Randolph, a name thoroughly intertwined with Lees. Among other names that indicate membership in the cousinage are Wickham (Mrs. Wickham of Hickory Hill was a Carter), Stribling, Wellford, and Williams.

Residents of the Tidewater, as the center of colonial Virginian power and government was called, were Episcopalian. Presbyterian Lexington was settled later, and the people of the two cities are usually considered quite separate. The list of food donors shows, however, that by the 1860s members of several Tidewater families were living in or near Lexington. The husband of Mrs. Burwell could have been Thomas S., who lived in town, or Nathaniel, in nearby Liberty. Jones was also a cousinage name, and Mrs. Jones may have been the wife of J. H. B. Jones, headmaster of Lexington's Ann Smith Academy for young ladies. Miss Jenny Bacon, her surname prominent in Tidewater history, lived where the Lexington cemetery is now.

December 1864 received 25 lb yarn

Sent to the army socks that came in bales

ll m one knit of government wool yarn   1,30
     of cotton   200

Sent by Mrs Dangerfield cotton yarn free   34

15th	30 pr free socks	30
For	20 pr government	20
Jan 1	20 prs socks 4 pr free	20
Received	50 pr gloves 30 prs=80	50
50 lb yarn	sent 60 prs socks	60
4 bales	sent 20 prs socks	20
cotton	sent 62 prs socks	62
200 „	sent 50 prs do	50
wool yarn	50 prs do	50
4 bales	30 prs gloves	
Cotton do		
February	58 prs & 100 prs	1 58 „
Received	100 71 prs & 5 prs gloves	74
131 lbs	80 prs 7 prs	87
grey yarn	50 prs 50 prs	1 00
Major	82 prs 50 prs 30, 18 pr 22	2 02
Ferguson	50 prs 50 prs 50 prs	

Other contributors from the Lexington area probably had no Tidewater or kinship ties to the Lees. Mrs. Lee, Agnes, and Mary had stayed during the war with Captain Buford, who sent a barrel of apples, a turkey, and twelve "fowls." After the war, General Lee and Mildred tried to reimburse him on their ride to the Peaks of Otter, but the captain not only refused their money but sent Mildred her rare Jersey cow. Like others—including John Stewart, owner of "the Mess" in Richmond, who declared he would accept payment only in the worthless Confederate money for which it was rented—Buford honored the general with what he had.

Food for the Family

When Mrs. Lee arrived in Lexington, people in the town, college, and countryside had already stocked her house with a dizzying profusion of edibles. Her list of donors and their gifts, headed "[illegible] Presents from 1st December 1865," includes the wives of the college's "big four" professors. Mrs. White, herself among the Lexington elite, contributed pickles, preserves, and rolls. Her husband, the Greek professor called "Old Zeus" (surely only behind his back), had led the little college's student body off to war and would become the new president's closest colleague; during their long rides together, Lee, who almost never mentioned the war, confided his conviction that if Stonewall Jackson had been at Gettysburg, the South would have won.

"Old Nick," husband of Mrs. Harris (jelly, blanc mange, butter, "etc. and other things"), taught Latin and, judging from his first name, Carter, could have been kin to the Lees. The second wife of the math professor, Mrs. Nelson (apples and jelly), raised eight children, four from a previous wife and four of her own. Mrs. Campbell, wife of the science professor and mother of nine, brought the Lees butter, lard, rolls, jelly, and salsify, a coarse, gray root vegetable also called

The Notebook

Cousin Julia Calvert Stuart of Cedar Grove. (Portrait by Thomas Sully, courtesy of the Robert E. Lee Memorial Association, Stratford Hall Plantation)

oyster plant because it tastes (only vaguely) of oysters. It was still common when I was a child, and I loathed it.

The only bottle of wine on the list and several other offerings came from perhaps the most talented and colorful lady in Lexington. At a time when most women derived their identity from marriage, Margaret Junkin Preston was known as the Poetess of the South, due to her popular heroic poem "Beechenbrook." Her father had been president of Washington College, and she was sister-in-law to Stonewall Jackson and Elizabeth Cocke (owner of Derwent). Her husband, Colonel J. T. L. Preston, founded VMI and for years constituted half of the Institute's faculty.

The husband of Mrs. Boude ("a turkey every Tuesday" and other contributions) was the business partner of the innovative photographer Michael Miley, a young Confederate veteran who learned the trade and moved to Lexington in order to photograph the general. The rest of the family sat for him too, including my mother and my aunt, and so did the townspeople. He also made photographic copies of Mrs. Lee's earlier daguerreotypes; and experimented with color photography.

Among the many college and town luminaries on the list are Mrs. Brockenbrough, whose husband took the college's invitation to Lee, and "Mrs. Senior White," mother of Old Zeus. Her husband, the Presbyterian minister, had urged Lee to accept the college's invitation and, as the town's oldest clergyman, swore in the new president and presided at his funeral.

While the supply lasted, the family must have eaten a lot of rolls, butter, and jelly and longed for fresh green vegetables, which the list shows were in short supply in December. They still were in January, when a third gift of food arrived from nearby Greenway. Among the contributors was the owner of the horse and wagon, and the accompanying letter explained that while the food was intended as a Christmas present, "the delay is perhaps for the better, in view of the

The Notebook

late burglary committed on your premises." The Lees were robbed again in May during that time of widespread hunger.

Mrs. Lee recorded a few gifts not meant to be eaten: "a splendid pair of blankets" from a factory in Fredericksburg, "a beautiful knitted counterpane" from Mrs. Gold (or perhaps Goldsborough) in Vinton County, "a box from Phoenix Cotton mills with cotton blankets," and "balls & 4 homespun hanks yarn, very [illegible]." In 1867, "Mrs. Higgins, Rockville, Md. sent a box of goods for the South."

"Old Zeus," James J. White, biggest of Washington College's "big four" professors. (Photograph by Michael Miley, courtesy of Special Collections, Leyburn Library, Washington and Lee University, Lexington, Va.)

Food for the Lord

"This is the night for the supper for the repairs of the Episcopal church," wrote General Lee, as punctilious about dating letters as his wife was lax, to Mildred on December 21, 1866. He added in good-humored irony, "Your mother and sisters are busy with their contributions. . . . and your brother, cousins, and father are to attend." Perhaps this was the occasion for the notebook's page that begins "[illegible] 18 hams, all of them cooked." The list included forty hams overall ("6 from Genl Lee"), two barrels of flour, one each of sugar and rice, and a suitably large amount of supplies, enough to raise a tidy sum for the church.

Lexington contributors to the hams list include Mrs. Bacon (again); Wm. Campbell, the father of nine; Mr. Harris (Old Nick); and Mrs. Witt, wife of a Lexington doctor. Another four hams came from Phoebe, Elizabeth Cocke's daughter, who had kinship links to both town and cousinage. Mrs. Lee may have asked for outside donations too, because contributor Mr. Whitcomb, a friend and railroad executive, lived in Richmond, and Dr. Bolling Haxall, related to Rob's first wife, Charlotte Haxall, and Rooney's second, Mary Tabb Bolling—the cousinage again—lived over 150 miles from Lexington.

The Notebook

Even before the war, the thrifty heiress of Arlington had kept a sharp eye on prices. During and after it, she jotted down more, providing glimpses of the rampant inflation in wartime Richmond. By far the largest expenses on the page headed "January 1865" are two designated "Mess bill." That month she had moved into 707 East Franklin Street, the house her husband used as his office in Richmond. It had been christened "The Mess" when Custis and other bachelor officers took up residence. Since the owner refused to accept rent, these probably represent outlays for housekeeping. According to Mrs. Lee's record, they rose from $800 in January to $1,160 in February, an increase of nearly 45 percent in one month.

Other expenses listed include $45 for shoes for a servant, Sally, and $15 to an unidentified Lizzie "for three days." Ever charitable, Mrs. Lee also gave $25 to "soldiers" and another $5 to "a poor woman," but the $70 labeled "Poor" could have been for Miss Poor, a favorite Arlington governess, or family friends by the same name. In addition, through March, she spent $20 each for "making bloomers," "cording a window," and subscribing to *Southern Churchman*, and another $35 for proofs, probably small likenesses of General Lee. He signed scores of these cartes de visite but drew the line at requests for hair on the grounds that it was too scant already.

Groceries

Mrs. Lee did not note the year of the food prices she recorded from April 18 through July, but chances are it was 1865, when the family was at Derwent. She would hardly have "received $35.00 in greenbacks" during the war, when Union money was illegal, and the prices are not as exorbitant as those represented by the $30 turkey that Mrs. Chesnut remarked upon in Richmond. Mrs. Lee's frequent

January 1865

	Dol	Cts
For Rob.	166	00
Paid for making drawers	20	00
servants for hauling	16	00
Paid Lizzie for 3 days	15	00
corduing a window	20	00
Churchman	20	00
Poor	70	00
Photographs	35	00
for washing	6	00
Sally & shoes	45	00
Mess bill $800 less	8 08	
Gave Poylen 6.00 a Margaret $5.00	11	00
for 10 Ches	25	00
a/c Bill	11 60	78
March Paid $30 for dogs meat $20 for table	50	00
poor woman $5.00		
April expences for house keeping &c	$133	10

green basket $4.00
Gave Mary $4.00
Gibson

21 gols at 30
30
6..30
60
90

7th April 2 weeks milk paid Myr C

purchases of fish, which were plentiful and relatively cheap during their spring migration up tidal rivers, suggests that the family was not yet living in landlocked Lexington, and the small amounts listed for supplies that were usually bought in bulk—ice, soap, cornmeal, brown sugar, vinegar, and coke (to burn)—suggest a temporary household. The large numbers and amounts of vegetables bought indicate that harvesting had not begun in the Lexington garden on which her husband prided himself. The two pages filled with tiny figures that were never added may be the least legible in the notebook.

After the war, many if not most southerners subsisted on fatback, cornmeal, and the occasional cabbage or mess of greens, but the Lee family continued to consume an abundance of vegetables, as they had before. Besides a peck (a quarter bushel) of greens, Mrs. Lee bought peas, lettuce, potatoes, asparagus, beets, "salad" (maybe more greens), and "snaps" (green beans).

The list shows growing seasons lasting two months at most, with prices sharply higher at the beginning and end. Asparagus, for example, appearing only in May, cost fifty cents at the first and last of the month and a nickel in the middle. During their three-week spring run upriver, shad and sturgeon—the latter plentiful until the turn of the century—varied in price from sixty cents to $1.25 apiece.

Mrs. Lee also bought veal, lamb, bacon, a little pork and "meat" (perhaps beef), but no chicken, eggs, milk, or cream. Since these ingredients are prominent in the receipts, the family must have kept hens and a cow. She did buy about ten pounds of butter in three and a half months. Perhaps their milk had little butterfat before Captain Buford gave Mildred the Jersey cow, a breed known for its rich milk, or perhaps they used a great deal in cooking and on the table, or perhaps both. As for the chickens, Lee teased his daughter Mildred about her pets at Derwent: "I suppose Robert would not eat 'Laura Chilton' and 'Don Ella McKay,' and still less would he devour his sister 'Mildred.'" But eventually they all must have become dinner.

The Notebook

Beginning of
the "Womans
Exchange" price
list, a three-page
list tucked inside
the notebook.
(Courtesy of Vir-
ginia Historical
Society)

Womans Exchange

Light Bread - - - - .5 cts per loaf.
Salt Risen - - - - .10 " " "
Beaten biscuit .12 " " doz
Wafers - - - - - .20 " " "
Chicken Salad - - .80 " " quart.
Potato " - - - - .50 " " "
Fried oysters .35 " " doz.
Deviled crabs - - .75 " " "
Croquettes - - - .35 to 75 cts per doz.
Stuffed eggs - - - .20 cts per doz.
Pickle - - - - $1.75 to 3.00 per gal.
Chow Chow - - - - $3.00 per gallon
Chilli Sauce - - - .40 cts " quart.
Cocoanut balls .25 " " doz.
Caramels - - - - .30 " " lb.
Grape Wine .50 " " quart.

The Notebook

No doubt the Lees ate better than many, but their food was not cheap. Ten-cent lettuce, nickel string beans, and butter at fifty cents a pound sound fine now, but not at an annual salary of $1,500.

Another brief list lets us glimpse travel prices in 1871. When Mrs. Lee returned "on the packet boat of Capt. Wilkerson" from a visit to Rooney, she paid $8.25 full fare and $5.50 for each servant.

Self-Help for Ladies

Stuck loose in the back of the notebook, written in a clear but unknown hand, is a long list of prices at the Women's Exchange. In her history of this Virginia organization founded in 1866, Suzanne Lebsock calls it one of the "creative experiments in mutual aid" to grow from the social ashes of war. (Others included a black women's insurance organization and an all-female, integrated labor union.) Through the Exchange, once-prosperous mistresses of households sold on consignment items made with skills acquired as genteel accomplishments. The organization was still going strong in Richmond in the 1940s, when it was the place to buy fine handwork and homemade baked goods, jams, pickles, and the like at very reasonable prices.

Perhaps the Exchange began by selling only food, for nothing else appears in the notebook list. The prices shown were close to pitiful even then: loaves of salt-rising or light (yeast) bread cost a nickel; twelve cents bought a dozen of that now-endangered species, beaten biscuits; the same number of stuffed eggs cost twenty cents; and a dozen fried oysters or baked custards went for thirty-five. Charlotte russe started at twenty cents apiece; the sixty-cent versions must have been extravaganzas.

The Notebook

THESE MISCELLANEOUS LISTS, scattered through a household note-book, are only fragments. Through them, though, we can catch glimpses of a family's intimate domestic life, for the most part during and immediately after the social cataclysm of the Civil War. Glimmers of everyday life and activities shine through scraps of household finances, details of community involvement, social events, and the like. And perhaps, through this one family, we can glimpse more vividly their time.

The receipts, which make up the bulk of the notebook, add a direct, sensory reality by allowing us to experience the Lee family's fare for ourselves. But to recreate the dishes as they were then requires understanding something of the circumstances, ingredients, and equipment of the time plus a few tips on how to approximate some of that yesterday today.

The Notebook

Recreating the Lee Table after the War

Luckily for most of us who want to explore the Lees' postwar cuisine in our own kitchens, the family dined and entertained modestly. The elaborate concoctions we usually associate with Victorian cuisine did not appear on the tables of many ex-Confederates—nor on those of more than a privileged few in the North, for that matter. Millionaires lived high during that era of extravagance known as the Gilded Age, when the Grants gave twenty-course dinners in the White House, but most home cooking of the comfortably well-off came closer to what we find in the notebook.

The notably lavish dining of the prewar South was, of course, also confined to a privileged minority. Such menus would have been impossible without large kitchen staffs such as the one George Clark headed at Arlington. Nor were establishments as elaborate as Arlington's common, even among large plantations. Ladies of such houses did prepare special dishes themselves, including, apparently, Mrs. Lee. Mr. Wickham of Hickory Hill once complained about the scant sugar in one of Mary Lee's desserts, at a time when the stuff was close to unobtainable. She was still making others the year she died. The receipts she put in the notebook to help her daughters with their new kitchen chores show that she also knew something of basics and was well acquainted with frugality.

Living patterns, like deeply held values, do not change automatically with outside circumstances. The family's meals and their schedule probably remained much the same after the war and their relocation to Lexington. Leftovers had appeared for breakfast at Arlington and no doubt continued to do so in Lexington. Dinner, the main meal, was served at three o'clock, after Lee returned from the office, the same hour as was customary on prewar plantations. It probably still started with soup and was followed by meat or fish, perhaps two kinds, with vegetables and perhaps salad, then dessert. A light tea, supper, or both, served in the early evening, ended the day's repasts.

The dishes may not have changed in some ways, either. The complexity of meals in great Southern houses before the war derived largely from the number and variety of fairly simple offerings from which people could choose. Afterward, the number of dishes shrank and their ingredients become more Spartan.

What Were the Ingredients Like?

A myth of the culinary golden age holds that before additives, preservatives, and long-distance shipping, ingredients were fresh, wholesome, and delicious. No doubt many were, if they were in season, but Mrs. Lee's grocery lists show how short a time that was. By spring, fresh produce must have dwindled to little more than tired cabbage, shriveled carrots, and withered apples and pears.

The Lee Table after the War

George Clark, Arlington's head cook, or possibly one of the other servants who came from Mount Vernon with Mr. Custis. (Photograph by a Union soldier, courtesy of National Park Service, Arlington House Collection)

The Lee Table after the War

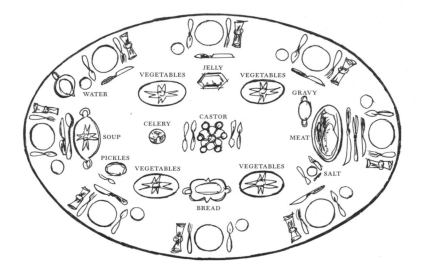

VEGETABLES JELLY VEGETABLES

WATER GRAVY

CELERY CASTOR

SOUP MEAT

PICKLES

VEGETABLES VEGETABLES

SALT

BREAD

And while cream really was cream colored and too gloriously thick to pour, cows did go dry. Then Mrs. Lee's water pancakes— still good, considering—were welcome. Butter served with them could have been resurrected from a bed of salt; Mrs. Tyree's *Housekeeping in Old Virginia* instructed housewives to work two pounds into each pound of butter, then cover the whole in brine. Even washed well before using, it may have stayed salty, and that may account for the receipts using butter with no added salt.

Also, since hens stop laying, eggs had to be stored. Once as a teenager I helped use a preservation method that was common then: sinking the eggs into a thick, slimy goo called water glass (sodium silicate). My hands still remember that awful, slippery feeling, but I have no idea how the eggs tasted later—I could not possibly have eaten them. Clearly, preservative-free breads and cakes can be delicious—and most made from the notebook's receipts are—but it's doubtful that they stayed fresh from one major chore of baking to the next; hence, Mary Custis's receipt for stale breadcrumb pan-

The Lee Table after the War

cakes—again good, considering—and the others utilizing bread and cake past their freshness.

Nevertheless, the last half of the nineteenth century was an exciting time in the kitchen. New tools were introduced that lightened the drudgery, and ingredients once made at home began to be manufactured. Through the notebook we can glimpse how (and whether) some of these innovations influenced the Lees' cuisine.

Vanilla, for example, had been available for a long time. Williamsburg apothecaries stocked its essence, and Mary Randolph sometimes used vanilla beans. Stonewall Jackson's household inventory even shows that commercial vanilla was available in Lexington before 1840. A few of the notebook's receipts do call for it, and others for the bean or for almond, presumably the manufactured extract. Yet an older flavoring, rose water, turns up more often than either of the other two. Introduced to England (along with sugar) by returning Crusaders, it perfumes almost all the sweets in the Washington manuscript. Roses grown at Arlington provided petals for distilling the flavoring, and very likely the Lees continued to prefer it.

In contrast, the Lee ladies took readily to techniques for raising dough quickly and chemically. "When eggs are scarce, a teaspoon of saleratus [close kin to baking soda] will supply the place of two," says another of Mrs. Lee's receipts. The notebook also calls for three other chemical leavening agents: baking soda, which was not widely available commercially until after 1867; baking powder, first manufactured in 1850; and the combination of cream of tartar and baking soda, which make up baking powder. Use of these leavenings took off throughout the United States after the Civil War, when the notebook's receipts were compiled, but even now Europeans prefer to use yeast and beaten eggs and consider chemical leavenings inferior.

Perhaps the American origin of these leavenings influenced their more ready acceptance on this side of the Atlantic. Indians first taught the early colonists to make cornbread light and salty by adding wood ashes. Mrs. Randolph and Mrs. Lewis both used a refined form of wood ashes, called pearl ash, which could be made at home or bought from an apothecary. Pharmacies stocked the next step of refinement, the saleratus used by Mrs. Lee, and they still do, as sodium carbonate. A precursor of baking soda, saleratus was also exported profitably to Europe.

Making the Receipts, Then & Now

Reproducing the notebook's dishes exactly as the Lee ladies made them means using exactly the same kinds of ingredients, cooking techniques, and equipment. That may be possible today, and on occasion worth the effort—to Civil War reenactors, for example—but for most of us most of the time, it is hardly practical. The food of the Lees is essentially simple, and authenticity, to borrow a phrase, is a sometime thing. Depending on time, ingredients, health, palate, and the occasion, we may want more or less of it.

That said, the closer one comes to how things were then, the more closely the results will resemble the Lees'. Knowledge of some of the differences between cooking then and now can make for a more informed decision about how to proceed with a receipt. But in passing it on, please include the original or at least note your deviations; then people need not wander away from it unwittingly, as has happened countless times to countless other heirloom receipts.

Flour

In an article titled "What We Found Out about Flour," based on much experimentation and consultation, *Washington Post* food writer Carole Sugarman concluded that "flour is far more complex than

The Lee Table after the War

that sack of white fluff lets on." Add historical change, and it becomes even more so.

The Lees' flour came from the same kind of wheat that supplied Mr. Custis's main income. Exported from his two working plantations along the Pamunkey River (my mother and my aunt grew up on one, Romancoke), it was, like the wheat in Britain and the other colonies, low in gluten, the protein that makes bread rise. We now call it soft wheat, or winter wheat, because it is sown in the fall and harvested in spring. (High-gluten, hard spring wheat arrived in Kansas from Europe, probably after the Civil War, with the opening of the Great Plains.) Baked goods made with low-gluten flour have a more tender crumb than those made with high-gluten flour. They do not rise as high or absorb butter quite as well, but southerners still tend to prefer the low-gluten variety; we say the North's bread and cake may look prettier, but ours taste better.

Today, a few small, water-powered mills, some predating the Civil War, still grind flour between large stones, and other such mills are being revived. Low-gluten wheat flour from them resembles the Lees' closely: slightly rough, creamy in color, and still containing the tasty, nutritious germ. Unfortunately, most of these mills turn out only specialty flours, not plain white wheat flour, which is the only kind used in the notebook. Two that do produce white wheat flour, and white cornmeal as well, are the Amherst Milling Company, established 1813 in Amherst, Virginia, phone 804-946-7601; and Wades Mill, established circa 1750 in Raphine, Virginia, 800-290-1400.

Ms. Sugarman also concluded that all-purpose flour is usually okay, and that bleached flour works better than unbleached for baked goods not raised with yeast, and I concur. But to approximate nineteenth-century flour more closely, look among mass-produced brands for unbleached flour with the lowest percentage of protein (85 percent of which is gluten) listed on the label. Cake flour, though low in gluten, has little taste and is too finely ground; best not to use it alone for the receipts here. Regional southern brands such as

White Lily and specialty flours such as Robin Hood are low in gluten, and some of the mass-produced national brands are said to be formulated with a lower proportion of protein below the Mason-Dixon line. You probably will not find the 7 percent protein flour typical of the period except wholesale or from a friendly baker, but you can bring contemporary white flour closer to the Lees'.

To approximate the earlier color and texture, use about a table-spoon of whole wheat flour per cup of white flour. To lower gluten (a consideration more important in tender cakes, cookies, and pie crust), use up to one-third cake flour. We had no trouble with lower-gluten flour not absorbing butter, but in a receipt that is high in fat, a high proportion of cake flour could lead to trouble. In general, the simpler and plainer the receipt, the more difference the kind of flour and the quality of other ingredients will make.

Cornmeal

Corn remains a staple in the Deep South to this day. This native American grain, which produces more nutrition than wheat for the same amount of land and labor, kept the early colonists from starving. It soon became the staple of Virginia's poor and was even a preferred food among the gentry, as Robert Beverley observed in 1705: "In Gentlemen's houses, some rather choose [over wheat bread] the Pone . . . made of Indian meal." More than 150 years later, Mildred Lee was making "corn *Pone* baked in the ashes" of her brother Rob's fireplace at Romancoke, where apparently he did not have a stove before he married my grandmother.

"Delicious . . . sweet-flavored but uneven" is the way an old cookbook describes meal ground by the small, old mills. To me, it compares to mass-produced cornmeal as good vintage wine does to jug. Since it retains the germ, it does not last indefinitely unless refrigerated or frozen. (The same is true for stone-ground wheat flour.) The best cornmeal and grits I know come from Stratford Hall

Plantation, where Robert E. Lee was born. (To order, contact the Robert E. Lee Memorial Association, Inc., Stratford Hall Plantation, Stratford, VA 22558, phone 804-493-8038.)

The notebook's five receipts for cornbread show that it remained popular with the Lees. All five are far more delicate than pone made from meal and water. (I haven't heard of adding wood ash these days.) They were probably made with white meal, noted in 1833 by a visitor to Shirley plantation, the home of Robert's mother. Describing the culinary opulence there shortly after the young Lees were married, Henry Barnard wrote that hominy, "made of their white corn," was "always at dinner." White was the only kind of cornmeal I knew while growing up, when a southern grande dame sniffed, "Yankees use yellow meal. *We* make *our* cornbread yellow with eggs."

The mill at Stratford Hall, rebuilt on the foundation that was there when General Lee was born. (Photograph by Richard Cheek, courtesy of the Robert E. Lee Memorial Association, Stratford Hall Plantation)

Sugar

"I was compared to sugar—clarafied at that," teenage Agnes Lee confided to her diary about a valentine. To Mrs. Tyree of *Housekeeping in Old Virginia*, clarified sugar was unsuitable for anything finer than gingerbread, but they may not have meant the same thing. Sugar became a complex, confusing subject in the nineteenth century, when this longtime luxury became more affordable, and granulated sugar made by a new process replaced cone-shaped loaves.

These cones weighed from five to fifty pounds. Eliza Chinn Ripley, born in 1832, remembered them from her Louisiana childhood as being "hard as stone. They hung (like hams in a smokehouse) from the closet ceiling." To be used, they first "had to be cut into chips by aid of carving knife and hammer, then pounded and rolled until reduced to powder." Iron sugar nippers were also used to cut the cones into the forerunners of sugar cubes, for tea and coffee.

The Lee Table after the War

The best sugar, triple-refined, went into preserves and onto the table; double-refined was for cakes. In Lexington, Mrs. Lee bought light brown, single-refined sugar by the barrel for the servants, describing it in a letter to Rooney as better than the "cheap brown sugar" she specified in the notebook's blackberry wine receipt. The latter, probably strong and perhaps runny, may have tasted more like Indian *gur* than our brown sugar. Last on the sugar quality scale came lowly, bitter molasses, the sweetener of the poor. With the possible exception of sorghum, botanically unrelated but tasting much the same, molasses was the only form of sugar available in Richmond in the months before the Confederate capital fell.

In her 1861 *Book of Household Management* (published in England but widely used in America), Mrs. Beeton explained how to make confectioner's sugar: white sugar was pounded "to the finest powder" and a little starch added to keep it from clumping, just as machines do now. The fineness must have varied with the pounder, and since the 1950s the machine process has changed enough to make the difference between disastrous and delicious in the Robert E. Lee cake (see page 132). Mrs. Beeton also advised replacing hard loaf sugar with granulated, but that innovation may not have reached Lexington by the time these receipts were collected. Although the kind of sugar to use is not always specified, no receipt mentions the new form, while several clearly imply the use of loaf sugar.

The Lee ladies could at least buy hard cone sugar already broken; before the war Lexington shops carried white sugar loaves in three forms—whole, cut, and crushed—and brown sugar, too. But prices must have been high, for when Mrs. Lee asked Rooney about the cost of sugar, she also asked about "nice *crushed* not *cut* white sugar, which latter is more expensive." If she bought the crushed form, she may have regretted it; Mrs. Tyree warned that "pulverized [sugar was] apt to have plaster of Paris or other foreign elements in it."

Fine sugar still comes in cones in Denmark, France, Germany, and maybe other countries as well. Those intrigued by working with loaf sugar can find small cones wrapped in traditional light blue paper at Colonial Williamsburg, at souvenir prices.

Milk, Cream, and Butter

Few purebred milk cows had crossed the Atlantic when Captain Buford sent Mildred her Jersey cow shortly after the war. Ours, when I was growing up, was no rarity, but it gave the same rich milk. Matt, who sometimes cooked for us, used to wait until everyone sat down to announce, "Milk ain't scum." Then a grownup would get up from the table and go to the pantry to remove the thick, yellow skin of cream from a huge bowl of milk, leaving a few flecks that I, for some reason, hated.

Home-skimmed milk is richer than machine-separated, so authenticity requires using at least part—some say all—half-and-half in these receipts. Regular milk will usually do, though. Today's commercial whipping cream is a pale shadow of what used to be skimmed off at home, but it will probably have to do, perhaps with increased butter added to compensate. I make up for the salt that must have lurked in even the best-washed butter by adding a pinch per cup to lightly salted butter, two pinches to unsalted. Since completely salt-free bread tastes flat, all the testers agreed, we added it even to receipts with no butter.

Eggs

Hens never have laid neatly sized eggs that I know of, but today's medium eggs come closest to their nineteenth-century counterparts, and the large size will usually do as well. Ironically, now that getting fresh eggs is not a problem, getting salmonella from them is. Even though only one egg yolk in 10,000 is infected, according to 1995

The Lee Table after the War

statistics, and the whites more rarely yet, the bacterium can be extremely dangerous, especially to small children, the frail elderly, and people with impaired immune systems.

Refrigeration retards the germ, so keep eggs thoroughly chilled. Heating egg yolks to 180 degrees kills salmonella, so baked goods present no risks. However, dressings, custards, meringues, and all other receipts that call for raw or barely cooked eggs or egg whites should be approached with extreme caution.

Flavorings

Even the wealthiest Victorians had comparatively few ways to flavor food, but they used them well. From the notebook I have learned the joy of a bitter touch of citrus pith and the pleasure of nutmeg and red pepper in nonsweet receipts. The quality of ingredients such as jelly, jam, and marmalade is important. Use the best available, and fresh or frozen lemon juice and rind. Grind all spices fresh, if possible; a small coffee grinder pulverizes even whole nutmegs, and a touch of spice left behind will perk up the next brew. Middle eastern and Indian grocery stores usually stock rose water.

Use black (or at least dark) rum and for wine, a medium-sweet, flavorful sherry or perhaps Madeira. Possibly with more Lee frugality than authenticity, I use good domestic sherry (imported Madeira, though) and SOP French brandy, not the pricier VSOP.

Calories and Cholesterol

In the Lees' time, no one had heard of either one of these C-words, and perhaps some day we can ignore them again. Meanwhile, sometimes the amounts in the receipts can be cut back—not out—satisfactorily. I actually prefer Mrs. Letcher's eggnog made with 3.25 percent, or even 2 percent, milk since I usually find the real thing cloying. In general, though, experiment first or make these receipts

The Lee Table after the War

in all their C-word glory (just, perhaps, not often). And let your taste buds and conscience, along with the comments on receipts, be your guide. You can often use all whole milk rather than at least part half-and-half for milk. Substitute two egg whites per egg for *half or fewer* of the eggs. To cut cholesterol and saturated fat, though not calories, substitute margarine made with nonhydrogenated vegetable fat for *half or less* of the butter or other fat.

Time, the Almost Intractable

Whatever Victorians lacked in conveniences, however hard they labored in the kitchen, they used our biggest luxury, time, lavishly. Nothing here can be made in minutes, but some receipts, as noted, can be fit into busy schedules when made in stages.

Equipment:
The Stove Revolution

Although cast-iron cookstoves had been manufactured in America since 1765, they were still uncommon when the Custises installed one at Arlington in 1830, the year before Mary and Robert Lee were married. By 1850, cookbook writers assumed their readers owned one, and after the Civil War the stove spread rapidly. But decades later, some discriminating cooks still scorned them.

Stoves used less fuel than cooking fireplaces; they were less likely to burn the house down or catch a cook's long skirts on fire; and they did not require such heavy equipment, and therefore so much muscle power. Nevertheless, fireplaces were thought to be more flexible. They could simmer soup, toast bread, and brown meringue at the same time.

Bread baked in the companion brick oven was considered so supe-

The Lee Table after the War

Keystone of the kitchen revolution of the 1870s: an early cast-iron stove. (Sketch by Fred Zimmer from an 1874 Prang chromo-lithograph at the Library of Congress)

rior that in 1861 housewives were still being urged to use them, even though this process meant building a fire on the oven floor, sweeping out the coals, and then washing the oven floor before putting in the loaves. After the bread came out, cakes, pies, and so forth were baked according to the fall in oven temperature. Well after the Civil War, Harriet Beecher Stowe of *Uncle Tom's Cabin* fame and her sister Catherine, a leading figure in the northern cult of domesticity, denounced stove-baked bread as "a specious substitute so easily made, and so seldom well made."

As for roasting, Mrs. Randolph declared that "no meat can be well roasted except on a spit turned by a jack, and before a steady clear fire—other methods are no better than baking." More than fifty years later Mrs. Tyree agreed, although she did deign to explain how to cook wild birds in a stove oven without "that stovy taste." (Use a rack.) She also subjected beef to steaming in the oven over water, which shows how tough it was before the turn of the century. As late as 1885, one cookbook still held out for the art of fireplace roasting, even while acknowledging that few cooks practiced it. Now Nancy Carter Crump, author of *Hearthside Cooking*, and other enthusiasts make a mouth-watering case for the crackling, caramelized crust and tender, juicy meat. I almost wish I had the time and equipment to try.

The cast-iron behemoth in our basement, as I remember it, had advantages much like those claimed for the cooking fireplace. It fried chicken, boiled vegetables, baked biscuits, simmered stew, and kept meals warm all at the same time, and it could have made crème fraîche if we had heard of it. But when the cook did not come to shake up the fire in the morning, we were lost. Nobody begged to chop wood, carry it in, or feed the fire, either. I suspect the Lee ladies enjoyed the convenience of their cast-iron stove, and that Progress does not march necessarily toward perfection.

The Lee Table after the War

Canning and a Hymn to the Eggbeater

Probably no gadgets in the gadget-happy nineteenth century received a warmer kitchen welcome than the rotary eggbeater and the screw-top canning jar. The latter made the all-important task of "putting up" so much easier that Mrs. Lee thought it worthwhile to have jar rings made in Canada while she was at a spa there, since they were not available at home. Their notes and letters show that the Lee daughters canned in Lexington, and it would be hard to explain the huge amounts called for in the notebook's receipt for tomato soup in any other way.

"If I could not get another," rhapsodized cookbook writer Marion Farland about her Dover eggbeater, "I would not sell mine for fifty dollars—not a hundred. With it I can . . . make the formidable 'snow custard' in less than half an hour with no after tremulousness of nerve or tension." The syllabub churn that whipped up the notebook's Snow Pudding (probably the same dessert) retreated to museums long ago, and the Lees may well have retired their own for the new marvel. Its descendants still live in many a kitchen drawer, useful any time and indispensable during power failures.

Translating Then into Now

Although occasional mistakes in these receipts caused problems when we tested them, more often it was vagueness that left the final dish in doubt. The ladies who contributed the receipts could, of course, explain what they did not write down. Beyond that, they could assume knowledge of techniques that have become obsolete now and a greater culinary background in general, for cooking was much more central to women's lives then.

Such casualness can be liberating as well as frustrating: receipts become friendly guides instead of straitjackets, and personal taste

The Lee Table after the War

more important than exactness. A kitchen is still not a chemistry lab, after all. Even standard measuring tools, thermometers, and ovens, as well as standardized ingredients, can vary. Developing a feel for *when* and *how* to change does indeed require experience, but words like "about" and "approximately" still have a place in many a receipt. While cooking with the Lee ladies, please consider "flavor as you will" an opportunity, not a hurdle.

Some kitchen techniques that were convenient then are not any longer, and modern equipment has rendered others needlessly laborious. Here are some changes we made in using the receipts and observations about them; purists may feel free to ignore.

Changing the Size of Receipts

Something mysterious is supposed to happen when the quantity of a receipt is altered, but when we made smaller sizes for today's smaller households, we didn't notice any problems. Perhaps simplicity and casualness combined to build in leeway.

A Source of Steady Warmth

Wood stoves, though hardly a blessing in hot weather, dried ingredients and raised yeast doughs set near them handily. To accomplish these tasks in a modern kitchen, set the oven at its lowest temperature (on mine, 100 degrees), put in the food, and leave the door cracked open.

Baking: Combining Doughs and Batters

Modern double-acting baking powder need not be added immediately before baking. Sifting it and small amounts of other dry ingredients with the flour distributes them more evenly and otherwise makes no difference. "Some of the best housewives," according to

Mrs. Tyree, creamed butter and flour together, instead of butter and sugar, and beat the sugar into the egg yolks, "as it produces yellow specks when you add the sugar sooner." The Lee ladies may or may not have been done so; we did not.

Otherwise, the sequence for mixing doughs and batters has not changed much over the years. By hand, with rotary eggbeaters, or light electric mixers: beat egg yolks and whites separately; cream butter, then add sugar and cream together until very light; fold in beaten yolks, then liquid and dry ingredients alternately; fold in whites last. To preserve the dense glory of the heirloom cake while taking advantage of a heavy stand mixer, drop whole eggs into creamed butter and sugar one at a time while beating on medium, then add liquid and dry ingredients alternately, on low or by hand.

Yeast Updates

For those who prefer to use today's commercial yeast, 2 cakes or packets, softened as instructed, equals ¼ cup homemade; however, be sure to count the liquid used to soften the yeast as part of the total liquid called for in the receipt. Either type will raise plain bread made from 6 cups flour (or sweet dough from 4 cups) overnight; with more yeast, the dough may fall and sour by morning. Begin about 8 P.M. in summer; 6 P.M. in winter if the kitchen is appreciably colder.

Overnight rising sentenced the cook to early rising to have hot bread ready for the breakfast table, a sacrifice that few people would make today. To fit such slow rising into a faster paced, servantless life, you can make your own brown-and-serve baked goods, although they won't be quite as good. Remove them from the oven when they have risen but are not yet browned (start checking 15 minutes ahead), freeze, and finish cooking just before serving. These receipts have not, by the way, been tried in bread machines. Nor have they been tested using super-quick (rapid-rising) yeast, since I came to

The Lee Table after the War

Table of Equivalents
1 tablespoon = 3 t.
1 wineglass = 2–4 oz.
¼ cup = 2 oz.
1 teacup = 6–8 oz.
2 cups = 1 pt.
 (can be scant)
4 cups = 1 qt.
 (also can be scant)

Abbreviations
c. = cup
oz. = ounce
pt. = pint
qt. = quart
T. = tablespoon
t. = teaspoon

agree with master baker Elizabeth David that the least yeast and slowest rising makes the best bread.

When Are They Done?

My mother used to say you have to eat a peck of dirt before you die. She didn't mean that literally, but many of her generation (and mine, including me) used to stick a broomstraw into cakes, which were cooked when the straw came out clean; a toothpick or wooden skewer does as well. Another test is to press a cake layer lightly with a finger; if it springs back, it is done, as it also is when it shrinks slightly from the pan's sides. It should be lightly browned, too. If in doubt, try several of the above tests. A knife blade inserted near the middle of baked custard also comes out clean when it is done, and the knife need not be silver, as my mother thought. Also, your nose knows when something is done and/or about to burn. Trust it before the timer.

Other baking constants to observe unless directed otherwise:

• Have ingredients at room temperature.
• Preheat oven.
• Butter and flour cake pans or use nonstick varieties.
• Butter bread pans or use nonstick varieties.
• Cool goods on a rack.

Measuring: Weight vs. Volume

Supposedly, the shift from pounds to cups happened when women could not take their scales west in covered wagons. The notebook uses both. Today's American volume measurements have been given with receipts, but weight is more accurate and can sometimes save such steps as preliminary sifting.

The Lee Table after the War

The Receipts

The 70 receipts selected here from the notebook's 120-some represent the outstanding, those that have dropped out of common usage and are thus newly new, and the best among minor variations. They also include the downright disasters—in the hope that someone, somewhere, may be able to interpret them better than we have. Outright duplications have been omitted, as have minor and less successful variations as well as some receipts that are still available in standard cookbooks.

In what follows, each original receipt is reproduced as it appears in the notebook, followed by an annotated list of the ingredients and recommendations on how to prepare the receipt today. The comments and notes on measurement equivalents are based on the results of home testing and on advice drawn from both historic cookbooks and contemporary scholarship on culinary history.

The notebook's six receipts for yeast demonstrate its importance. Before the war, five different kinds of bread, mostly hot, might appear at breakfast, and the necessity for hot bread lingered through the Depression and beyond: "We serve cold baker's bread only to our enemies," declared southern writer Marjorie Kinnan Rawlings in the 1940s. And while I don't remember what we served enemies, or that we had any to dinner, I will never forget the glee of the grown-ups when brown-and-serve rolls arrived on grocery shelves. They were so convenient that people hardly noticed that they weren't as good.

An unsigned receipt inscribed "July 1st 1865 for dear Mrs. Lee" shows that the family started collecting yeast receipts before they left Derwent that November; the other five could all stem from their days in Lexington. (Though Superneat did not attribute the one written in her copybook-perfect script to anyone, most of the other receipts she put in can be traced to Lexington days.) Formulas for yeast came from family, friends, and Charlotte Haxall, a friend who became family; she sent her Aunt Anne's receipt "because it is better," presumably than her own.

The general had pleaded playfully with "beautiful Lottie" to marry his youngest son Rob long before the two became engaged. Then Lee wrote her prophetically, "I already love you as a daughter. I . . . beg you quickly to become so, for I have little time to wait." His death three months later postponed the wedding for a year, and Charlotte lived only one year after that, but ties between the families continue.

Dutiful Mildred, who did not like to cook, wrote in the other yeast receipts. One came from Mrs. Dabney Maury, born Nannie Mason and, judging from her name, a member of the cousinage. Her husband was the nephew of Matthew Fontaine Maury, famed as the first to chart the ocean's currents. Like Lee, Matthew Maury resigned from the Union forces, in his case the Navy, when the Civil War

The Receipts

began. He became a commodore of the Confederate fleet and, like many other fellow officers, left the country after defeat. He returned in 1868 and became a professor at VMI. Mildred probably collected this and other receipts from his niece-in-law while she was visiting in Lexington, and when, incidentally, commercial yeast was already widely available.

Two yeast receipts came from "Tabb," Rooney's second wife, Mary Tabb Bolling, who belonged to the cousinage. She was known, according to my aunt, as "a *Petersburg* beauty, and Petersburg grew beauties like ordinary people grow cabbages." Although still lovely in old age, she grew very deaf; my mother and aunt were "terrified to speak to Aunt Tabb in her ear trumpet."

The best and longest-lived yeast came from one of four Nannie Lees. The first, Anna Maria Mason, sharp-tongued and vivacious, married the general's brother Smith, whom diarist Mary Chesnut considered the handsomest of the three brothers. Nannie thrived on society. With secession, wrote Mrs. Chesnut, she "says she was dragged away from Washington . . . kicking." Her grandfather, George Mason, though a drafter of the Constitution, had refused to sign it without a Bill of Rights; added later, it was modeled on the earlier Virginia Declaration of Rights, which Mason had drafted. That first Nannie Lee lived until 1898, her son Dan married another Nannie (a Burwell), and two granddaughters were named for the first. Any one of them conceivably could have contributed the receipt.

Yeasts, with Their Breads

The yeast receipts all begin with a "starter" of old yeast, showing the importance of having a good strain to keep going. They could represent a cutting edge of cooking history too, because all depart sharply from the kind made by Nelly Custis Lewis, which was still being recommended in an influential 1855 cookbook. Based on rye flour, the older style was dried and cut into cakes and supposedly

Breads

Top: Charlotte Haxall, who became Rob Lee's first wife. (Courtesy of the Lee family)

Bottom: Anna Maria "Nannie" Mason Lee. (Portrait by John Neagle, owned by Mrs. Fitzhugh Lee, print courtesy of the Robert E. Lee Memorial Society, Stratford Hall Plantation)

Right: Mary Tabb Bolling, Rooney Lee's second wife. (Courtesy of Virginia Historical Society)

The Receipts

stayed active for a year. All the yeasts in the Lee notebook, however, are liquid, made from wheat flour, potatoes, and hops. The best of them lasts seven months and then turns gradually into good sourdough starter. Since contemporary bread expert Elizabeth David considers two months an exceptional lifetime for liquid yeast, the Lee ladies may have found something extraordinary, even for today.

Although hops can cause off-flavors, they do not do so in any of these receipts, another indication that the Lee ladies chose well. Food writer Waverly Root calls this ingredient a preservative, but it seems to be more than that. Two loaves made using yeast with the hops omitted rose—and fell—unevenly, but the same yeast made with hops produced smooth, light loaves from the same receipts. Beer-making stores and some health food stores carry this perhaps crucial ingredient.

Since the viability of homemade yeast could be uncertain, cooks tested it by making sponges first, to keep from wasting flour. To adapt receipts that contain no instructions for making a sponge, subtract flour, sugar, and liquid from the receipt to make one. The bread in the receipt below is little more than a footnote to the yeast and sponge, where its ingredients are included. Close-grained and delicious, it has a purity that is hard to describe but easy to appreciate.

· NANNIE LEE'S YEAST, SPONGE, AND BREAD ·

Yeast

Take 2 teaspoonfuls of pressed hops in a small bag—add 3 pts boiling water to this with 2 teaspoonfuls of white sugar & salt, have 3 medium sized potatoes or 4 if small, creamed nicely with ½ teacup of flour—gradually add the hop tea to the potatoes—return all to the fire & cook for a few moments. When cool add a good teacup of old yeast, & set in a cool place to work—12 hours after, bottle in two glass jars.

Breads

Yeast:

2 t. pressed hops, in a small bag
6 c. boiling water
2 t. sugar
2 t. salt
3 medium or 4 small potatoes, cooked and mashed
½ c. flour
1 c. yeast (to substitute commercial yeast,
   see "Yeast Updates," page 105)

Steep hops in boiling water with salt and sugar. Cream together potatoes and flour. Gradually add hop tea to potatoes and place over medium heat for 2–3 minutes. Cool mixture to lukewarm before adding yeast. Cover and set aside to work for 12 hours. Transfer to two sterilized quart jars, cover, and refrigerate. Keep it going by making a new batch with 1 cup of the old after a few months.

Sponge for rising bread

To one pound and ¾ flour—you will put together 2 tablespoonfuls of mashed potatoes—2 teaspoonfuls of sugar—a teacup of flour—& 2 tablespoonfuls of good yeast—when well risen make up yr bread with it, & a little cool water. Add an egg or two if you wish small breads.

Sponge and Bread:

7 c. flour *total* for both (1 c. for the sponge, 6 c. for bread)
1–2 eggs, if desired for rolls, or about ½ c. water
   (less if eggs are used)

Make sponge as directed and allow to rise. Add rest of flour, eggs if desired (they make rolls more tender), and enough water to make a soft dough. Grease top and let rise overnight in greased bowl covered with a towel. Divide into two greased bread pans or make into rolls and place on greased tins. Allow to rise, about 2 hours. Grease tops with butter or lard (preferred). Bake loaves 40–45 minutes at 350°; bake rolls at 425° about 15-20 minutes, depending on size.

When she crammed fourteen receipts in her tiny, cramped script onto three notebook pages, Mary Lee was not concerned about punctuation, legibility, or posterity. She probably meant them to help her daughters cope with their new kitchen chores in Lexington, where she could explain and interpret, but the nearly telegraphic directions here and in many other receipts (some have none) underline the fund of knowledge cooks were presumed to bring to their craft.

Since the "new milk" called for in this receipt meant milk that had not been skimmed, half-and-half with a little cream best achieves the original's richness and lusciousness, but whole milk will do. This large receipt, which can be halved or quartered, makes about three dozen large rolls or nearly 100 of the tiny Parker House kind. They freeze well and stay fresh in the refrigerator for about a week. Then, when past their prime, split the rolls raggedly, dab with butter, and toast under the broiler until the edges brown and crisp and the middles are soft and yellow. Splendid.

To shape Parker House rolls, follow instructions in a standard cookbook. Or make "pulled rolls," survivors from colonial times to the present, by forming dough into smooth balls and placing them, touching, in circles on a greased tin.

Boil a qt of new milk stir in a qt of flour when nearly cold a spoonful salt 2 tablespoons of lard & half a teacup of good yeast set in a warm place to rise for 2 hours when light work in flour on the cake board quite smooth mould into rolls & put in a greased baking pan set in a warm place for a second rise.

Breads

4 c. milk (half-and-half or whole)

10–12 c. flour, divided

2 t. salt

2 T. lard .

⅓–½ c. homemade yeast (to substitute commercial yeast,
    see "Yeast Updates," page 105)

Butter or lard (preferred) for greasing bowl and tops of dough

Heat milk to barely simmering and cool to lukewarm. Sift 4 cups
flour and salt and add. Knead on a floured breadboard to a soft
dough. Grease a large bowl, turn dough to grease top, cover and let
rise until almost doubled, about 2 hours. Work in 4–6 cups more
flour, kneading to a soft dough. Make up rolls and put into greased
muffin pans or on greased baking sheets. Grease tops (lard preferred) and allow to rise until almost doubled. Bake at 325° 15–20
minutes, depending on size of rolls.

Who or What Was Sally Lunn?

Mrs. Lee put two receipts for Sally Lunn among the basics for her
daughters, and a third was stuck into the notebook loose. The family must have loved it. Certainly my mother did; she considered it her
quintessential company bread, both immutable and old-fashioned.
Hers was coarse and eggy like this receipt and the rest I knew while
growing up, but they all had a crucial difference from this: they were
sweet. This receipt is not, and after getting used to it, I'd rather put
good jam on the bread than sugar in it. But that is only one of many
changes Sally Lunn has undergone.

    Some say the name began in France, as Soleil et Lune (Sun and
Moon) and underwent a sound-alike change after crossing the English Channel. Some say, too, that settlers made it at Jamestown to
remind them of home. Others call it the invention of a cook of
George Washington's, which it probably was not.

The Receipts

Molasses sauce

Put half pint of Molasses to boil in a skillet with a piece of butter the size of an egg when it has boiled a few minutes pour a tea cup of cream & grate in half a nutmeg or any spice you like

Crisp Ginger cake

3 lbs flour 1 sugar one butter or lard 3 table spoonfulls ginger one cloves & aniseed & wet it with molasses roll it thin, cut in shapes & bake with quick heat —

Wheat flour Muffin bread

pint of Indian meal sifted, a cup full of wheat flour [Indian meal] a lump of butter or lard 4 eggs beaten light mix all about the consistency of pound cake [with milk] & bake in a cake pan —

Boiled Milk rolls

boil a qt new milk stir in a qt of flour when nearly cold 2 tea spoonfuls salt 2 table spoons of lard & half a tea cup of good yeast set in a warm place to rise for 2 hours then light & work in flour on the cake board quite smooth mould to rolls & put in a greased baking pan set in a warm place & let them rise

another recipe for Sally Lunn

Sift into a pan a good qt of flour, make a hole in the Middle & put in two oz of butter warmed a pint of milk a spoonful salt 3 well beaten eggs 2 table spoonfuls of good yeast mix all well & put in a tin pan that has been greased & cover it, set it in a warm place & when quite light & bake in a Moderate oven

I prefer the *Oxford English Dictionary* version, for personal reasons as well as its widely recognized authority. The *OED* traces the bread to a late-eighteenth-century teacake vendor in Bath, England, by that name. There years ago, supposedly in her shop, I enjoyed a Sally Lunn, made supposedly from the original receipt, which I still have. It was a plain, delicate, light, shallow mound about six inches across with a thin, sweet glaze, and quite unlike Mrs. Lee's. So is the feathery, brioche-like Sally Lunn baked in an angel food cake pan, sold by at least two bakeries in Richmond, Virginia. And some English friends call currant buns Sally Lunn. Wherever and however the lady started, she has evolved.

Mrs. Tyree's book shows that by 1879 the bread could be raised with baking powder as well as the yeast I considered inevitable, and could be either sweet or not. The angel food cake pan that I thought indispensable is not mentioned.

Some contemporary purists say to beat the batter only by hand — 100 strokes, 400 strokes, or until the dough blisters, depending on the purist — but a five-minute workout in a heavy stand mixer set on medium works fine for me and is infinitely easier. Even more than most southern hot bread, this one suffers from being served cold, but it takes well to the brown-and-serve treatment (see "Yeast Updates," page 105). Leftovers can be sliced, buttered, and broiled, as in the receipt above. Made fresh and devoured hot, it can be the showpiece of a special brunch or tea. A 10-inch tube pan serves 10–12.

Of the notebook's three extremely similar receipts for Sally Lunn, Mrs. Lee's second has a bit more butter and probably for that reason is the best. She called it "another recipe for Sally Lunn."

· SALLY LUNN ·

Sift into a pan a good qt. flour, make a hole in the middle & put in 2 oz. of butter warmed in a pint of milk a spoonful of salt 3 well-beaten eggs,

The Receipts

· 116 ·

2 tablespoons of good yeast mix all well & put in a tin pan that has been
greased Cover set in a warm place & when quite light bake in a moderate
oven

¼ c. (½ stick) butter plus more for greasing pan and top
4 c. sifted flour
1 t. salt
2 c. whole milk or (better) half-and-half
3 eggs
2 T. homemade yeast (or see "Yeast Updates," page 105)

Melt butter in milk. Add salt, cool to lukewarm, and add yeast and
beaten eggs. Stir in flour. Batter should resemble a thick pancake
batter and will double in about 2 hours. Bake in a greased angel food
cake pan in bottom third of oven preheated to 350° about 30–40
minutes. Makes one loaf. *Do not serve cold.*

Spas and the Staff of Life

Before the war, spas known familiarly as "the Hot," "the Sweet," "the
White," and "the Warm" served as gathering places for widely scattered rural southern society. There, besides taking the waters, families discussed politics, made financial deals, renewed friendships,
conducted flirtations, and contracted marriages. Mrs. Lee often
sought their healing waters for relief from her rheumatoid arthritis,
and after the war, her husband sometimes took her to a spa for a
cheering change of scene.

In the summer of 1867, the two journeyed to the preeminent
"White" (White Sulphur Springs) by slow train and jolting stagecoach. There Christiana Bond, a young southern belle, wrote a
charming memoir about their stay. While Mrs. Lee remained mostly
in their cottage, took treatments, and saw old friends, the general cut
a wider swath. He chatted with, among others, philanthropists William Corcoran and George Peabody and ex-Lexington industrialist

Breads

Cyrus McCormick; all three contributed to struggling little Washington College. While bantering with young ladies, a favorite pastime, he noticed a party of Yankees who were being snubbed and sent Christiana to welcome them. Then he asked her to tell her friends that such hostility "grieves me inexpressibly . . . I implore them to do their part to heal our country's wounds."

· WARM SPRINGS MUFFINS ·

Mary Custis, the eldest Lee daughter, visited Virginia's Warm Springs ("the Warm") before the war, during it, and afterward, in 1868, when Mildred contracted typhoid fever and prolonged the family's stay. During one of her visits, she took down this receipt for lovely, light muffins; it makes about 24, each 2 to 2½ inches across. The milk to be added in winter was needed to counteract the drying effect of cold air on flour; now modern home heating makes it unnecessary. The "skillet with a top" suggests they could also be baked in a fireplace, but we were not equipped to try.

To a quart of flour put 2 eggs, a spoonful of butter, 2½ spoonfuls of yeast, and in winter some milk. Add a little salt. Put into greased muffin tins or baking cups. Allow to rise overnight. Bake them in an oven or a <u>skillet with a top</u>.

4 c. sifted flour, plus enough to make a soft dough
2 eggs
1 T. butter plus more for greasing baking tins and top of dough
2½ T. homemade yeast
½ t. or more salt

Sift salt with flour. Beat eggs well, add yeast and butter, melted and cooled. Mix into flour to make a soft dough. Raise overnight, covered, tops greased, in greased baking cups or muffin tins. Bake tins about 20 minutes in preheated 375° oven, longer in cold cast-iron or larger earthenware cups.

Waffles

*"Waffles—Pussy—*and *Mr. Harrison* are temptations too strong to resist . . . *but* Mrs. Hay asked me to come to night . . . for a game of whist," begins Mildred's note to Lella Pendleton, daughter of an ex-Confederate officer who had urged General Lee to accept the college's presidency. Through it we can catch glimpses of the Lees' modest postwar social life, a fad of the last half of the nineteenth century, and perhaps a change in attitude by the elder Lees, who had looked with disfavor on card games some thirty-five years earlier at Fort Monroe.

These descendants of medieval *gauffres* (called French Wafers in the Washington manuscript) became an entertainment with the invention of the waffle iron, which was in turn spawned by the popularity of cast-iron stoves. Instead of simply being cooked over an open fire, exulted cookbook writer Mrs. S. C. Lee (no known relation), "the waffle is put in, locked up, baked on one side to a lovely brown [then] turned over prison and all until the other side is still lovelier brown, and then released steaming but ready for the table."

Mildred must have liked them; she entered three receipts. One came from Mary T, or Tabb, Rooney's second wife, the "Petersburg beauty" (who, according to my aunt, struck a minister dumb in mid-sermon with her beauty when she arrived late for church one Sunday). The Mary Cocke who contributed another waffle receipt was probably a younger relative of the Mary Cocke with whom Mrs. Lee stayed on her way to Richmond, the latter the mother-in-law of Elizabeth Cocke, who gave the family sanctuary at Derwent. In 1897, the youngest Lee daughter sent this younger Mary Cocke mementos of her parents. Until then, to get Mildred to part with any of these had

Breads

been "as hard [as] to get blood out of a beet," her brother Custis had teased her. But by then both their lives had grown increasingly melancholy. "We are just about to break up our home—I am too weary & tired & sad to write about it," says a note from Mildred that accompanied a Bible of her father's, a paper cutter "constantly used by my Mother," and other remembrances.

The receipts from Tabb and Mary Cocke are raised only with beaten eggs and are weighed down by that Victorian standby, cooked rice—creditable early efforts, perhaps, but by today's standards, heavy, rubbery, and chewy. The third, though, Evelyn Krumbacker's, is a real find.

· EVELYN KRUMBACKER'S WAFFLES ·

I know nothing about Miss or Mrs. Krumbacker, but her waffles — crisp, tender, and slightly perfumed with yeast—have recalled several waffle irons from basement exile. They are easily made, and served with Chicken Terrapin and/or Mrs. Lee's Molasses Sauce, they constitute a fine Lee brunch or Sunday breakfast.

The "yeast powder" called for may be some early, now-forgotten manufactured product or a throwback to Nelly Custis Lewis's, but today's granules work fine. Lumps in the batter dissipate overnight, and the waffles (better when the eggs are not separated) are ready to pour in the morning. They freeze well and can be reheated.

Evelyn Krumbacker— delicious Waffles

1 pint flour
1   "   milk
2 eggs
2 teaspoonfuls yeast powder
1 table spoon melted butter

The Receipts

salt—
Bake in waffle iron very quickly

2 c. sifted flour
2 c. milk
2 eggs
2 t. commercial granular yeast
1 T. melted butter
¼ t. or more salt

Sift salt with flour. Beat eggs. Combine all ingredients. Refrigerate overnight. Next morning cook 4–5 minutes in hot waffle iron. Makes 8 waffles.

Pancakes

The Washington manuscript has many receipts for this food, which may be as old as ground grain and fire. Of the notebook's three, Mrs. Lee's Water Pancakes sufficed when the cow went dry, and Stale Bread Pancakes, in daughter Mary Custis's writing, used up a frequent leftover. Both, though remarkably palatable considering the ingredients, have little to recommend them today. The third, which Mrs. Lee called simply Pancakes, makes the standard crepes widely available in cookbooks.

Mildred sent a dessert based on these thin pancakes to a fundraising cookbook of receipts from notables, in which she and the Bishop of Virginia represented their state. Though it is not in the notebook, she called A Quire of Paper Pancakes "an old-fashioned Virginia receipt, which we used to use at Arlington." It also appears word for word, title and all, in her kinswoman Mary Randolph's *The Virginia House-wife*. To make it, sprinkle sugar on crepes, stack them, and cut into wedges.

Breads

The Lloyd sisters:
above,
Miss Minnie;
opposite,
Miss Jeanie.
(Courtesy of the
Lee family)

The notebook's four receipts for Laplands and Lapland Cakes have imaginative titles compared to most in the notebook. However, they have little else in common beyond a high proportion of eggs and the shape of a muffin. I suspect they were trendy at the time, but their identity had not yet settled down. (Another, from the same period, is raised with whipped cream.) The receipt that Mary Custis wrote in makes a pleasant but unremarkable yeast muffin, with or without the cornmeal she suggested adding. The three others seem to be early attempts at popovers. Of these, the version attributed to Mrs. Maury has too much milk in the batter and collapses. The other two, the best and only marginally different from each other, Mildred attributed to Minnie Lloyd.

The Lloyds were kin, and close. Before the war, Lee used to leave his carriage in their yard while he went to services at Christ Church in Alexandria. Years later, Mary Custis was staying with the Lloyd family when she learned of her father's death, and the families kept in touch afterward too. My aunt remembered that during summers at White Sulphur Springs her father (Rob) called on Miss Minnie and her widowed sister, Miss Jeanie (pronounced "Jinnie") Yeatman every day. Once a season she and my mother had to visit, too. "I thought they were terrible old ladies," she said, "but I was only three or four."

Certainly the sisters became peculiar later. When Miss Jeanie's husband died shortly after Prince Albert, she followed the fashion set by Queen Victoria and took to her bed. There, after she received her visitors' condolences, she would hop out, fully clothed, and everyone had tea.

An old-time Virginian calls Miss Minnie's second receipt for Laplands (which she titled simply "or") "the best batter muffins I ever

The Receipts

ate." These airy clusters of bubbles have more inside them than popovers, and they do resemble the notebook's Batter Pudding—a good, though less unusual, Yorkshire pudding. Half the receipt makes 18 if baked in regular muffin tins, fewer if earthenware cups are used, depending on their size.

· MISS MINNIE'S LAPLANDS ·

4 Eggs—1 pt flour 1 pt milk—add the whites
last—baked in earthenware cups

4 eggs
2 c. flour
½ t. salt
2 c. whole milk or half-and-half
Butter for greasing tins or cups

Separate eggs. Beat whites and yolks separately and well. Sift salt with flour. Combine thoroughly with milk. Fold in yolks, then whites. Fill greased or nonstick muffin tins half full. Bake immediately in preheated 275° oven about 35 minutes or until lightly browned.

Cornbreads

I, like most Virginians, have innumerable ways with cornbread, but all four in the notebook were new to me. I suspect the Lee ladies had their own more extensive repertoire and entered only those outside it. Three are delicious, but the fourth, Mrs. Lee's Muffin Bread, has nowhere near enough milk. Whether baked as muffins, corn sticks, or a loaf, and made with and without baking powder, it crumbles like damp sand or becomes so dense a soldier could live off one piece for a week.

Breads

I was curious about the Anne Carter who contributed Rice Bread, essentially a cornbread with rice incorporated in it, since I share her name. A likely candidate did not present herself, and so I braved the briarpatch of Lee and related genealogy, to find Anne Carters all the way back to seventeenth-century England, where one married a Lee before the families left for Virginia. Mrs. Wickham of Hickory Hill, where Agnes Lee and Orton Williams parted dramatically, was another Anne Carter. And a cousin Anne Carter lived next door to Lee's sister Anne in Baltimore. The niece of *that* Anne Carter, Charlotte Haxall, became Rob's first wife. It was all quite a tangle.

Finally I realized I had known the most likely donor myself—my grandmother's younger sister, Anne Willing Carter Dulany. She was a good friend of Mildred, who wrote it in, as the baking powder suggests, fairly late. This Anne Carter oversaw my mother and my aunt after their parents died. We children called her Nannee, and when I knew her, she was a regal presence. Her dresses, as I remember, were black and reached the floor. I loved her sparkly jet throatband (and now that I know what such bands can do for an aging chin, I covet it). After she broke a hip, she used to pay calls in a hearse, or maybe an ambulance. I remember how we all went outside to say hello.

I wouldn't have dared say so to the lady I knew, but in this receipt either the baking time or the number of pans is wrong. Spread over two pans, the batter is too thin; it almost always burns in spots, but between the spots is an unusual hors d'oeuvre. A single pan needs more cooking time and makes a thinnish, good, moist cornbread, more usual and probably more authentic. Cooked in a single pan, the rice, which Virginians had been combining with cornmeal since colonial times, remains noticeable and becomes crisp bits in the top crust. Cooked my mother's way (detailed below), the rice retains the right amount of water. If it is drier, particularly if reheated in a microwave, it may need to absorb a few tablespoons of hot water before it is added. Double-acting baking powder need not be added last as the receipt directs.

The Receipts

· RICE BREAD (ANNE CARTER) ·

1 tea cup of raw rice—boiled well done—drain off all the water—stir in a table spoon full of butter—when rice is hot—& one teaspoonful of salt. Then stir in a good tea cup of meal—½ pint of new milk—2 eggs well beaten together—& last of all 2 teaspoonsful of baking powder—Grease with butter the baking pan & bake in a moderately quick oven about 15 minutes.

¾–1 c. raw rice
1 T. butter, plus more for greasing the pan

Breads

1 t. salt
¾–1 c. white water-ground cornmeal
1 c. part half-and-half, part cream
2 eggs
2 t. baking powder

In a large pot of water, boil rice about 20 minutes until soft. Drain in a colander. Preheat oven to 400°. Stir butter into hot rice. Stir baking powder and salt into meal. Butter well 1 or 2 (see above) shallow baking pans about 8 × 10 inches in size (glass or heavy iron pans give the best crust). Combine cornmeal mixture with rice. Add milk to beaten eggs and stir in. For 2 pans, bake about 15 minutes in top quarter of oven, or until lightly browned; for 1 pan, bake in middle of oven 25–30 minutes. Cut in squares. Serve hot.

You Say Batterbread, and I Say...

Until I read that the term "spoonbread" did not see print until 1906, I had assumed that it and batterbread were the same bland, succulent, heavy, down-home background for other food. Since baking powder had become common by the time the name "spoonbread" came in, maybe the slightly fluffy stuff made with it is spoonbread? And the more solid stuff made without baking powder, with the cream-of-wheatish texture of period receipts served in Williamsburg and in the notebook, is batterbread?

Maybe, but like the *Iliad* and *Odyssey*, many receipts circulated widely long before they were written down. Many accomplished cooks could not read, and some still cannot; the man who served as our cook in Pakistan had learned an extensive repertoire from his illiterate grandfather. Closer to home but further away in time, laws in Virginia against teaching slaves to read all but guaranteed that many cooks learned more by ear and by watching and doing than by book. Mistresses routinely read receipts to their servants. Even now,

The Receipts

when we are deluged with printed receipts, who does not make a casserole or dessert or two from memory?

At any rate, the notebook has two soft breads that taste predominantly of cornmeal. The one Superneat attributed to Mary Cocke, with no baking powder and the title Batter Bread, contains cooked rice in addition to cornmeal. The rice adds heft and moisture and disappears in the baking. The other receipt is much the same, but "small hominy" takes the place of rice and gives it more corn taste. Its name, Owendaw Cornbread, raises another issue: where did it come from?

Southern chef and food writer Bill Neal identifies Awendaw as a Native American settlement outside of Charleston, South Carolina. Daughter Mary Custis, who wrote in the receipt, loved to travel, but she may never have gone there. The receipt she recorded is word for word the same as Sarah Rutledge's in her 1847 *A Carolina Housewife* (which borrows heavily from Mrs. Randolph). Even the spelling—or misspelling—of Owendaw is the same. Chances are good that Mary Custis copied it from there or from someone else who already had.

Nowadays we call small hominy "grits," for reasons history has left behind in language. Like pone, made with cornmeal and water, hominy comes from an Indian word for corn, *opone*. The hominy used in the Lees' time was dried corn ground somewhat coarser than cornmeal. In colonial times, both meal and grits were made by pounding; a huge hollow log used for that purpose is still at Stratford, where Lee was born. When mills took over the task, hominy became the coarser grain left behind when cornmeal passed through a finer screen. Sometimes it was produced at home, too, as the "hominy mill" in the 1840 inventory of Stonewall Jackson's house shows. At some point, grain on the way to and from larger mills became known as "grist," an old word for gnash or grind. It took only one slight change to turn "grist" to "grits."

Some say Indians were already making the moist kind of hominy we know today before white settlers arrived; certainly something

Breads

close survives in modern Mexico. But Williamsburg food researcher and hominy authority Patricia Gibbs traces this wetter process to the middle of the nineteenth century. The grandfather of a friend, herself now past eighty, would have agreed; he called it "the modern way." As Mrs. Algie Norton explains in *The Foxfire Book*, whole corn is first soaked in lye water for eight or nine hours, then washed about a dozen times to get rid of the hulls and poisonous lye, and the kernels boiled "about all night." The result, I understand, is delicious, and tastes only vaguely like canned hominy.

Back when people had more time and ate more calories, my mother built a special Sunday breakfast on soft cornbread. In it, simple dishes combined into a complex whole—somewhat, perhaps, in the manner of plantation meals. Beyond the zone where the menu is just good home cooking, this meal earns gourmet points as a brunch or supper. But do not invite those who, like the Duchess of Windsor, cannot be too rich or too thin or those who are seriously cholesterol-challenged.

To pull out all the stops, I start with mint juleps in silver cups. Then come tastes that are salty, sweet, acid, peppery, and bland, and textures from soft to crisp and from smooth to sharp. It goes like this: On each plate, place a base of steaming batterbread. Add butter, then creamed oysters in season or creamed chicken. Then comes salt roe herring, both fish and roe rolled in cornmeal and fried in bacon grease; those who balk at all those tiny bones may substitute thinly slivered country ham or lean country bacon. For sweet, slice apples skin and all, sprinkle with brown sugar, and fry in, yes, bacon grease. For acid, dredge semiripe tomatoes in cornmeal seasoned liberally with pepper and, yes again, fry in bacon grease. Serve a light dessert, if any—perhaps the notebook's Wine Jelly or Pineapple Ice.

Owendaw cornbread is heavy and solidifies when cold. You can fry leftovers like mush or sprinkle the cold cornbread with water and reheat in a microwave oven or double boiler. Make this, as always, with white water-ground meal and grits. The test and best part of good batterbread is the brown, shiny crust that forms when the batter is poured into hot cast-iron (authentic) or ovenproof glass. For softer bread, use the lesser amount of grits and/or add a few more tablespoons of milk, half-and-half, or cream. For a fluffier texture, use baking powder. This should serve fifteen, but eight have finished it off.

· OWENDAW CORNBREAD ·

Owendaw Cornbread (Very Nice)

Take about 2 teacups of small hominy boil it, and while hot mix with it a very large spoonful of Butter. Beat 4 eggs very light, and stir them into the hominy; add about 1 pint of milk, gradually stirred in, and at least ½ pint of cornmeal. The batter should be as thick as a rich boiled custard. If thicker add a little more milk. Bake with a good deal of heat at the bottom of the oven, and not too much at the top, so as to allow it to rise. The pan it is to be baked in should be a deep one, so as to allow space for rising. When cooked it has the appearance of a baked Batter Pudding.

3–3½ c. hot cooked grits
2 T. butter, plus more for the pan
4 eggs
2–2¼ c. milk or half-and-half
1–1½ c. white water-ground cornmeal
2½ t. baking powder and 1 t. salt may be added, if desired

Stir butter into hot, cooked grits. Grease a 10-cup or larger baking dish and put into an oven while it preheats to 400°. Stir salt and baking powder, if desired, into cornmeal. Beat eggs very light. Fold eggs into cooled grits, then milk, then meal. Carefully pour batter into hot pan; it should sizzle. Bake in lower third of oven about an hour, until well browned.

Breads

Oats

This grain does not seem to have been important to the Lees, but the notebook does have a newspaper column extolling its virtues that contains two receipts. The one for Bannock, a sort of Highlander C-ration made from oats and water, is portable but barely palatable unless heated and smothered in enough good jam to make anything taste good. The other, Porridge, when made with either imported Scottish oatmeal or the supermarket kind, explains why cold oatmeal was a punishment in Dickens novels; hot, it is not much better. Since the clipping is clean, perhaps the ladies did not make either of them.

Cakes' Progress

A true heirloom cake is said to be a prize from the past. Certainly the notebook suggests that Progress has been hard on cakes. As they have grown airier and more moist, they have lost that special succulent solidity I enjoyed even in my own childhood. They were, as a cousin remembers, "not much for looks but hell for substanch," a description that fits the Lees' cakes well. Even the sponge cakes in the notebook have "substanch," and sometimes icing can make appearances a problem. Everyone who tried these loved them all, even a husband who had given up on modern cake.

Looking for the Robert E. Lee

The general's favorite cake is not in the notebook, presumably because the ladies already knew how to make it. Nevertheless, it kept popping up—in modern books of period receipts and from friends who sent more, unsolicited. And only two were the same. What was going on? Little did I know where finding out would lead.

According to one authority, the Robert E. Lee Cake was not in-

The Receipts

vented until the 1890s or even as late as the 1920s. However, Mrs. Tyree published two receipts for it in 1879. One of these adds only one sentence of instruction to the version Miss Edmonia Lee identified as "Mrs. Lee's Cake" when she contributed it to *Virginia Cookery—Past and Present*, a compendium cookbook published in 1957 by the Women's Auxiliary of Olivet Episcopal Church (reproduced below, with permission). And Miss Edmo should have known how to make the authentic cake. Her father, Dan, was the son of the general's brother Smith Lee and "kept the door" with Rob after Appomattox, shielding the defeated general from his admirers. Years later, my aunt remembered the two men visiting back and forth on horseback, and she remembered Miss Edmo well.

The other receipts varied wildly, and one house museum I promised anonymity serves defrosted Sarah Lee (definitely not kin) as the general's favorite. But most of the other receipts I saw have sponge or very light layers and soft, citrus-flavored filling and frosting—except for the one that calls for grape jelly between the layers; we will return to that later.

Food historian Karen Hess calls many so-called historic receipts "modernized beyond recognition," and certainly most of the versions I came upon bear only a distant relationship to Miss Edmo's. But how did these changes happen, and why? Slowly I began to realize that receipts are a kind of folklore. Like folktales, they are recreated each time they are made or told, and each time they can be—and often are—changed by the taste and times of the maker. That is a very different process from reproducing either one mechanically; frozen in print, each tale or receipt becomes identical to the next.

On a less theoretical level, cooks change receipts all the time, without thinking much about it. Say you lack the canned cherries your mother used before freezing became common. Frozen cherries taste better, anyway, so you use them. Then you pass the receipt along, listing fresh or frozen cherries as an ingredient.

Cakes

I had no desire to collect the tremendous number of examples that would be needed to trace the twists and turns of this cake's journey from cook to cook through changing culture. But in the few receipts I did examine I could see traces of what probably happened.

The *Virginia Cookery* committee intended to be faithful to Miss Edmo's receipt when they made it, and compared to other later examples, they were. Nevertheless, the 1950s crept in. The ladies baked basically a simple sponge cake batter in layer cake pans, which are close to Miss Edmo's jelly cake tins but thicker. For "nice 'A' sugar" in what they called "icing" (a word not in the original) they used confectioner's sugar, a reasonable choice, since people had been pounding hard loaf sugar into powder for a long time. But foodways professionals Walker Allard at Stratford Hall Plantation and Dennis Cotner of Colonial Williamsburg think that "A" sugar meant the finest grade, closer to granulated or superfine. In addition, the receipt for the nearly identical "Gen. Robert Lee Cake" sent to Mrs. Tyree calls simply for sugar, neither powdered nor confectioner's.

No one would mistake what went on top of the Lee cake for nineteenth-century icing, which was generally white and hard. "You can write on it with a pencil," one lady commented on her receipt approvingly. By the 1950s, though, at least among the southerners I knew, "icing" meant whatever went on cakes. The committee followed Miss Edmo's directions, but what they called icing actually sank into the cake. Granulated and superfine sugar left a thin, gritty, brittle crust. Powdered sugar turned into a sort of penetrating glaze.

Meanwhile, over time, as other cooks followed their own ideas about icing, most of the other examples of the Robert E. Lee cake developed soft frosting and filling while keeping the distinctive lemon-orange flavor—except for the renegade made with grape jelly.

Most people prefer Miss Edmo's version of the cake made with confectioner's sugar; the result is certainly prettier, and it could be correct. Personally, I like the gritty crunch left behind by superfine,

The Receipts

so I follow the sugar experts, even though the mixture never becomes "perfectly smooth," as the receipt says it will.

As for the layers, a receipt of Mrs. Tyree's allows only two-and-a-half tablespoons of batter to a jelly cake layer. Authenticity buffs may feel free, but thicker layers—split or not, depending on you and the occasion—are much easier to handle. Stacking a full receipt is tricky, too; use skewers until the "non-icing" sets. Or dodge the problem and halve the receipt to make three or four layers, to serve six to eight.

Perhaps restoring heirloom receipts (maybe heirloom anything) is inherently an uncertain pursuit, like restaging ballets from written notations, only less strenuous and more fattening. Just be sure to mark "improvements" clearly as such when you pass on this original—if, indeed, it is that.

· MRS. LEE'S CAKE ·

Twelve eggs, their full weight in sugar, a half weight in flour. Bake it in pans the thickness of jelly cakes. Take two pounds of nice "A" sugar, squeeze into it the juice of 5 oranges and three lemons together with the pulp. Stir in the sugar until perfectly smooth, then spread it over the cakes as you would jelly—putting one above another till the whole of the sugar is used up.

Mrs. Robert E. Lee

Half quantity:

Cake:
6 eggs, separated
1½ c. sugar
1½ c. flour

Non-Icing:
1 1-lb. box confectioner's sugar, sifted, *or* 2 c. superfine

Cakes

4 T. orange juice plus 1 T. rind
4 t. lemon juice plus 1 T. rind

Preheat oven to 350°. Grease and flour bottoms only of layer pans. To mix by hand, beat yolks light, add sugar gradually, beating until very light; fold in flour, then beaten whites. To mix with a stand mixer, beat *whole* eggs 15 minutes in all, starting on low and increasing to high; when soft peaks form, fold in flour. Bake about 20 minutes for 3 layers, less time for more, thinner layers. To ice, follow directions in the original, reserving slightly more of the juice-and-sugar mixture for the top.

The Notebook's Sponge Cakes

The notebook has six receipts for what is essentially sponge cake, although some titles vary, marking this as a decided family favorite. Two of them demonstrate this cake's close relationship to Jelly Cake: a receipt with that name has exactly the same ingredients and proportions as one Sponge Cake, and only the quantities differ. Jelly Cake makes one layer to spread with jelly, while Sponge Cake fills a tube pan. Since sponge cake remained small and ladyfinger-like until whips were developed to increase the volume of eggs, Jelly Cake may well be the precursor of Sponge Cake; if not, the two are close kin.

A variant, Butter Sponge, reminds me of a heavy, succulent genoise. The rest are all very much alike. Superneat attributed one to Sarah Compton, among the large Lexington Presbyterian contingent, who in 1877 lived where the Robert E. Lee Memorial Church stands now. Like the Lee sisters and many other white southern women after the war, she never married.

Two of the three other receipts came from unknown donors. Mildred wrote them in merely as lists of ingredients, which shows how familiar she was with making sponge cake. Although Mildred did

The Receipts

not attribute any of them, Mrs. Lee identified one as Mrs. Hay's. It is marginally the heaviest, and to my mind the best, except that it calls for lemon juice. I prefer not to disguise the purity and egginess of the Lee sponge cakes, but other cooks, particularly younger ones, prefer the taste of brandy and mace, vanilla extract, or lemon juice that flavor all but one receipt.

Mrs. Hay was probably Emily Hay, a widow who kept a boarding house near VMI. She was an intimate friend of Mildred's, and considering the family's multigeneration friendships, she could have been a connection of the Mrs. Hay to whom Mary Anna Randolph Custis wrote some thirty years before announcing her engagement to Lieutenant Robert Lee.

Mildred sent Emily spritely word sketches from her travels with Mary Custis, on subjects ranging from Queen Victoria's Diamond Jubilee to icebergs in the North Sea. Having been boosted up on a camel once myself, I suspect her account of being pushed up a pyramid is more amusing than it felt. And Mildred confided deeper feelings as well, confessing "the need for someone to take care of me." From Romancoke, where the youngest Lee daughter said she was happiest staying with her brother Rob and his children (my mother and my aunt), she wrote, "be thankful that you have your own little home—anything can be endured if you have that!"

· MRS. HAY'S SPONGE CAKE ·

1 lb sugar
½ lb flour
9 eggs
Juice of one or two lemons according to size

2 c. sugar
2 c. flour

Cakes

9 eggs
Juice of 1½ large lemons or to taste

Preheat oven to 350°. Butter and flour bottom only of a 9- to 10-inch
tube pan. To mix by hand, beat lemon juice into yolks and beat until
light; add sugar gradually, beating until very light, fold in flour, then
beaten whites. To mix with a stand mixer, beat lemon juice and *whole*
eggs 15 minutes in all, starting on low and increasing to high; when
soft peaks form, fold in flour. Bake 45 minutes to 1 hour, until an inserted skewer comes out clean.

The Fall of the Great Cake and Rise of the Layer

The gigantic "great cakes" of the Washington manuscript, which
were raised with yeast and eggs beaten tediously with a rod, lasted
for months and resemble sweet bread. Many could be boiled as puddings as well. The cakes in the Lee notebook, however, except for a
few of the sponge cakes, are made in the now familiar but then probably new layers. The change toward lightness had already begun in
the Great Cake receipt "wrote by Martha Custis for her Grandma,"
Martha Washington, which is now at Mount Vernon. Though raised
by eggs only and not baked in layers, it is substantially lighter and
cooks in only two hours instead of six or even longer.

If layer cakes did not arise from earlier jelly cakes, the two were
inseparably intertwined. In Mrs. Tyree's book, sponge cake baked in
layers is called jelly cake, layer cakes are baked in jelly cake pans, and
jelly cake layers are stacked, with jelly spread in between. The jelly
could, of course, be any flavor, and in one jelly cake receipt it has
been supplanted by a lemon-flavored filling. Finally the Robert E.
Lee cake with grape jelly between the layers is not so strange after all.

Shrinking households, the proliferation of the cast-iron stove, and
manufactured leavenings all played their part in the rise of the layer
cake, too. Forty eggs went into Martha Custis's receipt and thirty

into Nelly Custis Lewis's Black Cake, a fruitcake and arguably the lone modern survivor of the Great Cake. (The "Mrs. L." who contributed it to Mrs. Lewis's cookbook may have been Mrs. Lee.) But after the Civil War fewer people needed or could afford such huge concoctions. The large brick ovens of cooking fireplaces gave way to the smaller ones in stoves. These, being more easily regulated, were better adapted to the quicker, more precise baking requirements of chemicals such as baking powder.

· MISS BETTY ALEXANDER'S ORANGE CAKE ·

The Lee ladies collected four of Miss Betty's receipts, and Mrs. Lee added a crucial instruction from Miss Betty to another. Snow Mountain, a layer cake receipt copied in by Superneat, has a good but not unusual batter and soft white icing made from beaten egg whites that may have been a revelation then (see Icing) but is a passé standard now. Its smothering of real, fresh coconut remains glorious, though, and now that frozen and even fresh coconut is often available already grated, it is possible even for the time-impaired.

Mildred entered Orange Cake as a variation on Miss Betty's Cup Cake. The latter seems dull and floury now, but an eighty-nine-year-old devotee of orange cake declares the former the best she ever tasted.

Miss Betty, who, like the Lee sisters, never married, lived most of her life at Clifton, still one of Lexington's loveliest houses, where the Lees called often. Her forebears had arrived when Lexington was a collection of log cabins and built a combined store and residence that survived a disastrous fire. By the 1850s her family was prospering in the manufacture of blast furnaces. As embedded in Lexington families as the Lees were in Tidewater genealogy, the Alexanders were also deeply involved in higher education. Miss Betty's great-great-uncle founded Augusta Academy, which grew ultimately into Wash-

Cakes

ington College, where Lee was later president. One of her uncles was a founder of Princeton. And a first cousin was the wife of "Old Zeus," the Greek professor who led the school's students off to the Civil War. The biggest of the college's "big four," he became Lee's closest confidant and later acted as president during Custis Lee's frequent illnesses. Another Alexander first cousin was the first wife of Colonel J. T. L. Preston, a founder of VMI and for many years half the faculty.

The Orange Cake receipt, at a culinary crossroads, calls for cream of tartar and soda, which together make baking powder, a chemical

The Receipts

leavening that was on the way in, and implies cone sugar, which was on its way out. (Substitute sugar cubes or grate the orange rind and use granulated sugar if you like.) Sweet milk simply means milk rather than buttermilk or sour milk; as usual, half-and-half is more authentic. This makes four regular 9-inch layers, more if they are thinner.

Cup Cake—Miss Betty Alexander

6 eggs—4 cups flour—1 butter—1 sweet milk—2½ of sugar.
One teaspoon cream of tartar—½ of soda—season as you like it.

Orange Cake—by the same

Take the above receipt—omit one cup of flour—rub the outside of
3 oranges on sugar & grate it into the batter. Bake as you do Jelly Cake.
Make an icing of four eggs (the whites) & add the orange juice.

Cake:
3 c. (*not* 4) sifted flour
2½ c. sugar
1½ t. baking powder *or* 1 t. cream of tartar and ½ t. soda
3 oranges (for orange cake only)

Icing:
4 c. sugar
Juice of 3 oranges plus enough water to make 2 c. liquid
4 egg whites

Preheat oven to 350°. Butter and flour cake pans. Grate rind or rub sugar cubes over it to absorb the essence, then crush and sift, adding granulated sugar if necessary. Sift flour with leavening. Cream butter, add sugar, and cream until very light. To mix with rotary or light electric: Separate eggs and beat yolks, then whites, until very light. Add grated orange rind to yolks and beat into creamed butter and sugar. Fold in flour, then egg whites. To mix with heavy stand

Cakes

mixer: Drop whole eggs one by one into creamed butter and sugar, beating on medium speed. Fold in flour mixture. Bake 35–40 minutes or until tops spring back when lightly pressed. For icing: Follow directions for Silver Cake (below), substituting orange juice for water.

· SPICE CAKE NORVELL ·

"You must thank Miss Norvell [Caskie] for her nice cake," Lee wrote to his wife from near Petersburg. "I . . . assembled all the young gentlemen around it & though I told them it was a present from a beautiful young lady, they did not leave a crumb." The Caskie-Lee friendship stretches back at least to Mr. Custis's death, when Mr. Caskie, a lawyer, helped settle the snarled estate. In Richmond the hospitable family housed Mrs. Lee and several daughters for months, both before and after the ill-fated Christmas at Hickory Hill. Generations later, the friendship continues. My friend Norvell Caskie Sharp Loughborough sent the picture of her grandmother as a seventeen-year-old belle.

In a playful attempt to marry off Rob while—perhaps not so playfully—retaining his daughters, the general encouraged his youngest son's "advancements toward Miss N," a good friend of Mildred, who considered Norvell the height of fashion. Stuck in provincial Lexington, the youngest Lee daughter asked Agnes, who was visiting in worldly Richmond, whether there "they gore the dresses as much as Norvell's." And at Rooney's second wedding, Lee wrote his wife, who was too crippled to attend, that Mildred was "perfectly happy as she had on last evg. a dress about 2 yds longer than Norvell's."

If this is not the cake Norvell sent, the officers missed a treat. Rich and redolent of spices, it is best when they are freshly ground, and the velvety crumb suggests that lard was more than a wartime economy. Excellent plain, it is even better with thin brown sugar icing,

The Receipts

Cakes

best of all with ½–⅔ cups chopped black walnuts in the filling and on top. You may sift spices and soda with flour and need not let the batter stand. To sour half-and-half or cream, add 2 tablespoons lemon juice or vinegar per cup and allow to stand 10 minutes.

1 nutmeg
1 tablespoonful of cinnamon, 1 of Allspice, 1 of cloves, 1 lb of flour, 1 lb of brown sugar well dried, ½ lb of butter, ½ lb of lard, 7 eggs, 1 wine-glass of brandy beat sugar till very smooth, add flour & eggs alternately & the brandy & spices. Dissolve 1 teaspoonful of soda in a tea cup of sour milk or cream— Add it just before baking & be careful to let it rise well before you bake— Bake in pans not more than two inches deep.

1 nutmeg pulverized in a clean coffee grinder or
   mini-food processor or 1–1½ T. ground nutmeg
1 T. each of cinnamon, allspice, and cloves
3¾ c. flour
2¼ c. dark brown sugar, well packed (1 lb.)
1 c. (2 sticks) butter
1 c. lard
⅛–¼ c. brandy
7 eggs
1 t. baking soda
1 c. sour half-and-half or milk

Preheat oven to 325°. Cream butter and lard, add sugar and cream until very light. You may sift soda and spices with flour. Add flour and eggs alternately, then the brandy. Dissolve soda in sour milk and stir in just before baking. Bake in 4 greased, floured layer cake pans 15–20 minutes. Layers may be thin.

This was the quintessential cake when I was young and cakes were wonderful. Our version undoubtedly had baking powder instead of the yeast specified in the receipt below, but it had the same taste, texture, and "substanch."

Well into the nineteenth century, dry yeast was stirred into flour used for baking cakes. Although yeast powder must have been different then, today's granulated kind raises the cake pleasingly, and anyone inclined to experiment further might try the newer rapid-rising yeast. The confectioner's sugar should be weighed rather than measured by volume. Makes three regular layers, more if thinner.

The icing may have developed from the hard kind given in the Icing receipt directly below. Popular in the 1940s, it is rare now, probably because beating it to the right consistency is tricky—and can be impossible in muggy weather. With two cooks, one to beat and the other to pour, and some luck, it develops just the right thin, smooth, slightly brittle surface, a touch gooey underneath.

Silver Cake

10 oz powdered sugar	(How to mix the cake)
" " flour	Cream butter & sugar
7 oz butter	Then mix in the whites (well beaten)
Whites 10 eggs	then the flour—milk—etc—
½ cup of milk	Bake in jelly cake pans—
2 teaspoonfuls yeast powder	
½ " of almond	For the icing
	Boil the sugar with a pint of water—
Icing	when almost candy—mix with the
1½ lbs powdered sugar	whites (well beaten) then beat all
whites 3 eggs	well & put in layers.

Cakes

Cake:

3¾ c. sifted confectioner's sugar
  (or preferably 10 oz. by weight)
2½ c. sifted flour
1 c. minus 1 T. butter
½ c. milk or half-and-half (preferred)
2 t. granular yeast
½ t. almond extract

Icing:

9 c. sifted powdered sugar
  (or preferably 1½ pounds sifted)
2 c. water
3 egg whites

Cake: Preheat oven to 375°. Grease and flour cake pans. Stir yeast into flour and almond into milk, then follow original directions. Bake about 25 minutes for regular layers, less for thinner, until a toothpick comes out clean. Cool on a rack.

Icing: Bring sugar and water to a boil, cover a few minutes, uncover, and boil to 238° to 240° on a candy thermometer, or until syrup spins a thin thread. Beat egg whites stiff. Pour syrup into them in a thin stream, beating constantly, until thick but spreadable. Use between layers, on top and sides of cake. Allow several hours to dry.

· ICING FOR THE LEES' CAKES ·

Judging from the cooking stains, the Lee ladies used the notebook's only separate receipt for icing often. It seems to be descended from one in *The Art of Cookery Made Plain and Easy* by Hannah Glasse, who may have been a male hack writer in London, but whose book was used extensively in America. It seems likely that Martha Washington relegated the Washington manuscript to the library and used

The Receipts

her copy of Mrs. Glasse in the kitchen. This excerpt, giving the ancestor of the version in the cookbook, comes from the 1805 edition, published in Alexandria, Virginia (quoted in *Virginia Cookery, Past and Present*, used with permission):

To Ice a Great Cake

Take the whites of twenty four eggs and a pound of double refined sugar beat and sifted fine; mix both together in a deep earthen pan, and with a whisk, whisk it well for two or three hours, till it looks white and thick, then with a thin broad board, or bunch of feathers, spread it all over the top and sides of the cake; set it at a proper distance before a good clear fire, keep turning it continually for fear of its changing colour; but a cool oven is best, and will harden it. You may perfume the icing with what perfume you please.

No wonder that icing died out. Although modern-day substitutes for hand beating and feathers make the notebook's version feasible, it remains tedious, and the result shatters at the touch of a knife. The secret to avoiding brittleness may lie in another of Mrs. Glasse's icing receipts, which calls for an unspecified gum that should make it less fragile. For flavoring, we found that rose water, instead of extract of roses, was strong enough, and almond or vanilla extract may be substituted. Each coat dried 2½ hours in a 150-degree oven with the door cracked open; the second coat stayed in overnight with the heat turned off. The receipt makes only enough icing for one coat. Make the second batch fresh, feel free to forgo the feathers, and pay attention to Miss Betty's advice.

Icing

A qr. lb of finely powdered loaf sugar, to one white of egg. Beat the white by itself till it stands alone. Beat the sugar hard into the white till it becomes thick & smooth. Flavor it with the juice of orange or extract of roses.

Cakes

Spread it evenly with a broad knife or feathers. If too thin, beat in a little more powdered sugar. Cover thickly tops & sides, taking care [illegible] to have enough [illegible]. When dry put on a second coat.
[Note by Mrs. Lee:] Miss Bettie Alexander says you should <u>well beat</u> eggs before putting in the sugar.

For each coat:
1½ c. or ¼ lb. sifted confectioner's sugar (better to weigh it)
1 egg white
¼–½ t. almond or vanilla extract *or*
   ¼ c. orange juice *or* 1 T. rose water.

Gingerbread over the Ocean

The notebook's seven receipts for gingerbread—and Mrs. Lee gave Mrs. Lewis yet another—mark it as a family favorite. Four (two of them Mrs. Lee's) make the soft, cakelike kind; three others are for what we now call gingersnaps. These supposedly arrived with the colonists from England, but in the Washington manuscript, which also arrived from England, only one gingerbread receipt is recognizable as such today. That one features treacle, roughly British for molasses, and is baked. The rest underwent as profound a sea change as did ballads and folktales on their way across the Atlantic. Most consist basically of breadcrumbs in sweet wine syrup and are "culler'd" red or purple, even left white.

These bizarre concoctions had an equally bizarre beginning. Karen Hess traces them to a medicine made from mashed parsnips, called *gingibrati.* Over time, the sound affected the substance, which became gingerbread, in somewhat the same way that the French Sol et Lune may (and may not) have crossed the Channel and turned into Sally Lunn.

Most of the notebook's gingerbread receipts taste lovely made with today's molasses. Chances are, though, molasses was stronger and more bitter then. We probably cannot duplicate the Lees' gingerbread, and we might not like it if we could. (Something closer than most is the blackstrap molasses available from the Virginia Honey Company, P.O. Box 246, Berryville, VA 22611.)

"Recipe for *my* gingerbread," Mrs. Lee wrote firmly on one of her two gingersnap receipts. It has significantly more brown sugar than molasses, and it leaves the spicing entirely to the cook. Since then, the receipt has kept her name but has spread and changed, much like the ones for her husband's favorite cake, though probably not as much. As molasses grew gentler, the proportions of it rose. The dough is usually chilled now, and so it can be rolled out with less flour, making more tender, flavorful cookies. However, it is highly doubtful that anyone fortunate enough to own a small ice refrigerator then gave space to cookie dough.

· MRS. LEE'S GINGERBREAD ·

6 cups of flour 1 of lard with a table spoonfull of butter, two tea spoonfuls salt, a cup of butter milk, teaspoonful of soda sifted with the flour, a full cup of brown sugar, as much molasses as will make a dough which must be rolled out and baked in a moderate oven. The dough should be well worked out & rolled with flour enough to make the cakes smooth but not to have any on the outside when baked.

6 c. flour
1 t. baking soda
2 t. salt
1 c. minus 1 T. lard
1 T. butter
1 c. brown sugar, lightly packed

Cakes

1 c. buttermilk

About 1 c. dark molasses

5 T. ginger *or* 4 T. ginger, 2 t. cinnamon, and 1 t. cloves

Sift flour with salt, baking soda, and spices. Cream together lard, butter, and brown sugar. Stir in flour mixture and buttermilk, adding alternately until well mixed. Stir in molasses until dough is the right consistency to be rolled. On a floured surface, roll out to a thickness of about ¼ inch and cut into 2- to 2¼-inch rounds or other shapes. Bake at 350° 12–15 minutes. Makes about 6 dozen. For serving and storing suggestions, see following receipt.

· MRS. LEE'S CRISP GINGER CAKE ·

Although the anise seed in this receipt seems unusual now, it is probably a holdover from the time of the Washington manuscript, where four gingerbread receipts call for "anny seed." The darker the molasses the better, and whether you use all butter or half lard makes little difference. When I misread Mrs. Lee's cramped "shapes" as "strips," the cookies I baked vanished more quickly than when they were plain rounds.

A fourth of this huge receipt makes about 120 small strips ¼ inch thick, ½ inch wide, and 5 inches long. The dough keeps for weeks when refrigerated and indefinitely when frozen, and the cakes themselves last for weeks in a tight tin box. Serve them for tea or with light desserts, such as Cold Jelly, Snow Pudding, fruit compotes, or ices.

3 lbs flour 1 sugar one butter or lard 3 tablespoonfull ginger
& some cloves & aniseed & wet it with molasses roll it thin,
cut in shapes & bake with quick heat.

The Receipts

...ps of flour 1 of lard with a spoonful of butter two tea spoonfu...

...cup of butter milk teaspoonful of soda sifted with the flour all

...more sugar is much molasses as will make a dough which

...he rolled out + baked in a moderate oven. The doughnuts

...Kee smooth worked out + rolled with the flour enough to mix like thi...

...smooth but not to have any on the outside when baked

Recipe in my gingerbread   M C Lee

One-quarter quantity:
¼ c. butter plus ¼ c. lard *or* ½ c. butter, at room temperature
½ c. sugar
About 3 c. sifted flour
About ½ c. dark molasses
2½ t. ginger
¼ t. cloves
¼ t. anise seed (½ t. if you like it;
    I don't, but here a little adds a lot)

Preheat oven to 350°. Grease cookie sheets. Cream shortening, then cream in sugar until very light. Resift flour with ginger and cloves. Add to sugar-shortening mixture in thirds alternately with molasses, beating after each addition. Stir in anise seed. Add more molasses or flour if needed to make dough the consistency of modeling clay. Roll out on lightly floured board. Cut in shapes or strips. Bake 8–10 minutes.

· CAKE GINGERBREAD ·

Soft gingerbread, which seems to have developed in the colonies, first saw print in the first American cookbook, Amelia Simmons's *American Cookery* (1796). Mary Custis's receipts for both kinds came from Carter Hall, where she was probably visiting with Agnes Atkinson Burwell, the widow of her cousin George Burwell, the first of three Burwell men in a row with that name. His father, one of even more Nathaniel Burwells, had left Tidewater and established the plantation in Clarke County, 150 miles or so from Lexington.

As the name Carter Hall indicates, the Burwells and Lees sprang from the same genealogical briar patch. A Burwell married a daughter of Robert "King" Carter, from whom both Lees were descended. (He had twenty-four children by two wives.) Generations later, another Burwell married a sister of Robert Lee's mother, Ann Carter. The Burwell family was so well-connected and powerful in colonial Tidewater that Royal Governor Spotswood objected to adding another to the King's Council, Virginia's highest governing body, because "[already] the greater part of the council are related to the family of Burwells." More, he declared, would make a fair trial for their connections impossible. Later, Spotswood's own grandson (his mother a Dandridge, Martha Washington's maiden name) married a Burwell, and the name Spotswood has been descending in the Burwell family ever since.

Mrs. Lee knew "Cousin Charles" Burwell well enough to invite him to stay in Lexington before their furniture arrived, offering "a bed if he comes after Robert leaves." In the same letter she inquired about a Nathaniel other than the one in nearby Liberty, whose welcoming haunch of venison appears in her notebook and with whom Lee and Mildred would spend the night on their way to the Peaks of Otter. Yet another Burwell, Thomas S., lived in Lexington.

The receipt labeled "My Mother's 'Molasses Gingerbread,'" however, is refreshingly free of family tangle, connected only by friendship and, indirectly, to Tabasco sauce. Mildred used to visit the family of Washington and Lee professor Col. William Preston Johnston and his first wife in Louisiana after he became president of Tulane, and the youngest Lee daughter died while staying with the widowed second Mrs. Johnston, the former Margaret Avery. Margaret probably jotted this receipt, which appears on notepaper headed "Petite-Anse-Island." Later called Avery Island, it is still in her family, and is the home of Tabasco, the famed hot pepper sauce. Her gingerbread is dry.

Another gingerbread receipt in the notebook calls for a full cup of ground ginger and is consequently inedible. The amount may be no mistake, though; both Mrs. Randolph and Mrs. Tyree prescribed just as much. If the three represent some last gasp of medieval spicing (which is known to have been heavy), knights and ladies must

Cakes

have worn armor on their tongues. At any rate, the newer, soft style of gingerbread had probably not quite settled down yet.

Another gingerbread, written in an unknown hand that appears only once, prompted an elderly friend to enthuse, "I haven't had anything like this for seventy years!" It carries me back pretty far, too, to a shadowy parlor shuttered against the sun, where a childhood friend and I played endless hands of Rook. Her grandmother fed us gingerbread cupcakes, and her grandfather, haloed in white curls, was the Reverend Edward Burwell.

So I always make this gingerbread as cupcakes, about four to four and a half dozen, or twice as many miniatures. The amount also fills two 9 × 13-inch pans, and can be halved, or all of it baked and part of it frozen. Mrs. Randolph called her own gingerbread raised with chemicals "plebian," but I call these wonderful. They are best made with unsulphured blackstrap molasses. No icing, please; the slightly gummy top is the best part.

· GINGERBREAD (ANONYMOUS) ·

5 eggs half lb sugar 1 lb flour light pint molasses
2 tablespoonfuls ginger and cloves together 1 teaspoonful soda
1 cup sour milk ½ lb butter creamed

4 c. sifted flour
1 t. baking soda
2 T. ground ginger *or* 5 t. ground ginger and 1 t. ground cloves
1 c. sugar
1 c. (2 sticks) butter
5 eggs
12 oz. dark molasses, blackstrap preferred
1 c. buttermilk or sour half-and-half

Preheat oven to 350°. Grease and flour pans or use nonstick pans. Resift flour with spice and soda. Cream butter, then cream in sugar until very light. Beat in whole eggs one at a time. Add flour and sour milk or buttermilk—plain yogurt in a pinch—alternately in thirds, beating after each addition. Beat in molasses. Bake until a skewer comes out clean, about 10–12 minutes for miniature muffins, 15 minutes for regular cupcakes, 25–35 minutes for large pans.

Cookies to the North, Small Cakes to the South

The Dutch brought the ancestor of the word "cookie" to America along with the beads that bought Manhattan, and Amelia Simmons in Connecticut used it in 1796 in her *American Cookery*. The term may have made its way south slowly, though. The Lees seem to have been more at home with the English term, "small cakes." These probably appeared at tea, which, as high tea still is in Britain, could be a light supper.

The notebook's small cakes are raised with soda, baking powder, and other chemical leavenings that, says Karen Hess, "all but drove out traditional forms of aerating cakes and quick breads" during the nineteenth century in America. They range from delicious to everyday.

Margaret Avery Johnston, who sent her gingerbread receipt from Petite Anse Island in Louisiana. (Courtesy of Special Collections, Leyburn Library, Washington and Lee University)

· CHOCOLATE CAKES ·

Someone spilled ink on this already strong contender for the notebook's most frustrating receipt. Whoever entered it probably forgot the flour, may have left out the butter, specified an overwhelming overdose of chocolate (which had not yet been standardized), and

Cakes

put in no directions whatsoever for combining the batter. But it is also historically intriguing: it is probably one of the earliest receipts for cake that contains chocolate as an ingredient. Before the mid-nineteenth century, chocolate cake receipts, such as Mrs. Randolph's from 1824, produced cakes that accompanied hot chocolate—in the same sense that we speak of coffee cake today.

. Here's a chance for culinary creativity. Whatever these cakes were then, they are good and unusual now in various guises *if* the chocolate is cut far back. They come out very spicy, not very sweet, and still very chocolaty. To experiment with different amounts of flour, butter, and chocolate, use proportions and instructions of standard receipts as guidelines (for example, sponge cupcakes call for 1 cup flour to 3½ ounces chocolate). My first attempt, using the original receipt's proportions but less chocolate, produced delicious little erupted volcanoes. Later efforts using only one-third the amount of bitter chocolate looked more presentable and still tasted lovely, but their superb silky texture seems more akin to contemporary flourless cakes than the sturdier creations of the Lees' era.

*12 eggs, 1½ lbs chocolate grated, 1½ lbs brown sugar, cinnamon,
cardamom seed, nutmeg and cloves to be used for seasoning.
To be baked small tins.*

One-third quantity (makes 18 regular-size cupcakes
   about ⅝ inch high):
4 eggs
3½ oz. unsweetened chocolate, grated
1 c. plus 1 T. brown sugar, packed firmly
2 t. cinnamon
½ t. cloves
⅛ t. (a generous pinch) cardamom

Preheat oven to 400°. Butter generously and dust with confectioner's sugar two cast-iron or nonstick muffin tins. Melt chocolate

The Receipts

2 minutes, tightly covered in microwave; stir in spices, all freshly ground if possible. Beat eggs until very light. Gradually beat in brown sugar and chocolate mixture. Bake about 14 minutes, then turn off oven and allow cakes to cool inside it. They will fall.

· TEA CAKES ·

This receipt—along with those for Miss Betty's Cup Cake, the two other Jumbles, and an anonymous entry called "Cookies"—makes wholesome, everyday sweets, the kind that stay-at-home mothers used to bake for children after school. I would have omitted them all as uninteresting had not a teenager fallen in love with these, the best of the lot. She made them by the hundreds, topped them with lemon–confectioner's sugar icing, and took them to school, where they were promptly devoured. You may want to add salt and substitute baking powder for cream of tartar and soda. And do use the lard. It helps, honestly.

> *2 qts. flour—1 lb. sugar 4 eggs lard & butter 1 teacup—*
> *2 teaspoons cream of tartar & one of soda—flavor with mace*
> *or nutmeg—add a little milk if necessary.*

Half quantity:
3½–4 c. sifted flour (best when 1 c. or more is cake flour)
½ t. salt (my addition)
1½ t. baking powder (see above)
1 T. mace *or* 1 T. nutmeg *or* a combination of the two
¼ c. lard
¼ c. (½ stick) butter
1 c. sugar
2 eggs
Up to ¼ c. milk (optional)

Cakes

Preheat oven to 350°. Sift baking powder, spice, and salt (if desired) with flour. Cream together butter and lard, add sugar gradually and cream until very light. Beat whole eggs until light. Fold in, then fold in dry ingredients. Stir in milk if batter is too stiff to drop in soft mounds. Drop by tablespoons onto well-greased or nonstick cookie sheets. Bake 18–20 minutes. Makes about 50 2-inch cookies.

· MARGUERITES ·

This star of the notebook, though complicated, rewards the effort. Mildred sent the receipt to *Housekeeping in Old Virginia*, where two more receipts for the dish testify to its popularity; who gave the receipt to the Lees I could not determine. The hard meringue that Mrs. Horry used on similar cakes in *The Carolina Housewife* (1847) makes them more portable, but the notebook's other meringues are clearly soft. Since I grew up knowing that kind only, soft seems right to me.

Later, marguerites were simplified into obscurity: mere sponge cupcakes sprinkled with powdered sugar, or cookies topped with melted marshmallows, or cake or crackers with soft meringue on top. But the standouts this receipt produces cause appreciative comments at festive luncheons and teas. I have also used them as individual birthday cakes, with sparklers rising from the crowns of meringue.

They are, conveniently, best made in stages. The bases ripen overnight and will keep about a week sealed in a tin box, longer in the refrigerator, and months in the freezer. Although lemon juice alone stabilizes meringue, cream of tartar adds shrinkage insurance. Smaller, thinner cakes may require using three or four egg whites for the meringue (instead of two to three), with other ingredients increased accordingly. The "pasteboard" called for in the receipt is, of course, a breadboard. And for a refreshing change, directions are detailed.

The Receipts

Rub together 1 lb of sugar & 1 lb of butter, till perfectly light—Beat the yolks of six eggs very thick. Sift 1½ lbs of flour into the eggs, butter and sugar. A teaspoon of mixed spices (cinnamon, mace, & nutmeg) ½ glass of rose water. Stir the whole well—& roll it on the pasteboard about ½ inch thick, then cut out the cakes & bake them a few minutes. When cold spread the top surface of each cake with marmalade or preserves. Beat the whites of 4 eggs [illegible] very light & add enough powdered sugar to make them as thick as icing. Flavor it with lemon & put it on top of each cake. Put the cakes in the oven, and as soon as they are of a pale brown take them out—

Half quantity (makes 25–30 2½-inch cakes
  or up to 50 thinner, smaller cakes):

Bases:
1 c. sugar
1 c. butter
3 egg yolks
3 c. sifted flour
½ t. mixed spices (cinnamon, mace, nutmeg)
¼ c. rose water *or* 1 t. vanilla *or* ½ t. almond extract

Filling and meringue:
2–3 egg whites
4–6 T. sifted powdered sugar
½ t. lemon juice
¼ t. cream of tartar (my addition)
¼–½ c. jelly, jam, or marmalade

Ahead of time: Preheat oven to 350°. Grease cookie sheets or use nonstick type. Sift spices with the flour. Cream butter and sugar and beat in eggs. Add rose water or extract to egg-sugar mixture, then follow mixing directions in the original. Roll bases to desired thickness and bake until barely colored, about 15 minutes for ½-inch cakes. Store overnight, refrigerate, or freeze.

The day of use: Bring bases and egg whites to room temperature.

Cakes

Either preheat oven to 350° or turn on broiler just before browning meringue. Put filling in center of cakes, leaving edges free. Beat egg whites until foamy and continue beating while gradually adding first the cream of tartar, then lemon juice, then sugar, until mixture is stiff but not dry. Spread meringue to edges of bases. Bake in top of oven or under broiler about 5 minutes, until light brown. Turn off oven, open door, allow cakes to cool before removing.

Twists in the Tale of the Jumble

In medieval times, jumbles were intricately interlaced shapes that could be made of almost anything sweet; the Washington manuscript utilizes meringue, marzipan, and fruit paste. By the time of the Lee notebook the name belonged to plain, sweet cookies, and as such they crossed back across the Atlantic, where the British Mrs. Beeton called her receipts for them "American" and "Californian."

The shape of a jumble was not important enough to Mrs. Randolph and Mrs. Lewis to mention, nor was it in the notebook's two receipts for sugar cookie Jumbles, one anonymous and one taken down by Mary Custis from Carter Hall. The third receipt, with the same ingredients and proportions as Mrs. Randolph's, is dated "Lauderdale, 12 March, 1890," the latest in the notebook. Mildred probably collected it on a visit to that Virginia plantation (Mary Custis was in Cairo at the time), but the writing is not that of Mrs. Thomas Henry Johnston, the plantation's mistress.

· LAUDERDALE JUMBLES ·

These dense little cakes may still qualify as plain, but they are luscious and unusual, with crisp edges, a texture between shortbread and pound cake, and the scent of butter and roses. (The nutmeg and brandy flavoring is good too.) Chopped rose geranium leaves work wonders as a rose water substitute, and who's to say the Lee ladies did not use them when they ran out of rose water? I enjoy these cookies most when they are warm and perfumey, straight from the oven, but some like them better after the flavor has developed overnight in a tight tin box. They freeze well and keep several weeks when tightly sealed at room temperature. The receipt makes about 60.

1 lb of butter
1 " " sugar
1 " " flour
4 Eggs. Cream the butter and the sugar. then the eggs beaten lightly <u>together</u>, not separating the whites from the yellow—. add the flour—& seasoning to taste—nutmeg & brandy—or rose water—as may be preferred—.

Bake in papers in small round cakes—in a flat pan—less butter can be used but this is the original receipt and in a colder climate is not too much.

2 c. (4 sticks) butter
2 c. sugar
3¾ c. sifted flour
2 t. nutmeg plus 2 T. brandy *or* ¼ c. rose water
   or 3 T. chopped rose geranium leaves
4 eggs

Heat oven to 350°. Have ingredients at room temperature. Line muffin tins with baking papers. Resift flour with nutmeg if used. Add rose water or brandy to beaten eggs, or sprinkle chopped rose geranium leaves onto baking cups. Follow original directions for combining. Allow 2 level tablespoons batter for each cake. Bake 15–25 minutes or until barely colored and a toothpick comes out clean.

Cakes

A Proliferation of Puddings

The British call just about any dessert "pudding," and they have good reason. The name descends, says Karen Hess, from *boudin,* a fresh French sausage. When this crossed the Channel, it mutated in many directions, accounting eventually for the Scots' beloved haggis—grain and organ meats boiled in a sheep's stomach (the Germans do much the same with a pig's). A cook here, a housekeeping book there, and casings made of innards turned into cloth and the meat into flour and breadcrumbs. Sugar crept in. Puddings began to be baked in inedible "coffins," the precursors of piecrust, and the filling of one pie, *croustarde,* probably became custard.

The Washington manuscript provides glimpses of this progression, with its cakes that can be boiled as puddings, crustless puddings called pies, and a custard pie called a pudding. Even today, fruitcake, plum pudding, and mince pie are distinguished mostly by the way they are cooked, and some mincemeat still contains meat.

Boiled Puddings

Colonists in Williamsburg boiled and baked puddings and pies in both crusts and crockery. The boiling process was hotter, more backbreaking, and more dangerous, for long skirts could catch fire. Gradually, as baking became easier, boiling lost out. Now boiled and steamed puddings (the latter slightly later but similar) may be ripe for a comeback. Making them with today's kitchen equipment is less arduous, and these good and unusual desserts are convenient too; as Cordon Bleu graduate Louise Sinclaire points out, they "keep warm indefinitely." Microwaving works surprisingly well, although it produces a somewhat lighter, drier texture—heresy to purists, but also an object lesson in how and why cooking changes with changing technology.

The Receipts

Although Mrs. Lee probably entered this receipt to help her daughters, it seems to need help itself. One experienced cook dropped out of testing in frustration over it, and my own attempts resembled giant white termites. Someone must like it, though; the receipt is very close to that nostalgic British nursery favorite, rolypoly pudding. Neither a dumpling nor an accompaniment for stew, this is basically dough spread with sweet filling and boiled.

Combining Mrs. Tyree's 1879 receipt for piecrust with Mrs. Glasse's eighteenth-century directions for boiling puddings (as updated by Nancy Carter Crump), this receipt produces a very rich, heavy, unusual dessert. I like a thin slice of it covered with copious sauce, but many others find it "interesting" at best. The receipt, which makes enough for 10 to 15, can be halved and probably quartered.

Roll out some paste thin in a long strip lay in preserves of any kind or stewed fruit well sweetened. Roll it up & close tight & pin or tye strip in a cloth boil 2 hours—Dip in cold water when taken out—

Dough:
1 c. (2 sticks) cold butter
3 c. sifted flour, plus more for rolling surface and pudding cloth
About ¾ c. ice water

Filling:
About 1 c. well-flavored jelly, jam, marmalade,
    sweetened stewed dried apricot, or other fruit puree

Sauce: see suggestions below.

Fill a large oval roaster with enough water to completely cover the pudding; bring to a boil and have more boiling water ready in a kettle. Work butter into flour as for pastry. Add ice water, a few tablespoons at a time, to make a workable paste. Roll out on a floured

Puddings

board into a rectangle about 12 × 14 inches. Spread thinly with filling to within ½ inch of short sides and 1 inch of the final seam on the long side (it will spread). Roll it up like jelly roll. Butter a thick cloth (clean dishtowel or, better, canvas) over the area of the roll and spread with flour. Roll up pastry tightly in the cloth, tie ends with string, pin seam securely. Immerse it completely in boiling water and boil 2 hours, moving occasionally to keep the pudding from sticking to the pan. Replenish with boiling water from the kettle as necessary to keep the roll covered with boiling water at all times; otherwise, pudding will be "sodden," as Mrs. Glasse predicted. After 2 hours, dip roll in cold water and turn out from the cloth. Slice about ¾ inch thick, and serve hot with warm sauce. Depending on the filling, use the notebook's Pudding Sauce or custard sauce, cider boiled down into syrup, or more of the filling itself, thinned. Wrap leftovers in plastic wrap and refrigerate. Reheat, covered, in microwave oven.

· DRIED CHERRY PUDDING ·

Superneat did not record who contributed the receipt for this boiled bread pudding. Today's dried cherries are made much the same as Mrs. Randolph's and work well in it. Though most authentic boiled, it comes out about the same when steamed and is good, though different, when microwaved. Microwaving changes the texture, but it allows you to start cooking it just as you clear the table after dinner. The notebook's Pudding Sauce (not Sauce for Pudding, which is different) is a close to necessary accompaniment. Half the receipt serves 6 to 8.

Grate a quart loaf of sweet stale bread, add a quart of fresh milk, eight eggs beat very light, pour the milk on the grated bread; let it stand four hours, then add the eggs and eighteen ozs of dried cherries. beat the whole together and boil—to be eaten with wine sauce.

The Receipts

Half quantity:
1 lb. firm, uniced spice, Madeira, or pound cake
2 c. milk or half-and-half
4 eggs
9 oz. dried cherries

Remove dark crust from cake. If fresh, slice and dry directly on an oven rack at the lowest oven setting with the door cracked open for a half hour or more, or overnight in the kitchen. Crumble cake into a mixing bowl. Add milk or half-and-half and allow to stand until absorbed, about 1 hour. Separate eggs. Beat whites stiff. Beat yolks thick and lemon-colored, adding any unabsorbed milk. Fold in crumb mixture, then egg whites, then cherries. To cook, see methods below. Unmold, pour Pudding Sauce over, and pass more sauce.

To boil in cloth, see directions above in Stew Dumpling receipt. Use a cloth about 18 × 24 inches, tie the pudding loosely, and if it is ugly when unmolded (mine was), mask it with sauce.

To steam in a mold: Put a rack about 1 inch high in a large covered pot. Fill with water one-third of the way up the mold. Bring to a boil. Butter a 6- to 8-cup mold and dust with sugar (tastier) or flour (more authentic). This can be a hinged tin (easiest) or crockery pudding mold with or without a center tube, a souffle dish, or even a mixing bowl. Fill mold; if lidless, cover with buttered or floured cloth. Tie the cloth securely under the lip of the pan, then bring edges up and tie on top to keep water from wicking into the mold. Put mold on the rack, cover pot, and simmer—2 hours for solid crockery open mold, 1½ hours if tin and lidded or with center tube. Add *boiling* water as needed to maintain water level. Pudding is done when an inserted cake tester comes out clean. Leave in hot water until needed. Dip in cold water before unmolding.

To microwave: Pour batter into buttered microwavable dish that holds at least 8 cups. Cover with waxed paper, plastic wrap, or a

Puddings

plate. Microwave 17 minutes on high for full-powered oven. Let stand a few minutes. Serve warm with sauce.

Puddings into Pies

Superneat attributed a page with the notebook's only two pie fillings to Lucy Campbell, who lived two doors from the Lees. One of the nine children of "big four" professor John Lyle Campbell and his wife, she was a good friend of the Lees' cousin Markie Williams. Both are best baked in what I consider Virginia piecrust (the English and Italians may disagree): rich with lard, very thin, and made beautifully flaky by chilling all the ingredients before combining them, then the dough before rolling it out.

· LUCY CAMPBELL'S LEMON PIE ·

This filling, thin and intense in flavor, verges on lemon curd. It is best cooked separately and added to prebaked shells.

> *Two cups white sugar. 3 eggs, rind and juice of 2 lemons —*
> *bake in a rich pastry — This quantity makes two pies.*
> *Lucy Campbell*

Filling:
2 c. sugar
3 eggs
Rind and juice of 2 lemons (yellow part of the rind only)

To prebake crusts: Line prepared piecrust with waxed paper or aluminum foil and fill with beans, rice, or other weights. Bake 5 minutes at 450°; lower temperature to 350° and bake 10–15 minutes more, until lightly browned. Cool. Remove weights. Prepare filling by mixing together rind, juice, sugar, and slightly beaten eggs. Cook in

The Receipts

double boiler over simmering water, stirring until thick and somewhat clear. Pour into pie shells.

To bake pie in crust: Mix filling ingredients together and pour uncooked into prepared crust. Bake at 350° until crust is browned and
a knife inserted near middle comes out clean.

· COCOANUT PIE ·

This receipt, written in below Lemon Pie, underlines the close kinship of puddings and pies; its filling has an almost identical twin in
the Cocoanut Pudding contributed by Mrs. Maury. The ingredients
of the two receipts are the same, except that the pie calls for butter,
which makes it better. Both have a much higher proportion of "cocoanut" (a usual spelling at the time) than the custardy fillings we
know today, which makes them more substantial and more intriguing.

One pound cocoanut, one pound sugar—
¼ pound butter—six eggs—½ cup cream
Lucy Campbell

For two 9 inch pies:
1 lb. grated fresh coconut
2 c. sugar
1 stick (½ c.) butter
6 large or medium eggs
½ c. whipping cream
Up to 2 t. coconut extract if needed (see below)

If you do not have fresh or frozen grated coconut (the dried variety
produces a more macaroon-like pie), prepare the meat as follows:
Preheat oven to 400°. Pound holes in two eyes of the coconut with a
large nail or screwdriver. Drain liquid. Bake the nut until the shell
cracks, about 15 minutes. Hammer open, pry out meat, and remove

Puddings

dark outer skin with paring knife or vegetable peeler. Grate the meat on the large holes of a hand grater or pulse in bursts in a food processor with steel blade. If the coconut yields only about ¾ lb. prepared meat, reduce sugar and butter by a quarter and use 5 eggs instead of 6. If the coconut lacks flavor, as one of our four test coconuts did, add coconut extract.

Prebake crusts about 5 minutes at 450°. Melt butter, mix in all other ingredients, and pour into crusts. Bake 10 minutes in an oven preheated to 400°, then lower temperature to 350° and bake 40–50 minutes more. (Beginning baking at 350°, which is more authentic, will take a few minutes longer.)

Custards

Crustardes, according to Karen Hess, were huge pies "into which . . . court fools leapt to amuse the guests at royal banquets in medieval Merrie England." The filling, says Sarah Belk in *Around the Southern Table*, consisted of "dried fruit, cream, eggs, sugar, parsley, and beef marrow." Fortunately, that combination of ingredients has died out, but echoes of the pie survive in the cakes beloved of cartoonists who draw girls jumping out of them at stag parties. Simpler custards survive all but unchanged, though, from the Washington manuscript. The notebook has two, along with sixteen pudding receipts based on custard.

"Only a *little* custard spilled," Mrs. Lee wrote to Mrs. McDonald, thanking her for one of those little edible gifts that ladies exchanged after the war, as they had seeds and cuttings before it. She offered "sprout turnip tops" in return, and through such notes we catch glimpses of a deep friendship developing.

The exchanges began before Mrs. McDonald arrived in Lexington, when her fiancé, VMI mineralogy and chemistry professor Col. Marshall McDonald, wrote to her, "I . . . was out hunting . . . & sent my game to Mrs. Lee." As the bride settled into their new home,

Agnes Lee sent over milk and honey, saying in part, "I suppose the cows & bees are hardly established yet." And when their baby daughter Rose became ill, Agnes dispatched for her "this morning's milk, which has been on ice ever since it was brought in," an important precaution before electric refrigeration.

The Lee ladies sent the McDonalds pears, peaches, oranges, and lettuce, and received from them pickles, lettuce, and tomatoes. One basket that arrived at the Lees' with ice cream and cake Mildred returned with biscuits and "a wee bottle of champagne." When the McDonalds made jelly for the family with the Lees' currants, sugar, and jars, the flurry of notes ended with Agnes's "won't you make Hannah [presumably the cook] sensible of our appreciation . . . by giving her this handkerchief 'all the way from Baltimore!'"

Mrs. McDonald, whose daughter Rose MacDonald became Mrs. Lee's biographer. (Photograph by Michael Miley, courtesy of Special Collections, Leyburn Library, Washington and Lee University)

Little Rose became a favorite of Mary Lee, who invited mother and daughter for a drive in the new pony cart her husband had given her, "as you admire the *grandeur* of my equipage." "Dearest little Rose" worked a doily for Mrs. Lee one Christmas; another year, Mrs. Lee made the child a doll, sewing the elaborate costume exquisitely with her arthritis-wracked hands. She made a lifetime admirer, too. Years later in her book *Mrs. Robert E. Lee*, Rose declared Mary Lee "a heroine . . . the inspiration in the life of the great Confederate leader . . . [a woman whose] name has passed almost into oblivion." Though more admiring than objective, the biography, published in 1939, remains the best single source of information about Mrs. Lee.

· BOILED AND BAKED CUSTARDS ·

What we used to call "runny custard" goes by the name French Cream in the notebook and Crème Anglaise (English cream) in the

Puddings

encyclopedic *New Larousse Gastronomique*, demonstrating that receipts, like folktales, do not respect political boundaries. The notebook's receipt for French Cream is in English, but that for baked custard, *Manière de faire une Crème Renversée*, is all in French. The latter
could have come from Blanche, the French wife of the general's
nephew, who lived in France. Blanche had visited in Lexington, and
Lee mentions in a letter that she had sent Mildred receipts for
creams. At any rate, this dish, which has spread around the world, is
often known as flan and often considered Spanish.

Both custards are excellent and essentially the same as today's
standard custard receipt. Using a good basic receipt, make them
with half-and-half or perhaps part light cream in place of milk. Do
not thicken the "boiled" custard with flour. And despite its name, it
should never boil, just simmer while being stirred constantly. To caramelize sugar for flan's distinctive topping, see Caramel Ice Cream.

The Receipts

By themselves, the receipts for these two thickeners, botanically different but culinarily the same, are gluey and tasteless. Mrs. Randolph combined sago with "rich boiled custard," and perhaps Mrs. Lee did the same with both sago and tapioca. Although I know of no modern uses for sago, the sumptuous blend of tapioca and custard puts commercial tapioca mixes to shame. The Lees must have used the pearl type; the smaller, more granular kind did not come in until about 1894, when a sailor complained about lumps in his pudding and a Susan Savors put dry tapioca through a coffee grinder.

Although the Washington manuscript mentions neither sago nor tapioca, by 1787 at least some of the Washington and Lee families knew sago well, and each other even better. Sixteen-year-old Lucinda Lee, who wrote this account of house-party high jinks, was a first cousin of Matilda Lee, Light-Horse Harry's cousin and first wife (the second was Anne Carter, Robert Lee's mother). Others in the escapade were a niece and nephew of George Washington: Milly, who went on the kitchen raid, and Corbin, the incident's "Mr. Washington." "Hannah," his bride of a few months, was a daughter of Richard Henry Lee, a signer of the Declaration of Independence and a cousin of Light-Horse Harry. The following year, Milly and Hannah's brother were married.

I must tell you of our frolic after we went in our room. We took it into our heads to want to eat; well, we had a large dish of bacon and beaf; after that, a bowl of Sago cream; and after that, an apple pye. While we were eating the apply pye in bed—God bless you! making a great noise—in came Mr. Washington, dressed in Hannah's short gown and peticoat, and seazed me and kissed me twenty times, in spite of all the resistance I could make; and then Cousin Molly. Hannah soon followed, dressed in his Coat. They joined us in eating the apple pye, and then went

Puddings

out. [excerpt printed courtesy of the Robert E. Lee Memorial Association, Stratford Hall Plantation]

Tapioca

*4 table spoonfulls of tapioca soaked for 5 hours then stirred in
a pint of boiling water & season to your taste when thick & clear*

4 T. tapioca
2 c. water

Follow directions for pearl tapioca. Mix with equal parts rich boiled custard and "season to your taste."

· BREAD AND RICE PUDDINGS ·

Today's plain bread and rice puddings have hardly changed since the Washington manuscript. In the Lee notebook receipts, bread pudding is titled Mérangue Pudding, and both kinds are crowned with the same jelly and soft meringue as Marguerites; the combination must have been a family favorite. Make either from a good standard receipt for bread or rice pudding, using half-and-half with perhaps some light cream in place of milk. Bake pudding in the pot you will serve it in, then spread with jelly, jam, or marmalade and seal with soft meringue and brown lightly (see Marguerites). A meringue made of two egg whites will cover an 8- to 9-inch pot. Serve promptly if your receipt, like the Lees' rice pudding, turns watery in about half an hour.

· EVY TUCKER'S DELICATE PUDDING ·

Superneat wrote in this receipt from Mildred's friend Evy, who lived in Lexington with her parents at Col Alto until, at the confirmed-spinster age of thirty-eight, she married and moved to Natchez, Mississippi. When Mildred visited her there, she reported, "Evy is very happy, & has married into a lovely family." Among the many virtues eulogized at Evy's funeral were the "vivacity, humor and dramatic power" of a sketch she wrote about plantation life. It still seems lively, but the life it depicts suggests now that the Civil War did not change the life of former slaves in Mississippi much.

Water replaces milk in this custard, which turns stale cake into a mysterious, lemony, light dessert covered in soft meringue. The most difficult part today may be finding stale, good-quality bakery pound cake.

Slice cake and put it in a baking dish — 12 wine glasses of water — Yolks of 6 eggs and a lump of butter the size of a goose egg. Add the juice of three lemons and the grated rind of one. Sweeten to your taste and put the mixture on the fire until it begins to thicken. Then pour it on the cake, and let it cool.

Make a méringue of the whites of eggs, put over the pudding and brown in the stove.

From Miss Evy Tucker

Half quantity:
1 lb. loaf, pound, or Madeira cake
1½ c. water
Juice of 1½–2 lemons and grated rind of ½, yellow part only
3 egg yolks
3–4 oz. butter (½ stick; minus 1 T., if desired)
½ c. sugar or to taste

Cut off dark crust and slice cake ¼ to ½ inch thick. If cake is fresh, arrange directly on oven racks and dry in oven at lowest setting, door cracked open, 45 minutes to an hour, or dry overnight on a rack in the kitchen.

Butter an 8 × 12-inch to 9 × 13-inch glass or glazed pottery bak-

Puddings

ing dish. Cover the bottom with cake, cutting slices to fit when necessary. Separate eggs. Combine slightly beaten yolks, water, rind, juice, butter, and sugar in a double boiler over simmering water or in a very heavy pot over very low heat. Cook and stir until thick and smooth, about 10–15 minutes. Pour over cake. Allow to soak in and cool. Preheat oven to 350 or 400°. For soft meringue, see Marguerites. Spread over cake and custard. Brown lightly, about 8–10 minutes. Serves 6 to 8.

· SWEET–MEAT PUDDING ·

Miss Evy Tucker, a close friend of Mildred and contributor of the receipt for Delicate Pudding. (Photograph by Michael Miley, courtesy of Special Collections, Leyburn Library, Washington and Lee University, Lexington, Va.)

Here "meat" harks back to the Middle Ages, when it meant food as distinguished from drink. At the time of the Washington manuscript, sweetmeats could be dry, such as candied fruit, or wet, like the jam or preserves called for here. The receipt, even sketchier than most, leaves much room for interpretation. It could be an intensely sweet soufflé (another form of pudding), easily made but quick to fall, since it lacks a stabilizer such as flour. Served with unsweetened raspberry puree, it is tasty and trendy, but probably does not resemble the Lees', which makes no mention of such a sauce. Fallen, I learned thanks to some very late dinner guests, it becomes sinfully sweet, delicious, and unlike anything any of us had ever tasted before. But whether that is what the Lees served I cannot say.

Use a light-colored jelly or jam (English marmalade adds a welcome bitterness); dark ones turn it grayish. Buttering and sugaring the dish adds a nice crunch. The nutmeg, though nice, is unnecessary; it gets somewhat lost. Half the receipt serves only 4 if everyone has seconds, as they did at my house.

To 10 Eggs allow 2 cups of sugar 2 cups of any preserves, & 1 cup melted butter.

Beat the yolks and sugar together & the whites separately—Add a little nut-meg & bake in a dish (bake quickly)

Half quantity:
5 eggs
1 c. sugar
1 c. apricot or other light-colored preserves
   or English marmalade, melted with ½ c. butter
¼–½ t. nutmeg, if desired

Preheat oven to 400°. Butter and sugar a 7- to 9-inch soufflé dish. Separate eggs. Beat egg yolks very light. If using nutmeg, sift together with sugar and add to yolks gradually, beating continuously. Fold in butter-and-preserve mixture. Beat egg whites stiff and fold in. Bake immediately until puffed and lightly browned, about 25 minutes. Serve immediately, as a soufflé with raspberry puree, or allow to cool and fall.

· CHARLOTTE RUSSE ·

Chef Marie Antoine Carême, crowned by *New Larousse Gastronomique* "the cook of kings and the king of cooks," invented this elegant use for stale cake in Paris around 1830. The Lee notebook's two versions are both simpler, but simply delicious. Someone unknown entered Mrs. McDonald's Gelatine Charlotte Russe, which replaces Carême's custard with "new milk," close to today's light cream. Superneat wrote in the other receipt without giving a source. It calls for custard, is spotted with cooking spills, and must have been Mildred's favorite of the two: she sent it to *Housekeeping in Old Virginia*, where five more (four of them using custard) demonstrate the dessert's popularity in the period.

Puddings

Charlotte Russe makes a spectacular Victorian-as-we-know-it finale to a dinner party. An expert can produce a fairy tale of piped whipped cream and fruit, but even when mangled by a novice (me) and masked in hastily improvised sauce, it calls forth admiring gasps. My version might have horrified Carême, but my great-aunts, who struggled in the kitchen, and their father, who encouraged them with teasing, might have treated it kindly.

The basic dessert keeps a week or more in the refrigerator, leaving only unmolding and decorating for the day it is served. A single 20-cup mold makes the most dramatic presentation, but two smaller ones are easier to handle. The receipt may be halved and probably quartered.

1 oz Gelatin—one quart rich cream—eight eggs—half pint new milk— sugar and flavouring to taste.
Whip the cream to a stiff froth.
Make a custard of the milk, gelatin and yolks of the eggs and— When entirely cool, add the whites of the eggs well beaten and the whipped cream.
Line up mould with sponge cake and if in Summer put it in ice.

Shell:
1 9 × 9-inch pan of sponge cake (perhaps one from the notebook) or 2–3 dozen ladyfingers (used by Carême and easiest). One dozen 3-inch ladyfingers will line a 10-cup Charlotte mold; for the 20-cup mold, have 3 dozen on hand to be safe.

For the mold, a charlotte pan with its flat bottom and outward sloping sides works best; next best is a torte pan with a removable rim. Almost anything that is easily handled and does not narrow above the bottom will do.

Custard filling:
3 packets unflavored gelatin
1 c. milk, half-and-half or light cream

8 eggs
4 c. whipping cream or heavier cream
1 c. sugar
2 T. brandy or 1 T. vanilla

Decoration:
Fresh fruit, whipped cream, or sauce (see below)

For custard: soften gelatin in milk. Separate eggs. Allow whites to come to room temperature. Combine yolks, sugar, and milk in double boiler over simmering water or in a very thick saucepan. Cook and stir until custard thickens. Cool, stirring occasionally. Stir in flavoring. If filling begins to set before shell is ready, return to very slight heat and stir gently to soften.

To line mold(s): Make a pattern with ladyfingers, placing cut sides toward the custard. If using sponge cake, put the darker bottom crust facing the outside of the pan to show off the pattern; the softer top crust should face inside to absorb some filling. For a simple top design, cut triangles of cake and lay them close together and pointing toward the middle of the pan; for the sides, cut thin, straight rectangles to match the height of the mold.

To fill mold: Just before filling the mold, beat cream and egg whites stiff, separately. Fold first the whites then the cream into the custard, incorporating them gently but thoroughly. Assemble top design on the bottom of the mold and pour on enough custard to keep in place. Add several side pieces, tilt the mold sideways, and add custard to hold them in place. Turn the mold and repeat until all side pieces are anchored. Fill mold with remaining custard. Refrigerate at least 5 hours.

To unmold: Hold mold in very hot water a few minutes and reverse onto serving plate; remove rim if removable. If charlotte does not unmold, dip dishtowel in hot water and wrap around mold; repeat if necessary. As last resort, run thin, flexible knife blade carefully around mold and repeat dishtowel treatment.

Puddings

To decorate: Pipe with whipped cream and add fresh raspberries, strawberries, or other fruit in season. Or pour fruit sauce over.

A good, quick, disaster-masking sauce:

2 lbs. frozen fruit, such as sour cherries
2 T. cornstarch
Sugar to taste, depending on fruit

Cook and stir in a heavy pot until sauce clears, 10 minutes or so. To brighten flavor, stir in 1 T. frozen concentrated orange juice or 2 T. orange liqueur per pound of fruit.

Frozen Custards

"Blanche [the wife of Lee's nephew, who lived in Paris] sent you some receipts for creams," Lee wrote to Mildred, trying playfully to lure her home from a visit. "You had better come and try them." Those creams could have been basically either cream or custard. They might have been whipped, plain, or frozen; in soft mounds or molded with gelatin or with rennet, the homely junket of my childhood. "Do beware of vanilla creams," Lee also warned, and not unreasonably. All forms of creams spoiled easily before electric refrigeration, and Martha Washington is known to have served as dessert creams that had soured.

In fruit ice creams, Mrs. Tyree preferred a cream base rather than custard, and Mrs. Randolph opted for cream in any flavor, but the two were interchangeable. Both of the notebook's probable ice creams (one simply designated "Cream") have a custard base, and since custard is pudding, even ice cream can be called pudding too, as I understand it still is sometimes in Britain.

This receipt appears word for word in Mary Randolph's *The Virginia House-wife*; presumably it came from there or one of the cookbooks that plagiarized that influential volume. Mrs. Randolph, too, called it a "cream," but she clearly meant it as ice cream, one among fifteen other flavors (including oyster). Actually, it is equally successful served frozen or not. Unlike Chocolate Cakes, on the same page and in the same hand, where the amount of chocolate is overwhelming, this has a light but agreeable taste. This cream may curdle softly, and perhaps purposely: sweetened curd desserts survived into Mrs. Randolph's book almost unchanged from the Washington manuscript. Since Mrs. Randolph had no cake flavored with chocolate, I assume this is an early chocolate receipt. It serves 6 to 8.

Scrape a quarter of a pound of chocolate very fine put it in a quart of milk, boil it till the chocolate is dissolved, stirring continually—thicken with six eggs and sweeten. A vanilla bean boiled with the milk improves the flavor greatly.

4 oz. unsweetened chocolate
1 t. vanilla extract or, better, a piece of vanilla bean
4 c. half-and-half, perhaps part light cream
6 eggs
1½–2 c. sugar

Grate chocolate by hand or pulse it in a food processor. Cook chocolate, milk or cream, sugar, and vanilla bean, if used, over low heat (in double boiler or heavy pan). Stir occasionally until sugar and chocolate dissolve, then constantly. Beat eggs lightly, stir in some hot milk mixture, then stir eggs into it. Stir and scrape sides and bottom of pan until mixture thickens. Add vanilla extract or remove vanilla bean. To keep the custard smooth, pour into a bowl as soon as it thickens. To freeze, follow directions in Caromel Ice Cream.

Puddings

Although Thomas Jefferson is sometimes credited with bringing ice cream back from France, the editors of *Virginia Cookery, Past and Present* note that George Washington bought a "cream machine for Ice" in 1784, the year Jefferson left for Paris. At any rate, the Lee daughters enjoyed the delicacy. Agnes entered it twice in her diary: The menu for "a grand party for juveniles" at West Point includes "turkey, oysters, sangaree [red wine and lemonade, mixed] marmelade ice cream, cake, mottoes [probably small sweetmeats wrapped with verses or riddles in fringed colored paper, seemingly precursors of party crackers] and all things nice." The next summer at Cedar Grove, Virginia, home of their Stuart cousins, where Mary Custis later holed up during the war, "we went bathing by moonlight and feasted on crabs, fried chickens, green peas, cake, strawberries & ice cream which latter was particularly acceptable."

This receipt and several others occur in the notebook twice, word for word, in the same order but in different handwriting; two people must have copied the same section from the same source. The ice cream has an unforgettable silky, rich texture and a gentle, true caramel flavor that is far superior to the synthetic. Like all those based on custard, it stays smooth in the freezer without turning grainy longer than cream-based ice creams do. The mixture looks alarming if the syrup or custard are not hot enough, but it smoothes out with reheating, as the receipt predicts.

Take a teacup of sugar, & put it on the fire until it acquires the consistency of candy. To a quart of custard with a stick of cinnamon in it put the above quantity of sugar. The custard and sugar when mixed must both be hot. At first you will think that the sugar has spoiled the custard, but when dissolved it flavors it delightfully.

The Receipts

4 c. hot "boiled" custard (it should never cook above a simmer) made with 1 stick cinnamon and half-and-half or perhaps some light cream in place of milk

1 c. sugar

To make custard, see Charlotte Russe (above).

To caramelize sugar: Heat sugar, stirring constantly, in a small, heavy skillet, about 10 minutes or until rich and golden, a few more for more pronounced flavor. Pour some hot custard into the hot sugar, stir, pour back, repeating with gradually larger amounts to dissolve and incorporate all sugar. If syrup crystallizes, reheat mixture gently, stirring constantly. Cool, chill. Freeze according to freezer directions. If using the freezing compartment of the refrigerator, stir custard well every 45 minutes, and when almost frozen, hand beat or whirl smooth in food processor and return to freezer.

Precious Jellies

For hundreds of years, cooks made elegant "jellies" of clear liquids stiffened with gelatin, blended gelatin with custard, and even combined the two into elaborate molded desserts. Well into the nineteenth century, people continued to extract Jello's ancestor painstakingly from deer antlers (hartshorn), sturgeon bladders (isinglass), and even powdered ivory, which was boiled all night. By 1824, the calve's foot jelly that still survives at least in conversation had become popular, and Mrs. Randolph noted further that "the feet of hogs make the palest coloured jelly, and those of sheep make a beautiful amber colour."

"Sirrop of violets or sirrop of gilliflowers" and currant, quince, and raspberry juice dyed jellies in the Washington manuscript. Later, saffron, beet juice, and spinach juice were also used, along with cochineal, a red dye made from dried cactus bugs imported

Jellies

from Mexico. Chocolate may have colored gelatinous castle turrets and imparted the proper "sad hue" to edible, molded hedgehogs before it became an ingredient in cakes. Mrs. Beeton advocated adding gold and silver flakes. All these were used to color elaborate tableaux that were displayed proudly on dessert tables at balls. Cream fish might swim in clear ponds and jellied hens sit on nests of jellied eggs surrounded by their jellied chicks.

Then a reaction set in. "Jelly is considered more wholesome when not colored by any foreign substance," declared Mrs. Tyree firmly in 1879. Some of her contributors stooped to using early forms of commercial gelatin, but she found the wholesome homemade kind worth the arduous preparation. It began with boiling "feet" for a long time; then some furniture rearranging was required.

> The best and most simple arrangement for straining jelly is to invert a small table, fold an old table-cloth four double, tie each corner to the leg of the table; set a bowl under the bag thus formed, with another bowl at hand to slip in its place when the jelly first run through is returned to the bag, as will be necessary, the first never being transparently clear. Catch a little in a glass. If clear as crystal, it will be unnecessary to return it again to the bag. You may then put a thick cloth over the bag to keep in the heat, and if in winter, place it before a fire. Shut up the room, and let it drip. The jelly will run through the bag more rapidly if the bag is first scalded.

No wonder the Lee ladies bought gelatin made by Cox, Nelson, and Cooper, all apparently wiped out after Charles Knox introduced his brand in 1890. May Wait's flavored Jello came a year later, and when electric refrigeration swept the country around the turn of the century, the stage was set for this epitome of elegance to begin its slide into banality.

Not that Jello wasn't a treat when I was growing up. When we children beat it, semiset, into billows, we were unknowingly creating

The Receipts

a descendant of "Snow Pudding," a grown-up and infinitely better dessert that Superneat entered in the notebook. The syllabub churn that frothed it, between 1840 and 1890, was a cylinder fitted inside with blades that whirled when the churn's handle was pumped. The cool, astringent result is welcome on a muggy summer night even now.

· SNOW PUDDING ·

This receipt makes eight or more cups of white foam. Less beating produces less volume and a pleasant, cloudy, more solidly jelled layer that forms on top. Along with custard made from the leftover egg yolks (I prefer it to cream), fresh fruit (blueberries and peaches are best) and/or gingerbread go well with it.

Soak one oz of gelatine in one pint of cold water for an hour. Place it over the fire, stir it and take it off as soon as it is dissolved. When nearly cold, beat it to a stiff froth with a syllabub churn.

Beat the whites of three eggs to a stiff froth, and add this to the gelatine froth, together with the juice of 3 lemons and pulverized sugar to your taste. Mix the whole well together, pour into a mould, and set aside to cool.

To be eaten with cream or custard.

2 packages unflavored gelatin, softened in ½ c. cold water
2½ c. boiling water
3 egg whites
1¼–1½ c. confectioner's sugar (or to taste)
Juice of 3 lemons

Add boiling water to gelatin. Stir to dissolve and stir in lemon juice. Refrigerate until syrupy but not set. Beat egg whites stiff; gradually beat in sugar, then jelled mixture. Beat all to desired volume. Pour into a nonstick mold (12-cup size for maximum froth) or one that has

Jellies

been sprayed with nonstick spray or rinsed in cold water. Refrigerate at least 4 hours. To unmold, dip in hot water and shake gently but firmly to loosen sides. Pass with cream or custard. Serves 6 to 8.

· WINE JELLY ·

My mother kept saying she wanted to make wine jelly, and I kept sending her receipts. But, ruby with Burgundy or pale from Riesling, they were never what she meant. What she wanted, it turned out, had been in her grandmother's and aunts' notebook all along. Far from the accompaniment for toast that I had assumed, wine jelly as the Lees knew it was and is an easy, make-ahead, all-season dessert. The "Jelly made of Cox's Gelatin" put in the notebook by Mary Custis is molded; I prefer "Cold Jelly," in Superneat's writing, which is about the consistency of Jello, but either version finishes a ladies' lunch or substantial dinner lightly.

I make mine stronger in flavor than the receipt, and for beauty I use a gold-colored sherry. Serve it in clear glass, as elegant as possible. I have used large wine goblets, finger bowls, and my favorite, small, old, gold-banded tumblers with silver iced-tea spoons.

· COLD JELLY ·

One box of gelatine makes one gallon of Jelly

To one box of gelatine put one pint of cold water, let it stand an hour, then add to it the juice of three lemons, 1¾ lbs of sugar, one pint of wine, a wine glass of brandy and boiling water enough to make with the other things a gallon of jelly—add citric acid if it is not sour enough.

Boil the rinds of the lemons in the water before pouring it on the gelatine, stir all together and strain through a coarse cloth.

The Receipts

Half quantity:
2 packages unflavored gelatin, softened in ½ c. cold water
1 c. sugar, or to taste
1¾ c. boiling water
Juice and rinds of 1½–2 lemons, depending on size
1 c. sherry (good quality domestic will do) or imported Madeira
¼ c. brandy (imported French, not necessarily VSOP)

Garnish:
About 1 T. whipped cream and/or a few fresh
   raspberries or 1 candied violet per serving dish

Boil lemon rinds in water about 10 minutes. Add softened gelatin and sugar. Stir to dissolve. Cool. Remove lemon rinds. Stir in lemon juice, wine, and brandy. Pour into containers. Refrigerate at least 4 hours or up to 2 days. Garnish with restraint. Serves 4 to 6.

· JELLY MADE OF COX'S GELATIN ·

To convert the receipt above to a close approximation of Aunt Mary's version, follow directions above but reduce water to 1 cup in all (soften gelatin in wine), omit brandy, and use only 1 lemon rind. Pour into individual molds—nonstick, sprayed with nonstick spray, or rinsed in cold water. To unmold, dip briefly in hot water.

Fruit—Frozen, Stewed, Sieved, & Fried

Like other Virginia gentry, the Lees relished fruit. Before the war, Arlington's orchard had supplied the Lee table and the stall at Wash Market as well. During the war, this health-giving delicacy grew

Fruit

scarce. When the general received news that his wife had become ill in Richmond on a meager diet, he wrote Mildred, "You must go to market every morning and see if you cannot find some fruit." Afterward in Lexington, a houseguest remembered a gift barrel of oranges to which, she reported, "we all did full justice at all hours." Though often eaten raw, fruit was also used in various ways to make desserts.

Water Ices

The notebook's very delicate pineapple and orange versions could have been palate cleansers for formal, multicourse Victorian meals. They may have been new, too, for sherbets in the Washington manuscript are still iced drinks, and neither Mrs. Randolph nor Mrs. Lewis mentions ices. Both of the notebook's versions are extremely subtle. The Pineapple Ice below, with water reduced by a quarter, makes a two-gallon freezerful, still gently flavored. The receipt may be halved or quartered and the water, of course, restored.

· PINEAPPLE ICE ·

This receipt and one in Mrs. Tyree's book use canned pineapple, which was not processed commercially in the United States until 1894 so far as I know. For such an exotic to be canned at home seems odd, but perhaps it was.

In "Shirley Plantation—Built on a Tradition of Heritage and Hierarchy," current resident Charles Hill Carter III, a descendant and namesake of the Charles Carter who built Shirley in 1769, writes that the pineapples ordered carved into the woodwork by the earlier Charles, Lee's maternal grandfather, were a symbol of hospitality, adopted by colonists who first encountered the fresh fruit tied to the houses of natives in the West Indies. The wooden pineapple topping

The Receipts

Shirley's roof, according to the later Charles, signaled to ships on the busy James River that his ancestor could afford to offer this costly rarity to his guests.

1 box of gelatine (Cooper's)
1 gal. water
2 oranges & 2 lemons &
1 two pound can of pineapple — 6 eggs —
Dissolve the gelatine thoroughly & mix in the yolks well beaten — Add the juice of the lemons & oranges — make it very sweet — add the juice of the pineapple & then the pulp, beaten to a jelly, in a wooden bowl. Then add the whites of the eggs beaten to a froth.

Freeze

4 packets gelatin softened in 1½ c. water, plus 10½ c. water
Juice of 2 oranges and 2 lemons
3 c. sugar or to taste (less if using pineapple in heavy syrup)
2 lbs. crushed canned pineapple, whirled in a food processor
    with steel blade or put through a food mill
6 eggs

Separate eggs. Allow whites to come to room temperature. Soften gelatin in 1½ cups water. Bring rest of water to a boil; add softened gelatin and sugar, and stir to dissolve. Cool. Beat egg yolks until light and add. Add lemon and orange juice, pineapple juice and pulp. Beat egg whites to stiff peaks and fold in. Freeze in refrigerator (see Caromel Ice Cream) or follow freezer directions.

An Epiphany with Pears

When a Washington College student admired the basket of pears a Lee daughter was carrying, she apologized for not offering him any, explaining she had only enough for dessert. Then, she added lightly,

Fruit

she wanted inscribed on her tombstone: "Although she was on pleasure bent / She had a frugal mind." When I read the account more than a century later, I heard my mother saying the same thing to me as a small child. Suddenly, Aunt Mildred—it must have been Mildred, whose pet name, Precious Life, I shared—seemed real, and close, and smiling.

The Washington manuscript has many names for stewed pears and apples. These were called "compotes" by Mrs. Randolph and in the Lee notebook, although now "compote" usually means the dish the fruit is served in. The amount of sugar determines whether these are side dishes or desserts. Although apples and pears are prepared almost identically, I, of course, prefer pears.

Nowadays cooks are routinely warned against using citrus pith, the bitter white part of the rind. Mrs. Randolph, too, excluded it from her apple compote, but I came to prefer its flavor over the wine more typically used for stewing fruit. The Apple Compote receipt calls for "pippins," any one of several kinds of apple grown from seed. One of the recently revived "antique" varieties would be particularly appropriate or, as the receipt says, "any other firm juicy apple." Boscs and other firm varieties do best for the pears.

Although whole cooked fruit may have been considered more elegant, halves are easier to handle. Depending on their size, four apples or pears serve 4 to 8. This is subtle but unmistakably *not* canned pears.

· PEAR COMPOTE ·

Manière de préparer une compote de poires

Peel some pears. Cook them in boiling water to which you have added the skin of a lemon, cinnamon, cloves or other flavoring you like. When the pears are halfway cooked, add as much sugar as you want. When your fork pierces the pears easily, they are cooked, put them one by one on a plate. Reduce your syrup and pour it over the pears. [tester's translation]

The Receipts

Manière de préparer
une compote de poires

~~~~~~

Epéluchez des poires, faites-les
cuire à l'eau bouillante,
ajoutez une peau de citron
canelle, clous de girofle ou autre
parfum que vous préférez,
a moitié cuison ajoutez le su
que vous désirez. Quand votre
fourchette entre bien dans les
poires, elles sont cuites, mettez
les une à une sur un plat,
laissez réduire votre sirop
et versez sur les poires

This recipe for
pear compote may
have come from
Blanche Childe,
the French wife
of the Lee daugh-
ters' first cousin.
(Courtesy of Vir-
ginia Historical
Society)

Fruit

· 187 ·

4 pears or apples
¼–½ c. sugar or to taste
1 cinnamon stick
Up to 3 cloves
1 lemon rind

Put peeled fruit, halved or whole, in one layer in a large, shallow pan. Barely cover with water and add seasonings. Weight with a plate, then cover the pan. Simmer fruit about 10 minutes and add sugar. Continue cooking until fruit is soft but still firm and translucent, in all about 20 minutes for soft Bartletts, 30 minutes for hard pears or apples. Remove fruit and reduce syrup by half or more. Discard rind and spices, pour over pears, and chill.

· APPLE FLOAT ·

Eventually this popular Victorian dessert of cooked apple and egg white atop cream or custard became a cliché and died, a victim of its own success. Mrs. Beeton called it Apple Snow, and Mrs. Tyree included it under three different names. When made with superbly flavorful apples, both notebook versions are pale, ethereal, and lovely on hot summer nights. The roasting and grating called for in Superneat's receipt intensifies the taste, adds texture, and may have been thought healthful: Lee instructed Mildred to roast the few he could find during the war for his ill wife. The applesauce called for in the second receipt must be thick and well seasoned with nutmeg. I combine the two versions and make it with applesauce and custard.

Six eggs, three large apples first roasted and then grated—use the yolks for a boiled custard and let it cool—beat the whites light with sugar—blob in the apples—pile it lightly on the custard

[Superneat's version]

The Receipts

The whites of 4 eggs <u>well beaten</u>. Mash a quart of cooked apples smooth through a sieve—6 tablespoonsfull of sugar—flavor with nutmeg—then add yr apples a spoon full at a time to yr eggs—put a pint of cream at the bottom of the dish, seasoned with sugar & nutmeg

[Anonymous]

1 qt. thick, homemade applesauce
1 t. nutmeg
1 t. lemon juice
6 eggs
2 c. half-and-half
6 T. sugar or more, to taste

Separate eggs and allow whites to come to room temperature. Make a custard with the yolks, half-and-half, and sugar (see Charlotte Russe or a standard cookbook). Cool. Beat egg whites stiff, adding lemon juice slowly toward the end. Fold into applesauce. Pour custard into large, shallow serving dish (clear glass is pretty). Drop the applesauce mixture onto it in mounds. Serves 12.

· MRS. LEE'S APPLE FRITTERS ·

Receipts like this go back to the Washington manuscript, which includes fritters made with beer, ale, or cheese. The family served at least one other kind: the Arlington Fritters that Tabb, Rooney's second wife, sent to a fund-raising collection from "the great colonial families of Maryland and Virginia"; these were shallow-fried, holeless doughnuts. Mrs. Randolph added wine, brandy, and cinnamon to her apple fritters, but even without such flavorings, Mrs. Lee's plainer ones are crisp-edged, homey, and extremely tasty as long as they are fried in at least ¼ inch of lard; otherwise, don't bother. Mrs. Lee's Molasses Sauce goes well with these, as does the cinnamon-sugar dusting recommended in the Washington manu-

Fruit

script. The receipt makes about 50 fritters and may be halved or quartered.

Allow 4 eggs to a qt of milk make a thick batter with flour & beat it well stir in a qt of apples chopped fine have a frying pan with hot lard & drop them in the more lard the better tho they can be fried in a little.

4 eggs
4 c. milk
About 5 c. flour
4 c. apples, peeled and coarsely chopped
Lard for frying

The apples may be chopped in a food processor by pulsing with the steel blade. Make the batter by mixing beaten eggs and milk then adding flour. Stir in apples. In a heavy frying pan over medium high heat, melt lard to depth of at least ¼ inch. Drop batter by table-spoonsful into hot lard, turning once to brown on both sides. Drain on paper towels. The batter keeps several days in the refrigerator.

Candies & Sweet Sauces

"I believe a great number would be sold at the fair" reads the final line of Mrs. Lee's receipt for "caromels," the only one in the notebook that she did not obviously intend for everyday use. This occasion, like the forty-ham supper mentioned elsewhere in the notebook, was probably a benefit for Lexington's Grace Episcopal Church with its tiny congregation, which Lee called "few in number and light of purse." He had joined the vestry on his arrival, and was presiding over a meeting hours before his fatal stroke. His wife headed the sewing society, which often met in her room, due to her infirmities "—that is," the general wrote in a letter one rainy January day, "if the members are impervious to weather."

The Receipts

On some days Mary Lee's arthritis was so crippling she could not even write; still, to raise money for the new church, she made "housewives" (sewing kits) to sell to VMI cadets and tinted "photographs taken from oil paintings at Arlington . . . of her grandparents, General and Mrs. George Washington," as a houseguest recalled. "I would sit . . . and chat with her. . . . She was very warmhearted and very sweet to me, calling me her dear young friend."

She even pieced a quilt. "How well I remember," Maza Blair Anderson reminisced, how as girls she and Lizzie Letcher watched "dear old Mrs. Lee sewing the squares, and when the work got too heavy for her to hold [others] took it lined it and finished it. . . . [They] priced it at twenty dollars," a sum so high it was raffled. Earlier her husband had bought an expensive pincushion to save the church from the taint of gambling associated with a raffle, but he does not seem to have stepped in again.

After his death the congregation decided to dedicate the new church to the general, and Mary Lee sold cherished Washington mementos to raise even more money. "[We] have only the basement story up," she wrote three years later, explaining why she could not give away the first President's autographs. She died that year, but in time the Robert E. Lee Memorial Church rose. Today it has a large and active congregation.

Her "caromels" and a similar receipt in Superneat's tidy hand are more like forerunners of fudge. Both, like Chocolate Cakes, have much too much chocolate, and while batches sometimes came out hard and grainy, others relaxed almost into puddles. When native Washingtonian Agnes Mullins heard about these problems, she smiled dreamily. "Velati's," she sighed, remembering a confectioner's shop of her childhood, with its Meissen china counter. It sold candy just like that, she told me. Was it gritty? "Yes." Sticky? "Oh, yes." Which did she prefer? "They were both wonderful."

More than half the Washington manuscript is filled with receipts for sweetmeats, from candied "Apricocks" to violets. Yet neither Mrs.

Candies & Sweet Sauces

Above: The R. E. Lee Memorial Church in 1897. (Photograph by Michael Miley, courtesy of Special Collections, Leyburn Library, Washington and Lee University)

Right and opposite: Three items made by Mrs. Lee to raise funds for the church: a sewing kit called a "housewife" (courtesy of Washington and Lee University); a quilt (courtesy of VMI Museum); and her receipt for caromels (courtesy of Virginia Historical Society)

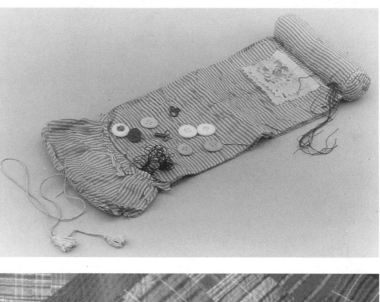

The Receipts

† table spoonfulls of Tapioca soaked for 4 hours then stirred in a pint of boiling water & seasoned to your taste then thick & clear

Beef tea
1 lb of lean fresh beef put in a wide mouthed bottle or jar place in a kettle of boiling water to remain one hour strain & there will be gill of pure nourishing liquid

Sago
To a teacup free a pt of water soak 2 or 3 hours then boil with Lemon peel till a clear Jelly or you may use milk.

Put in a stew pan 2 lbs nice brown sugar half lb grated Chocolate quarter lb butter a a cup of cream, boil all slowly over the fire 20 minutes stirring it one way all the time, When you take it off add Vanilla to your taste & pour it in a buttered dish, while warm mark it off in small squares — This is a simple & I should think excellent recipe. I beleive a great number would be sold at the fair — Caromels.

Lewis nor Mrs. Randolph put sweetmeats or candy in their house-keeping books. Perhaps by then the urban well-to-do bought confectionery; seven shops sold it in Washington City between 1822 and 1830. And if Nelly Custis Lewis's daughter did not take other cookbooks to the wilds of Louisiana, she must have satisfied her family's sweet tooth by other means.

About the time of the Lee notebook, the caramels in Mrs. Beeton's book came in raspberry, strawberry, coconut, and chocolate flavors. Mrs. Tyree's book calls a damson plum pie Caramel Pudding, and her Caramels, too, are early chocolate fudge, although she did not use the word. Very likely the two candies went their separate ways and acquired their different identities after her book was published in 1879 and before the turn of the century, when making fudge at home had become fashionable.

· MRS. LEE'S CAROMELS ·

Here is Mrs. Lee's receipt, in case others have more successful ideas about how to treat it. In our trials we cut the chocolate in half. It may help to know that the caramel receipt in *New Larousse Gastronomique*, which goes back far enough to specify loaf sugar, calls for glycerine; and in Mrs. Beeton's 1861 cookbook, one Chocolate Caramel receipt uses glycerine and golden syrup and the other, glucose—all of which promote chewiness.

Put in a stew pan 2 lbs nice brown sugar, half lb grated chocolate, qtr lb butter, cup of cream, boil all slowly over the fire 20 minutes stirring it <u>one way</u> all the time, When you take it off add vanilla to your taste & pour it in a buttered dish, while warm mark off in small pieces—This is a simple & I should think excellent recipe. I believe a great number would be sold at the fair—

The Receipts

Sweet Sauces

The three earlier family housekeeping books and Mrs. Randolph's cookbook have no sweet sauces, which had arrived in full force by the time of Mrs. Becton and Mrs. Tyree. That may be happenstance. Or perhaps today's old-fashioned hard sauce was not old-fashioned when Mildred wrote in what she called Sauce for Pudding.

· SAUCE FOR PUDDING ·

The lemon in this supplies a sharpness that is a welcome contrast to rich plum pudding and, combined with brandy, makes the nutmeg more subtle. I grew up with—and love—gritty hard sauce, which seems intended here, since powdered sugar is not mentioned specifically. Those who prefer fluff to grit should use confectioner's sugar and weigh, not measure, it. The receipt makes more than a quart and can be reduced.

1 cup of butter
3 " of sugar   *creamed well together*
nutmeg
1 wine glass brandy
juice and grated rind of a lemmon

3 c. granulated sugar
   or 1½ lbs. confectioner's sugar, sifted
8 oz. (2 sticks) butter
1 t. nutmeg or to taste
4 oz. brandy
Juice and grated rind of 1 lemon

Stir nutmeg into sugar. Cream sugar into butter, then beat in other ingredients in the order listed.

This simple sauce has a happy combination of ingredients. The spice, cream, and butter gentle the molasses, which was probably stronger then and could have been sorghum (botanically different but with much the same taste). To me, dark molasses is authentic enough, but for a source of blackstrap, see Gingerbread. Serve over pancakes, waffles, or bland desserts such as vanilla ice cream. Yields about 2 cups.

Put half pint of molasses to boil in a skillet with a piece of butter the size of an egg when it has boiled a few minutes pour in a teacup of cream & grate half a nutmeg or any spice you like.

¼ c. (½ stick) butter
8 oz. (1 c.) molasses
6–8 oz. whipping cream
1½ t. nutmeg or 1 t. ginger plus ¼ t. cloves

Bring molasses and butter to boil for 2–3 minutes, then add cream and spices, stirring to blend.

· PUDDING SAUCE ·

Superneat copied in this receipt. Good on hot puddings, it is close to essential with Dried Cherry Pudding.

Six heaped table spoons of loaf sugar—half pound of butter worked to a cream—then add one egg, one wine glass wine, one nutmeg—let it boil fast ten minutes.

½ c. sugar
8 oz. (2 sticks) butter

The Receipts

1 egg
¼ c. sweet sherry or Madeira
1 T. nutmeg

Cream butter well. Cream in sugar. Beat egg well, stir in wine, and fold into butter-sugar mixture. Boil as directed. This sauce separates easily; take it straight from the stove, whisk mightily, and serve immediately.

Alternatively, whisk the mixture in a double boiler over boiling water until it reaches 160° on a candy thermometer (this temperature kills salmonella). Remove from heat and whisk over ice water until cooled. Made this way, the sauce does not separate quickly.

The Main Meal: What a Difference a War Makes

In the early 1700s, Nomini Hall, the plantation of Robert Carter, son of "King" Carter, employed six oxen to haul firewood and, according to an account by family tutor Philip Fithian, in one year consumed "27,000 pounds of pork, twenty beeves, 550 bushels of wheat, besides corn, four hogsheads of rum, and 150 gallons of brandy." Roughly a century later, a year before the young Lees were married, large-scale opulence still prevailed at Shirley plantation, where Robert's mother had grown up. A young Yale graduate describing "the princely hospitality of the *gentle* born" wrote of "Mrs. Hill Carter at one end of the table with a large dish of rich soup, Mr. Carter at the other with a saddle of mutton, ham, beef, turkey, duck, innumerable vegetables. Then champagne." After two more equally bountiful courses came sherry, Madeira, and "a sweet wine for the ladies," who left the table to the gentlemen after a glassful.

Although the Civil War swept away that life forever, its patterns, including eating, lingered. In Lexington, the Lees took their main meal after the general returned from his office, at three o'clock, which Rob called "the old-fashioned dinner hour." Many of the dishes may not have changed much either. Since colonial times Virginia's cuisine had been distinguished by the number and variety of fairly simple offerings, and its complexity derived from their combination. Dinner probably began with soup and went on to meat and/or fish or poultry, vegetables, perhaps salad, and then dessert. But the number of offerings and often their sumptuousness diminished sharply after the war.

Soups

Before the war, soup took pride of place at dinner. The hostess served it to all, from tureens now prized as antiques. Then guests might choose from among the other dishes and help themselves; they rarely partook of all the profusion.

Some day I hope to feel rich enough to make Mrs. Randolph's oyster soup: first you simmer for a long time a large batch of the bivalves with quantities of ham (Virginia, of course) and seasonings; then you throw away everything but the broth, add fresh oysters, egg "yelks," and heavy cream and just warm it through. But I am probably too much of a Lee—too frugal—to try it, though like the others, I am immensely fond of oysters.

These shellfish were so plentiful in colonial times that slaves rebelled at eating so many. Into the mid-1800s, 20 million gallons a year were harvested in Virginia alone, most of them canned and many exported. The gift barrel of fresh ones that General Walter Taylor, Lee's ex-adjutant, sent the family in 1868 "converted our Easter celebration into a feast," Lee wrote to him in thanks, adding those of his neighbors "for the pleasing knowledge you have given them of so excellent a shell-fish. . . . We live so far up in the mountains that they do not flourish here." Later the general spent the then sizable sum of $15.50 on eight gallons of oysters to mark the New

Year of 1870, his last. They arrived by packet boat, "finely flavored and plump as eggs . . . enough for everybody."

· TURKEY SOUP ·

Unlike Mrs. Randolph's extravaganza, this soup begins with left-overs—and would have been welcomed after the war by the many southerners, black and white, who were subsisting mostly on corn-meal, fatback, and molasses. It still makes a good informal company supper.

Quantities and cooking times can be casual, but the right ingredients are essential. Use half-and-half, not milk. The ham can be scraps but must be dark red and country-cured; supermarkets in country-ham country often sell them. Though not as good as ham, lean country bacon may be used for "lean midling," but not regular fatback or salt pork. Leave plenty of meat on the turkey bones you begin with. If, like me, you save the "liquor" from cooking a country ham, add a cupful or so to the water.

The carcass of a turkey, a few pieces of lean midling or ham, a few onions & perhaps a carrot,—an hour before dinner pour in a pint of milk, having brought the milk to the boiling point & stirred in a tablespoonful of flour made to a paste with a little milk if the milk is thin. Herbs if you have them, & season with pepper & salt. If you have celery put it in after the onions, if parsley put in the tureen & pour soup on it—let it simmer

Remains of a 20-lb. turkey
About 3 qts. water
About 1 lb. country ham (scraps will do) or bacon
2–3 medium onions, roughly chopped
1–2 carrots, roughly chopped
1–2 ribs celery with leaves, roughly chopped

The Main Meal

About ½ c. parsley, chopped
About 1 c. ham liquor, if available
2 c. half-and-half
1–2 T. flour, if desired as thickening

Break up carcass. Cover with water and ham broth if used. Add onions and carrots and simmer at least 1½ hours. Add celery, simmer about 1 hour more. Strain off broth. Discard vegetables. Pull lean ham and turkey to shreds and reserve; discard bones. If broth is not intensely flavored, cook down. Before serving, return turkey and ham to broth and add half-and-half. If thickening with flour, stir in cold water to make a paste and stir into soup. Simmer, stirring occasionally, at least 20 minutes. Correct seasoning. Put chopped parsley in bottom of tureen or bowls and pour soup over. Serves about 10 to 12.

Descendants of Portable Soup

Although commercial bouillon cubes did not arrive until the twentieth century, Virginians had been concentrating soup since colonial times. In 1737, William Byrd recommended for traveling a complex stock made from several kinds of meat, bone, vegetables, and anchovies, boiled down and dried in the sun to a stiff glue. Dissolve a piece of "portable soup" in water, he wrote, and "a bason of good broth [can] be had in a few minutes." Thanks to ice refrigeration and perhaps canning, the Lees did not reduce their broths and soups to glue, but they did make soup bases and concentrates.

Three of the notebook's soup receipts appear on two facing pages—Turkey Soup on the right, and Soup (Preparation) followed by Preparation of Tomatoes for Soup [illegible] Tomatoes on the left—all written in a florid, scrawling script that cannot be identified. Even Mrs. Lee's tiny, cramped hand is more legible. The testers assumed that Soup, a rather undistinguished meat broth, and the tomato soup were separate receipts, but on closer inspection they may have been two parts of the same receipt. At any rate, the concentrated tomato preparation, though excellent when thinned with water, could only be improved by using this broth instead.

· MEAT BROTH ·

This part of the receipt calls only for meat, bones, and water. Make it by barely simmering ½ pound lean meat and 2 medium soup bones, covered, to each quart of water all day, most conveniently in a crock pot. Cool, refrigerate, and when cold, degrease. The writer notes that the broth will keep a week, and the last line reads, *"take out* what is needed," suggesting it was made in quantity, when soup at dinner was an everyday occurrence. It certainly makes a suitable addition to more kinds of soup than just the tomato written in below it.

· TOMATO CONCENTRATE ·

On very little evidence, namely this receipt and others in the same hand, I nominate daughter Mary Custis as the author of its maddening scrawl. She and Mildred both visited in Louisiana, where slaves brought okra, one of the notebook's few identifiably African touches, via the Caribbean. Mildred's handwriting remains consistent throughout the notebook and her letters to my aunt, but over time Mary Custis's varied greatly. Some samples from other sources are roughly similar to this receipt, although the handwriting definitely identifiable in the notebook as Mary Custis's differs greatly from it. Besides, she seems to me the type to write in such a big, impatient hand.

The okra I remember from my childhood was boiled to a stringy, gluey, grayish mass, but here it thickens the soup deliciously. Even cooked down as directed, the quantity given here is enormous. I

The Main Meal

suspect the family made it before frost hit the garden, canned it, and welcomed it during the vegetable-scarce winter. One-eighth of the receipt makes about a gallon and a half of concentrate, which "serves so many I couldn't keep count," the tester confessed. But the Parisian family she served it to raved about it. (It is, however, much less distinguished made with canned tomatoes.) Frozen, it revives splendidly.

Peel 1 bu. of tomatoes after pouring hot water over them, a few at a time, add to them 1 peck ochre cut up and 1 peck onions cut up, season with 2 cups of salt, 1 cup bk pepper, boil down to a marmalade, [illegible] takes about 1 cup of this to the soup just before it is taken up.

One-eighth quantity:
4 qts. (8 lbs.) ripe tomatoes, fresh or frozen whole at home
1 qt. (2 lbs.) okra, stemmed and chopped
1 qt. (2 lbs.) onions, peeled and chopped
3 T. salt
1½ T. black pepper, or to taste

First, peel the tomatoes. If using fresh tomatoes, submerse a few at a time in boiling water 1–2 minutes, then slip off skins; frozen tomatoes peel easily while thawing. Chop roughly. Cook vegetables in enamel or stainless steel pan; otherwise okra turns black. You may start cooking the tomatoes while chopping the onions. Add onions and simmer an hour before adding okra. Stir occasionally, then frequently, to prevent burning. Simmer 1 hour or more, add half to three-quarters of the salt and pepper. Simmer at least another hour, to desired thickness. Adjust seasoning. To reconstitute, add broth or water as needed.

"My dear Genl," Mrs. Lee wrote on October 10, 1870, to Francis H. Smith, superintendent of VMI, "the Drs. think it would be well for Genl Lee to have some beef tea at once and as I cannot get it at the market before night I send to beg a small piece." General Smith undoubtedly sent the beef if he had it, but it could not have healed General Lee's heart. "Robert . . . always welcomes me with a pressure of the hand," said Mary Lee as she sat behind him in her rolling chair, and two days later he died.

Foodways expert Kathryn Arnold calls beef tea "the early IV" (intravenous feeding) and adds that Mann Valentine—brother of Edward Valentine, who sculpted Lee's recumbent statue in the chapel at Washington and Lee—mixed liver extract with beef tea essence, bottled it, sold it, and made a fortune. As late as World War II, tuberculosis patients still received this concentrated source of sodium and protein; it is at least as health-giving as chicken soup. The receipt, entered by Mrs. Lee, remains much the same in the *Joy of Cooking*, and yields half a cup, so concentrated it tastes of iron.

1 lb of lean fresh beef put in a wide mouthed bottle or jar
place in a kettle of boiling water to remain one hour strain
& there will be a gill of most nourishing liquid.

Grind beef in grinder or food processor or dice fine. Put in a jar, cover, and place upright in boiling water. Cook one hour, strain off broth, discard meat.

· BOUILLON ·

This receipt, pinned in and probably from the same lady who provided Mrs. Lee with the one for yeast at Derwent, produces an ele-

gant, delicious, nonfattening, all-but-forgotten taste of the past. A crushed egg shell may replace the egg white. Soup bones, needless to say, have gone up in price.

A 10 ct beef bone & 2 lbs beef put on in ½ gal of cold water, boil thoroughly, remove the meat, put in a cool place for the night.

Next day remove every particle of grease, and add 3 carrots, 3 turnips, 1 onion, celery seed, salt & pepper. Boil 3 hours. Clear with beaten white of an egg after it is cold. Strain through a sieve first, then a thick cloth. Add wine before serving.

1 large soup bone
2 lbs. lean beef in chunks
8 c. water
3 carrots, roughly chopped

The Receipts

3 turnips, roughly chopped
1 onion, roughly chopped
1 t. celery seed, or celery seed, salt, and pepper to taste
1 crushed eggshell or egg white
1 T. medium sherry or Madeira per cup of bouillon served

Cook bone and meat in water at least 2 hours. Strain broth, discard meat and bone. Refrigerate overnight. Degrease. Add vegetables and boil 3 hours. Strain through a large sieve, return to pot, stir in egg white or crushed eggshell and heat. Skim off coagulated foam as it forms. Line a sieve with a clean, wet dishtowel and strain stock through. If still not clear enough, drip broth through a jelly bag. Cool. Add wine. Reheat or serve cold. It should jell when cold (for insurance you may add to hot stock 1 to 2 packets unflavored gelatin, softened in water or broth according to package directions). Serve hot or jelled.

The Heart of the Dinner: Meat

The customary British-derived emphasis on meat, fish, and poultry probably survived at the Lee family's main meal after the war. Two kinds may have been customary, down from many more, and leftovers no doubt reappeared in one form or another until finished.

What Mrs. Trollope called "the sempiternal ham," cured with salt and smoked, was well suited to such encores. This most prized part of the pig came from animals whose ancestors may well have landed at Jamestown and were semiwild and lean from foraging. A famed Virginia export by 1700, hams were consumed in quantity at home: one a day was boiled at Mount Vernon, and Mrs. Lee listed forty donated for a Lexington church supper. Some connoisseurs claim the quality has gone down in these days of mass production and tamer hogs, but I love these hams still and mourn the passing of the "sempiternal" into the realm of rare treat, even in Virginia, now that we

The Main Meal

have so many other choices and lack the long hours needed to prepare them.

The general's favorite fried chicken, though out of fashion, was no doubt served often. Presents of game also appeared, and probably the notebook's Boiled Leg of Mutton, which, alas, went untested (tough mutton was unobtainable, and Mrs. Tyree argued persuasively that boiling ruins lamb). Only some unspecified "meat" on Mrs. Lee's grocery lists might represent "the mammoth consumption of beef" that amazed Anthony Trollope, novelist son of the acerbic Mrs. T. Since beef was extremely tough until the turn of the century and the rise of specially bred beef cattle, perhaps the family preferred veal, which Mrs. Lee did buy.

Keeping raw meat fresh in hot weather was a chore. Every day, wrote Mrs. Randolph, each piece should be washed in cold water, dried, rubbed with bran, and hung in the coolest place available. Mrs. Tyree directed people who lacked icehouses to put meat "in a cool dark cellar, wrapped around with wet cloths, on top of which lay boughs of elderberry. The evaporation from the cloths will keep the meat cool and the elderberry will keep off insects."

Roasting

Although this cooking method needed no receipt, how best to accomplish it was another matter. By 1885, Mary Stuart Smith, while acknowledging that "epicurism has given way to convenience," still considered fireplace roasting superior to cooking in the oven of a cast-iron stove (see "Equipment: The Stove Revolution," page 101).

So did Mrs. Tyree, but by 1879 when *Housekeeping in Old Virginia* came out, fireplace roasting seems to have disappeared from the lives of her contributors. Virtually all their receipts for oven roasting— whether beef, pork, veal, lamb, turkey, or even chicken—involved water. Tougher cuts were often parboiled (simmered until partially cooked) first; others were cooked in or over water. Nowadays, purists

The Receipts

scorn such methods, but they do not have to contend with such tough meat, either. (Also prominent in the book is "lardering," or larding, a technique for making meat more tender by threading fat through it.)

In any case, this practice may have grown eventually into the school of low-heat, moist, gray roasting during the Depression. It held that high heat shrank precious meat and poultry, which some cookbook writers now discount.

Fish

We know that Mrs. Lee bought sturgeon, a fish that during the settlement at Jamestown grew up to twelve feet long and was so plentiful men killed them with axes. The United States exported caviar (sturgeon roe) to Russia as late as 1900 and still has a tiny caviar industry. Thanks to it, sturgeon turns up occasionally on coastal restaurant menus, but I have seen it only once, long ago in Tehran, where it was firm, white, succulent, and altogether lovely.

· BROILED SHAD ·

"Fresh shad caught in the river form our frugal repasts," Mildred wrote from Romancoke, where her brother Rob and his family lived along the Pamunkey River. My aunt remembered spring nights there, when fish swam upstream to spawn, and shadowy boats stayed out all night catching them in nets. Before the boats returned to port, her mother would choose fish that were "the best thing in the world."

Perhaps shad were saved from the fate of sturgeon by their bones. Though not so abundant now, shad may exist at all because only people lucky enough to grow up eating them will brave the needle-sharp, multitudinous bones of this largest member of the herring

The Main Meal

Romancoke, on the banks of the Pamunkey River, family home of the Robert E. Lee Jr. household: (left to right) the author's mother, Mrs. R. E. Lee Jr., R. E. Lee Jr., the author's aunt, servants Leanna and Mammy. (Courtesy of the Lee family)

family. The bones are said to dissolve with long, slow, cooking, but they never have for me.

The directions labeled "Broil shad," minimal even for the notebook, say only to cook the fish on one side and then the other until done. About fifteen minutes in all per inch of thickness (measured at the thickest part) should do whether under a hot broiler or on an outdoor grill.

Better yet, go to a shad bake, where at night men nail split shad to oak boards and stand them upright around a blazing fire. While the fish cooks to a smoky brown, bourbon flows (though alcohol isn't strictly necessary), stars shine, the women admire, the men work, and I don't remember bones. The roe, rolled in cornmeal and fried in bacon grease, is heaven. Civic associations put on these feasts along the Eastern Shore of Virginia and Maryland and probably in other states in the shad belt.

The Receipts

· DRAWN BUTTER ·

This simple, unassertive sauce begins an almost illegible double page in the same unidentified scrawl as the tomato soup. The receipt has an affinity for broiled shad, written in below it, and adds a little unction to other simple fish preparations and vegetables, particularly broccoli and asparagus. The flour keeps the sauce from separating, and the only taste is butter. Since Mrs. Randolph's Drawn Butter has no water and less flour, the Lee receipt could represent a drop in living standards—or just canny thrift. Makes about a cup.

*Have ready on the fire ½ pint of water, in which put
a large spoonful of butter, creamed with a teaspoonful of flour.
Let it boil until it thickens. It must be perfectly smooth.*

The Main Meal

1 c. water
1 rounded T. butter
1 t. flour

Knead or cream together butter and flour. Cook and stir or whisk constantly after adding to hot water.

Poultry, Bloody Poultry?

The roasting times that follow Drawn Butter, though headed "Meat," are all for poultry, and none are long enough to cook even the youngest, tenderest birds thoroughly by today's standards. Even when first brought to room temperature and then roasted at 450° for the times specified, red joints and pink patches remain. Could the timings be meant for fireplaces? Mrs. Randolph, arguably the best cook in Virginia, roasted chickens only 15 minutes, presumably over a very hot fire and perhaps with the help of a "tin kitchen," an open metal reflector box that intensified heat. Or did people enjoy underdone poultry? Wild duck is still served rare, and when asked how she liked her beef, my mother used to say, "just walk the cow through the kitchen." Why not poultry?

Another possibility is that, as of this writing (although calls for change have begun), poultry in the United States can legally be and is sold as "fresh" when it has been held chilled just short of freezing almost indefinitely. Truly fresh birds cook much more quickly, a fact I learned the year my Christmas turkey from a nearby farm was roasted through long before the rest of dinner was ready. It was also unbelievably better than the usual "fresh" bird.

Here are the timings given in the notebook, whatever they represent: "A moderate size turkey should take 1¼ hours to roast; ducks ¾, chicken ½."

Other Main Dishes

The notebook has three receipts for more elaborate preparations, which might have been served as part of a light supper.

· CHICKEN SALAD ·

The large proportion of celery in this receipt seems to have been a luxury, not a filler. Years later a then–Washington College student recalled, "Miss Mary [Custis Lee] sent for me and told me if I would go out to Dr. Ruffner's farm for some celery to be used in the salad at the Episcopal church fair[,] . . . I might ride old Traveller." Superneat entered this receipt. For a change, it is complete to the point of pedantry. Though it sounds bizarre and takes time, effort, and guesswork, it rewards them all. The testers and I reached no definitive answer to the question, how big was "a bottle of oil," but assuming that this was olive oil, the bottle was probably small. In the Northeast, Italian and Greek immigrants had created enough demand for the oil that it was imported in quantity, but in the South, chances are it remained expensive.

The region did grow at least a little of its own olive oil, for when Lee visited his father's grave on Cumberland Island, off Georgia, in 1862, he wrote his wife about a grove that had been planted by General Nathanael Greene, "from which, I learn, Mr. N[ightingale, the present owner] procures oil." However, if there were an olive oil industry in the South at that time, I doubt that the yield was enough to affect the price, just as today's U.S. caviar crop does nothing to moderate the price of those precious imported eggs.

Fannie Farmer's standardized measurements would have been more than welcome in this receipt; unfortunately, they were not published until 1896. I decided pragmatically that the bottle held the right amount for making mayonnaise, which this sauce resembles.

The Main Meal

As it happens, the Chinese way of boiling chickens to keep them juicy resembles Mrs. Randolph's, so I used it. Further tips: as the receipt says, a wooden spoon is preferable to silver, which both mustard and eggs will tarnish; and surrounding the chicken salad with frenched green beans makes a lovely one-dish luncheon.

To a pair of chickens (boiled tender) and cut into pieces (<u>not</u> minced) and about the same bulk of celery, take ten (10) eggs— Boil them <u>very</u> hard, rubbing their yolks to a <u>fine</u> flour and mixing in them two tablespoonsfull of water—Mix about two tablespoonsfull of mustard with as little water as is necessary to make a smooth mixture of it—and beat the eggs and it <u>thoroughly</u> together with a silver tablespoon. (A wooden spoon however is preferable)

Add to this the oil, by <u>small</u> quantities at first <u>beating</u> it in well. —till you consume the greater part of a bottle of oil. Towards the last you can add <u>larger</u> quantities of it—When all is in beat for <u>fifteen</u> minutes longer— Then take the yolks of five (5) new eggs which, when <u>well</u> beaten must be mixed <u>well</u> into the primary mass. Then season to taste with red pepper and salt adding the juice and grated rind of two lemons or about two small tablespoons full of vinegar.

2 chickens
1–1½ bunches (not stalks) celery
10 hard-boiled egg yolks, plus 2 T. water
5 raw egg yolks
2 T. dry mustard
About 2 T. more water
¾ c. olive oil
Rind and juice of 2 lemons
Salt and red pepper to taste

Stage 1: In a large pot, cover chickens with cold water, bring to a boil, reduce heat, simmer 15–20 minutes, and allow to cool in liquid (it may be boiled down for stock). Chickens may be refrigerated, covered, overnight.

Stage 2: The day before serving, skin, bone, and cut up chicken. Chop celery; grate rind and squeeze juice of lemons. Boil 10 eggs and mash or sieve yolks. (Reserve whites for another use; Mrs. Randolph put boiled egg whites in green salad.) Mix mustard and sieved cooked egg yolks with water separately, then together. As in making mayonnaise, beat in olive oil steadily by hand, at first drop by drop, then gradually increasing to a fine stream. Continue beating well. (Or follow directions for making mayonnaise with a blender or food processor.)

Stage 3: The day of serving, beat raw egg yolks until light. In a large bowl, fold the beaten yolks into the mustard-yolk sauce mixture, add lemon juice and rind and salt and pepper to taste. Add chicken and celery, mix well, and refrigerate. Serve on lettuce to 10–12.

· MISS COLEMAN'S CHICKEN TERRAPIN ·

The handwriting and identity of the donor of this pinned-in receipt remain mysterious, but through it we may glimpse a bit of culinary evolution: the path from giant sea turtle soup to creamed chicken. "The Larder Invaded," catalogue of an exhibition of nineteenth-century food, says that giant sea turtles, those widely relished ocean leviathans often weighing up to 500 pounds, made popular pièces de résistance at large public banquets until overly enthusiastic consumption made them scarce. Then terrapin, the "common marsh turtle"—once, like oysters, so plentiful that slaves rebelled against being given so many to eat—took their place. When these too dwindled, calf's head, tongue, veal, and chicken were often substituted and called "mock turtle," just as then-cheaper veal was called "city chicken" during the Depression. (Now we substitute pork, turkey, and chicken for veal, because it costs more.)

The Main Meal

General Lee's sketch of a diamondback terrapin, a frequent companion during his first assignment after graduation from West Point, supervising the construction of Fort Pulaski near Savannah, Georgia. (Courtesy of the Jessie Ball duPont Memorial Library, Stratford Hall Plantation)

Meanwhile, when and where I grew up, the name "terrapin" descended to the land, or box, turtle, and that in turn was served at least once during the meat rationing of World War II. When my mother asked an elegant French lady where she found the main ingredient of her delicious luncheon main dish, Madame answered sweetly, "under the kitchen steps, my dear."

The earlier family cookbooks and Mrs. Randolph's do not mention terrapin. By the time of Mrs. Tyree's, veal and tongue were used in mock terrapin dishes much like this one. And with more cream sauce (already in place in an 1860 Maryland cookbook) added and hard-boiled eggs subtracted, this becomes chicken à la king, or everyday creamed chicken. I suspect the dish was new and exciting when the Lee ladies gathered this receipt, and then, like Apple Float, became a culinary cliché.

The dish demands the flavorful sherry or Madeira that the Lees would have used, not the white wine prevalent today. Mace and red pepper combine well; I now use them often. A ten-year-old taster declared the hard-boiled eggs "weird" but "not bad for over a hundred years old." Do not overcook or refrigerate them, or they will become tough. This receipt makes a lovely supper or Sunday brunch for 4 to 6 when served with Evelyn Krumbacker's waffles, plus, perhaps, more cream sauce or cream.

The Receipts

Cut up a cold chicken (roasted or boiled) into very small pieces, being careful to take off all the skin, put it into a skillet with a wine glass of cream, a good sized piece of butter rolled in flour & season to taste with cayenne pepper, a little Mace & salt. Have ready 3 hard boiled eggs cut into small pieces & a wine glass of wine. When the chicken has come to a good boil, stir them in & in two or three minutes it will be ready to serve.

3 T. butter at room temperature
2 T. flour
2 c. chicken (or turkey), cooked, skinned,
　　boned, and cut in small pieces
½ c. or more whipping cream
¼ t. mace
⅛–¼ t. red pepper
Salt to taste
3 hard-boiled eggs
¼ c. sherry or Madeira

Bring eggs to boil in cold water, simmer 12 minutes. Shell them under cold running water and chop into small pieces. *Do not refrigerate.* Cream together butter and flour. Heat and stir in cream, seasoning, and chicken. Before serving the sauce, stir in wine, then chopped eggs. Heat briefly, stirring carefully so as not to break up eggs. (To subtract some calories and cholesterol, use only the whites of the hard-boiled eggs; the yolks can be used in the Chicken Salad receipt above.)

· GUMBO FILÉ — NEW ORLEANS ·

Mildred took down this receipt, one of the few with a recognizable African influence, no doubt on one of her visits to New Orleans. She and Mary Custis unveiled a statue of their father there in 1884, and later she died on nearby Petite Anse Island.

The Main Meal

Kingombo means "okra" in Angolan, which shows how closely the dish and vegetable were associated when they arrived in Louisiana. Stewed okra was "gumbs" to Mrs. Randolph, and her Ochra Soup (cooked in an "earthen pipkin") was on the way to gumbo. But by 1847, as Sarah Rutledge's *The Carolina Housewife* shows, yet another culture was influencing the dish: instead of okra, Choctaw Indian filé powder thickens her gumbo and that in the Lee notebook as well. The Louisiana contributor of a more Creole-style receipt in Mrs. Tyree's book explained, "*Filit* is only sassafras leaves, dried and sifted together; you can make it yourself." Perhaps, since the powder seems to have been unfamiliar in 1879, the notebook's was among the first gumbos thickened by filé to travel so far north.

This easy, basic, flavorful gumbo has none of the now all-but-obligatory tomato. It can be made with fish or shellfish as well as with chicken, which I skin and bone. Increasing the amount of flour allows decreasing the cooking time without affecting the flavor. Cooking makes filé powder ropy; heed the receipt and add it at the end, then reheat only briefly. Although some receipts call for both filé powder and okra, it is safer to use only one; otherwise you could end up with glue. Served New Orleans home-style, in soup bowls over rice, one chicken is enough for 4 to 6.

Take a good size piece of lard—about half as large as a goose's egg—to which when hot add a tablespoonful of flour—which keep turning until brown—put in the chicken which has been cut in pieces, & let it fry until brown—also an onion cut in small pieces. When the onion is cooked—& the chicken fried—pour over-all two qts of water—let all <u>simmer</u> for 3 hours. When about to be served after it is taken from the fire—put in 1½–2 tablespoonfuls of Gumbo-Filé, which keep turning for a while. Put in the bouillon all necessary herbs. When oysters are used—the water of the oysters should be added to the bouillon.

The Receipts

1 chicken
3 T. lard (best) or other fat
1–3 T. flour
1 large onion, chopped
8 c. water
2 t. thyme
Salt and red and black pepper to taste
1½–2 T. filé powder

Skin and bone chicken, if desired. Heat fat and stir in flour until smooth and browned. Fry chicken and onion until browned, then add water, thyme, salt, and pepper. Simmer up to 3 hours, not less than 45 minutes. Just before serving, remove from heat and stir in filé powder to thicken. If using oysters (2 c. or more), add the liquor before simmering, and poach the oyster briefly just before adding filé.

Vegetables

"In our garden nothing is up but the hardy plants, pease, potatoes, spinach, onions, etc.," Lee wrote his son Rob in April of 1868. "Beets, carrots, salsify, etc., have been sown a long time . . . I cannot put in the beans, squash, etc., or put in the hot-bed plants."

Along with his salary of $1,500 a year, the president of Washington College received the use of a house and garden, both of them devastated by war and neglect. With Sam, a man-of-all-work, "my father at once set to work improving all around him," Rob recollected, "laid out a vegetable garden, planted roses and shrubs, set out fruit and yard trees, made new walls and repaired the stable."

The Virginia colonists had arrived carrying a variety of seeds. By 1737, William Byrd, extolling "the Newly Discovered Eden" (and trying to encourage settlement) praised the vegetables, listing among others several different kinds of potatoes and cabbage and numerous varieties of peas and beans, as well as the native corn and pumpkins. From the start, says Williamsburg food researcher Patricia Gibbs, the colonists ate more vegetables than their counterparts at home.

Elizabeth Calvert, a Custis cousin who visited Arlington as a child before the war, recalled Arlington's vegetables lyrically: "There is pleasure . . . in a dish of asparagus just from the earth white tender & sweet. . . . There is joy . . . in the young peas that know no pause between the gathering, & the being placed upon the table, young, green, sweet & buttery. And what emotions of delight green corn that is fifteen minutes from the stork [*sic*], & fifteen minutes in the pot, inspire."

More prosaically, the chronically cash-strapped Mr. Custis paid many of the estate's running expenses with proceeds from vegetables, fruit, and dairy products raised there and sold at Washington City's Central Market. Lawrence Parks, a servant, used to row the produce across the Potomac and man the stall; sometimes on the way home he caught a nap on a mud flat before the tide rose and lifted the boat off. When Mrs. Lee left Arlington, she all but ordered the commander of the troops occupying her home to allow "my market man" to go back and forth to Washington, where his family lived.

Before the Civil War only a privileged few Southerners may have consumed as wide a range of vegetables as the Lees. Afterward, cabbage boiled in "pot liquor" from cured pork was "the daily and favorite [vegetable] dish of nine tenths of the [Virginia] country people," Mary Stuart Smith observed in her cookbook as late as 1885. Nevertheless, Mrs. Lee's grocery lists and her husband's garden show that the family continued to enjoy a variety of vegetables. Yet the notebook has only three receipts for cooking them. Most were simply boiled—interminably, we have come to assume.

This tendency toward overcooking persisted through World War II and in some places still does. Karen Hess traces its origins to home canning, widespread in the last half of the nineteenth century, which required long cooking to sterilize the jars' contents. Before

The Receipts

that, Mrs. Randolph did indeed cook spinach just a few minutes, but her other vegetables were not exactly *nouvelle cuisine*, perhaps with good reason. People then thought raw and undercooked vegetables caused cholera, typhoid, and other dread diseases, and they boiled them long enough to kill the real culprit, germs in contaminated water. Mrs. Randolph may have just been lucky with spinach.

Some but not all times for cooking vegetables did rise between her 1824 cookbook and Mrs. Tyree's in 1879. Both give peas and asparagus 20 to 30 minutes, but the latter sentences cauliflower to two hours on the stove, up substantially from Mrs. Randolph's 15 to 20 minutes. Mrs. Tyree's "snaps" (green beans) and corn take an hour, versus Mrs. Randolph's 15 to 20 minutes. The account of 15-minute corn at Arlington suggests that the Lee ladies stayed with their cousin's shorter timings.

Two vegetable preparations in the Lee notebook, along with two receipts for cooking oats, came from the weekly *Baltimorean* in 1873. Since none have telltale kitchen stains, none may have been used. Afterward, one vegetable receipt became commonplace and the other, undeservedly, all but extinct.

"When a girl," Mrs. Lee drew a sketch of Lawrence Parks about to embark for Wash Market, where he sold the estate's produce, including these cabbages. (Courtesy of a private collector, print courtesy of the National Park Service, Arlington House Collection)

· FRIED POTATOES ·

Through this newspaper cutting we catch a glimpse of a time when french fries were exciting. The writer, inspired to cut potatoes into strips, exclaimed, "Try it; you will think them delicious." By now, we consume so many we must agree. Except for frying the strips in tasty but now-suspect lard, this receipt has nothing to detain us.

Vegetables

In my husband's home state, Ohio, Thanksgiving demanded a wonderfully nutty, Shaker-style dried corn, which is now available under the brand name John Cope. (You can dry your own in an oven set at the lowest heat with the door cracked open; a food dryer works well, too.) The Lee receipt for corn is altogether different, closer to cream-style, and equally delectable.

I gather the corn when it is large enough to eat, and cook about fifteen minutes; then, with a sharp knife, cut the top of the kernel, scrape off the rest, leaving the hull on the cob; spread thin on plates and dry in a warm place near the stove; it will dry in six hours; when thoroughly dry place in a tight sack (a paper flour sack is good), hang in a dry, cool place; this needs no airing to keep it from getting musty. When wanted for use, take a sufficient quantity, place in a pan with plenty of water, cold or warm, not hot; let it soak over night; set on the stove with the same water it soaked in; let it cook slowly for 1½ hours; when nearly done, add a piece of butter, salt and pepper and sweet cream, if you like. If you want succotash, add to the corn about half as much well cooked beans. Beans are better soaked over night in cold water, then parboiled, and cooked slowly in fresh water; when nearly done add salt, and season to taste.

Yields about ⅔ c. dried corn:
6 ears corn
¼ c. whipping cream
3 T. butter
Salt to taste
Liberal grinding of pepper

Drying and storing: Scrape corn from cobs as described above. Spread a thin layer of the resulting rough paste on each of 3 large dinner plates or nonstick cookie sheets. Dry in oven at lowest temperature with the door cracked open. Stir occasionally, especially at

The Receipts

first, to keep corn from sticking. Corn should be dry in about 4 hours. Tie dried corn in cloth and hang out of reach of possible small marauders.

Soaking and cooking: Soak corn in water to cover well. Leaving it overnight does no harm, but about 1½ hours will do. Cook corn in soaking water for 20 minutes. When nearly done, add cream, butter, and seasonings and heat through. Serves 4 to 6. For succotash, soak and cook dried limas according to package directions and add about 1 part limas to 2 parts corn, increasing butter and cream proportionately.

· MUSHROOMS ·

"Mushrumps," the Washington manuscript calls them, and here mace and red pepper enhance their pure mushroom taste, which Mrs. Randolph called "too delicious to require aid from any thing"— though she in fact allowed a little red wine. My mushrooming friends could not identify what the receipt calls "flaps," but they think any wild, nonpoisonous kind would be good. In my youth, unpeeled mushrooms were considered uncouth, but apparently the Lee ladies did not think so. Skipping that tedious nicety saves nutrients, too.

This makes a good late breakfast or brunch with bacon or country ham and Owendaw Cornbread or Evelyn Krumbacker's Waffles. For a more substantial meal, top them with Cornish game hens, squabs, guinea hens, chickens, or partridges. Served in that way, a pound of mushrooms will do for four. Drained, they make an unusual hors d'oeuvre, and the juice enriches soups or gravies.

Mushrooms au Beurre (delicious)

Cut the stems from some fine meadow mushrooms—buttons, & clean them with a bit of new flannel & some fine salt; then either wipe them dry with a soft cloth, or rinse them in fresh water, drain them quickly, spread

Vegetables

*them in a clean cloth, fold it over them, & leave them ten minutes, or more
to dry. For every pint of them thus prepared put an ounce & a half of fresh
butter into a thick iron saucepan, shake it over the fire until it just begins to
brown. Throw in the mushrooms, continue to shake the saucepan over a
clear fire, that they may not stick to it, nor burn, & when they have simmered three or four minutes, strew over them a little salt, some cayenne, &
pounded mace; stew them until they are perfectly tender, heap them on a dish
& serve them with their own sauce only, for breakfast, supper or luncheon.
Nothing can be finer than the flavor of the mushrooms thus prepared, & the
addition of any liquid is far from an improvement. They are very good
when drained from the butter & served cold & in a cool larder may be kept
for several days. The butter in which they are stewed is admirable for flavoring gravies, sauces or potted meats. Small flaps, freed from the fur &
skin, may be stewed in the same way & either those, or the buttons served
under roast poultry or partridges, will give a dish a very superior relish.*

1 lb. (4 pts.) mushrooms
6 T. butter
1 t. salt or to taste
¼ t. mace
⅛–¼ t. cayenne

This detailed receipt needs little in the way of additions. If necessary,
cut mushrooms to make them roughly equal in size. You may clean
with wet paper towels and dry between dry ones. (The methods in
the notebook show the ladies guarded against the mushrooms' absorbing moisture, as they are wont to do.) Sauté over medium heat in
a 10- to 12-inch heavy skillet.

Salads & Dressings

"For nearly a generation after the Civil War," says Sarah Belk in
Around the Southern Table, "the average Southerner probably did not

eat many salads, if any at all." The notebook has no receipts for them, and "salad" on Mrs. Lee's grocery lists may mean greens for cooking. The lettuce there and in the general's garden might even have been wilted with hot dressing, although that strikes me as more a midwestern practice. Nevertheless, the notebook's two dressings for specific simple salads, along with the family's love of vegetables, convince me that when Mrs. Lee wrote Mildred, "you must not starve your brother and sister. I suppose the garden now furnishes you with plenty of spinach & lettuce," at least some of that lettuce went, raw, into salads.

People had been eating salads at least since the time of classical Greece. Tudor salads verged on edible art, with primroses, violets, and marigolds in among the greens. When William Byrd promoted the Virginia colony, he listed plenty of salad makings: three kinds of lettuce, two of garlic, several of cabbage and cucumbers, radishes, and many suitable herbs.

At first salads in the colonies were dressed with imported and expensive olive oil, although Thomas Jefferson tried raising benne (sesame) seed as a substitute. Green salads must have been confined to the wealthy before people turned to "boiled" dressings, probably brought by German and other North European immigrants. Nowadays we often consider boiled dressings more economical than gastronomical, but both of the ones in the Lee notebook, tangy with mustard and vinegar and with no filler, are a treat. They not only dress tossed salads nicely but also bind potato and other substantial salads and perk up salmon and vegetables such as asparagus and broccoli as well.

Deadly Nightshade on the Table

"Dressing for Salad o Tomatoes," in Mildred's hand, shows the family enjoying a vegetable long considered poisonous. Perhaps because Jefferson grew them at Monticello, Virginians took to tomatoes early;

Salads & Dressings

Mrs. Randolph put them raw into salad at a time when all uncooked vegetables were suspect. The Salad o Tomatoes dressing is good, but a very similar one, Dressing for Cold Slaw, from an unknown donor, seems less subject to curdling. The "Cold" of this Slaw began as the German and Dutch word for cabbage and is another instance, like "gingerbread" and perhaps "Sally Lunn," where a term changes to something that sounds familiar but has a completely different meaning. The receipt, which makes about ¾ cup, needs no elaboration.

· DRESSING FOR COLD SLAW ·

3 eggs beat light — butter size of an egg — tea spoon salt —
2 of mustard — ½ of pepper — vinegar — boil it like custard.

3 eggs
¼ c. butter
½–1 t. salt
½ t. pepper
2 t. dry mustard
2–3 t. vinegar
2–3 T. milk or cream

In the top of a double boiler or in a very heavy pan, whisk eggs until light and place over simmering water or very low heat. Whisk in other ingredients, continuing until sauce thickens. If too thick, whisk in a little more milk or cream.

Along the Mayonnaise Trail

Richard Hellman bottled and sold the first commercial mayonnaise in the United States in 1912, but we can see its beginnings long before. In 1669, John Evelyn's receipt for salad dressing said to mash oil, vinegar, pepper, and mustard seed with a cannonball and add "squashed" hard-boiled egg yolks. Mrs. Randolph dropped the cannonball, but otherwise it had not changed much by 1824. This version, the one in Chicken Salad, and one of Mrs. Tyree's all add raw egg yolks to the hard-boiled. Yet another in Mrs. Tyree's book leaves out the boiled yolks, calling only for raw. With that change, mayonnaise as we know it had arrived.

· SALAD DRESSING ·

A small, old mustard pot in a tester's mother's kitchen closet seemed to hold the right amount of mustard called for in this receipt, but again we yearned for Fannie Farmer's standardized measurements. Use a good olive oil, since "sweet oil" meant a superior one from the Mediterranean. This dressing does nice things for stuffed eggs and tomato aspic, makes an excellent base for tartar sauce, and on salad, says a tester, "makes even awful iceberg interesting." The amount of mustard is up to the individual.

If the threat of salmonella continues, perhaps we will return to John Evelyn's way. Meanwhile, premium mustard, several mashed egg yolks, and a little vinegar added to high-quality commercial mayonnaise comes close. Yields a scant half cup.

The yolks of 3 hard boiled eggs mashed well—add the yolk of a raw egg & mix well together—add 3 salt spoons of salt, some red pepper & half a mustard pot of mixed mustard. Stir all up then add sweet oil very slowly! & stir briskly til it becomes thick, then add half a tablespoonful of vinegar.

3 hard-boiled egg yolks
1 raw egg yolk
¼–½ t. salt
⅛ t. (a pinch) cayenne
1½–2 T. premium prepared mustard

Salads & Dressings

¼ c. plus 1 T. olive oil
1 ½ t. vinegar

Mash the hard-boiled egg yolks thoroughly with a fork, then combine with beaten raw yolk, salt, cayenne, and mustard. As in making mayonnaise, beat in olive oil steadily by hand, at first drop by drop, then gradually increasing to a fine stream. Continue beating well. Whether the vinegar is added before or after the oil does not seem to matter.

Drinks with & without Alcohol

The Virginia colonists arrived carrying wine, brandy, rum, and beer or ale. Soon they began making apple cider and brandy with just about any fruit from peaches to "Pissimonds" (persimmons). Although Southern men reputedly drank heavily before the war, Mr. Custis and his son-in-law were not among them. The convivial Custis imported fine spirits in quantity, but he banned intoxicants from Arlington Spring, the park he established to honor Washington, and only by coincidence skipped making the main St. Patrick's Day speech the year the celebration went teetotal.

At his first post, Lee commented about seeing soldiers' "minds formed for use and ornament degenerate into sluggishness and inactivity" from alcohol (and cards). When he could not politely refuse a "bottle of fine old brandy" before the Mexican War, he carried it with him throughout the war and returned it unopened. He went through the Civil War with two more, also gifts, but afterward he wrote the donor that he had used them for medicine "in a severe illness of one of my daughters."

Mrs. Trollope disdained the heavy drinking of the men she saw in the boardinghouses where she stayed in the late 1820s, but the tem-

The Receipts

perance movement was gathering steam: between 1820 and 1850, consumption of 200-proof (pure) alcohol dropped from seven barrels per capita to two.

Lee family members must have taken alcohol from time to time, and the notebook shows they served it when they entertained. Wine they likely regarded as good for health. This attitude may antedate the Roman Pliny, who pronounced blackberry wine good for kidney stones, and it remains evident in the Washington manuscript, which, like the notebook, has receipts for blackberry and currant wine. If these did not retain more specific healing properties in the Lees' time, they no doubt remained salutary.

Mary Lee had several wine receipts. Mrs. Tyree, who identified other donors only by initials, attributed directions for making currant and blackberry wine to "Mrs. Gen'l R. E. Lee copied from a recipe in her own handwriting." The blackberry could be the same as the notebook's; both are too vague for certainty. The currant, though different, is the same receipt that Miss Edmo Lee identified as Mrs. Lee's in *Virginia Cookery—Past and Present*. And Mrs. Tyree called another, Fox Grape Wine, "an autograph recipe of Mrs. Lee's, kindly furnished by her daughter," no doubt conscientious Mildred.

"Boy! Does that stink!" reported a distinguished academic scientist and volunteer winemaker describing a bottle of Blackberry Wine that blew up in his basement. Perhaps he should have strained it through a barrel of straw and sticks, as Mrs. Tyree directed. Later it matured into a simple, sweetish cordial, of more interest to history buffs than connoisseurs.

· BLACKBERRY WINE ·

To every quart of blackberries well mashed add the same quantity of boiling water. Let it stand in an open vessel 24 hours; then strain it. To every gallon of the liquor put 3 lbs cheap brown sugar. Put it into an old brandy

Drinks

or wine cask Do not stop it tightly for 48 hours or more—Leave it in an airy cellar until March—then bottle it if preferred.

If you try this, *please* supplement the directions with a home wine-making manual and safer, easier, more modern equipment. Best wishes to the basement.

The Hard Stuff

Mrs. Trollope did approve of juleps, and these were served at least once at Arlington. "When Sister [Mary Custis] went to carry her [Old Mammy, a servant from Mount Vernon] julip," fifteen-year-old Agnes wrote in her diary, "she was cold & lifeless, but O I trust her spirit is in heaven."

The first written reference to this celebrated potion comes in 1774 from a traveler who noted that his planter host began each day with one. It could not have been made with the bourbon now considered indispensable, though. Not until 1790 did Scotch-Irish distillers fleeing taxation in Pennsylvania move to what is now Kentucky. There they substituted local corn for rye in their whiskey, which did not become bourbon until about 1835, when either the Reverend Elijah Craig or Dr. James C. Crow, depending on the account you believe, standardized and named it. Incidentally, the notebook has no receipt using bourbon; brandy is the only distilled spirit.

The Punch in Punches

The Lees served a mild punch made with light wine at a student reception at Washington College. The Reverend S. H. Chester called such punches "a practically universal feature of Virginia hospitality" when he recalled his first encounter with one later. Before arriving in Lexington as a student, he had never heard of that innovation of the 1860s, cold tea. When his companions jokingly called the sherry

The Receipts

cobbler (a light sherry punch) at the president's house "cold tea," he wrote, "I thought it was . . . the best cold tea I had ever tasted." Soon he could not stop talking, and a young lady walked him around outside until he sobered up.

The notebook's two punches, though, are the kind that gave rise to the saying, "Ladies didn't take strong drink, just punches, and you could float out the door on them." You could get pretty far on an untitled potion related to fish house punch contributed by Mr. S. H.— perhaps "big four" Latin professor Sidney Harris, whom students called Old Nick. The other, contributed anonymously, leaves potency to the taste of the maker. Both, judging from the numerous similar receipts in Mrs. Tyree's book, were popular.

· ROMAN PUNCH ·

This, the more unusual of the two, could have been served frozen in small glasses at multicourse Victorian meals as a palate cleanser, as sorbets sometimes are today; perhaps the Lees did not always entertain so simply after all. The cassis flavor comes from currant jelly. Black rum gives it depth, while sugar adds smoothness; the sweetness diminishes with cold. Since I give few multicourse dinners, I vary the proportions in this receipt to suit other occasions, always remembering that alcohol is an antifreeze. Made with 70- to 80-proof rum (35 to 40 percent alcohol), this receipt becomes a smooth, soft sorbet, a delightful summer dessert. More alcohol and less sugar produce a daiquiri-like cocktail that semifreezes. Or still-freeze it to a slushy consistency and pour it without more ice into a punch bowl—sensational.

Unsweetened peach brandy is best, but a medium-priced regular French brandy will do. Black tea can substitute for green. Make it ahead to allow time to ripen (see Mrs. Letcher's Eggnog, below). The quantity may be multiplied or divided.

Drinks

Make a very rich lemonade 1 quart—add spirits to taste
(brandy and rum) 1 quart of strong green tea—half a pint of currant
jelly 1 lb & a half of white sugar—do not freeze it too hard—

Juice of 5–6 lemons
3 c. sugar
1 c. (8 oz.) currant jelly
2 qts. minus ½ c. water
1 c. brandy
⅔ c. black rum
About 5–6 T. or bags of green (or black) tea

Heat about half the water with sugar and jelly, stirring to dissolve.
Make tea with the rest. Combine the two mixtures. Cool, add lemon
juice, brandy, and rum. Ripen overnight at room temperature or up
to 3 days in refrigerator (see Eggnog), then freeze if you like. Makes
about 3 quarts.

· MRS. LETCHER'S EGGNOG ·

"Honest John" Letcher, the Confederate governor of Virginia, put
Lee in command of the state's forces at the start of the Civil War.
After the war, the two were exchanging letters about the future of
the South when Washington College invited the general to become
its president. Letcher, who had returned to his home in Lexington,
urged him to accept, writing, "You can do a vast amount of good in
building up this institution, and disseminating the blessings of education among our people."

Lizzie, one of the governor's daughters, belonged to the Lexington sewing society while Mrs. Lee was piecing a quilt with her
gnarled, arthritic hands. Finished on the Letchers' quilting frame, it
was auctioned to help pay for the church that became a memorial to

the general. Mary Custis spent her last summer, 1918, with Jennie, another of the Letchers' daughters (by then Virginia Lee Letcher Stephens), and Greenlee Letcher, her godson, was an executor of her estate.

A nephew described Mrs. Letcher as "an ideal house-keeper . . . and an ideal wife and mother." Her spirited eggnog was a hit of the final tasting, held in the basement of that same Robert E. Lee Memorial Church, and proves, wrote the minister, that "Mrs. Lee was obviously an Episcopalian, not a Baptist or a Methodist." (Some people called us Whiskeypalians when I was growing up.)

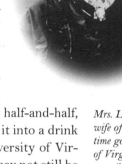

It is also the only receipt in the notebook that I like better with a lightened calorie load. Although in Mrs. Letcher's time it would have been made with at least half-and-half, perhaps with some heavy cream, 2 percent milk turns it into a drink that far outshines the Sunday milk punch at the University of Virginia as I remember it, admittedly a long time ago. It may not still be eggnog, but it need not be limited to the strict confines of Christmas either.

Mrs. Letcher, wife of the war-time governor of Virginia and contributor of a dynamite eggnog receipt. (Courtesy of Virginia Historical Society)

The "nog" in eggnog comes from an East Anglian beer, and while the name does not appear in the Washington manuscript, many of its kin do, where they are called syllabubs, caudles, and possets. None of them calls for distilled spirits, so perhaps the stronger stuff sneaked in on this side of the Atlantic.

Mrs. Letcher's eggnog, made with whatever kind of milk, requires black rum and ripening. This latter technique, practiced in Mrs. Tyree's time, was one of the keys to the best-ever eggnog made by an uncle of mine; he left it outside, covered and isolated on an upstairs porch "as long as people will stay away." Instead, leave this five days or so in the refrigerator, where it mellows; the alcohol preserves the eggs and cream.

Drinks

Beat the yolks of 10 eggs <u>very light</u> add 1 lb of sugar—
stir in slowly two tumblers of French brandy—¼ tumbler of rum—
add 2 qts new milk—& <u>last</u> the <u>whites</u> beaten <u>light</u>.

10 eggs, separated
2 c. sugar
2¼ c. brandy
¼ c. + 1 T. dark rum
8 c. (½ gallon) milk or part half-and-half, part cream

Beat the egg yolks until light, then stir in all but ½ c. sugar. Add liquors and milk, taste, and add part or all of reserved sugar, according to sweetness desired. Beat egg whites until light and fold into nog. Ripen (see above). Makes 4 to 5 quarts.

Everyday Drinks

Although the family partook of alcoholic potions on occasion, in their day-to-day lives drinks without spirits were much more important. Besides the notebook's lemonade and coffee, they took tea, and the general, if no one else, his favorite buttermilk. By midcentury, only a suspicious few refrained from drinking water, and that may have been their most frequent thirst-quencher.

· LEMONADE ·

The new bride who tried this receipt did not, as she feared, flunk lemonade; even though she made something very different from the simple summer refresher of today. The newspaper clipping containing this receipt is titled "The Wholesomeness of Lemons" and begins, "When people feel the need of an acid, ..." What follows seems more dose than delight, and is best understood as a descendant of the medicinal syrups in the Washington manuscript. In Mrs.

The Receipts

Tyree's book, lemonade, acids, vinegars, and syrups made from fruits all seem to be tonics; all are listed under Wines, which still retained a remedial overtone. A lemon-flavored vinegar, the book advised, "will make . . . a very nice beverage (very much like lemonade)."

Lemons were luxuries before the war, grown by wealthy planters in special orangeries. Lemon trees lined the superb, unsupported staircase at Shirley Plantation for a prewar New Year celebration, and when Lee was superintendent of West Point, Agnes told her diary about the "splendid lemon tree" in the greenhouse there. The family may have kept lemons in the Arlington conservatory, where tourists enter now, and in the glassed-in section of the porch next to Mrs. Lee's bedroom in the new president's house in Lexington.

Perhaps the sour citrus was considered more health-giving than other fruit. When Mrs. Lee and Mary Custis fell ill in Richmond while living on dried peas, rice, and salt pork, Mildred wrote her father asking for lemons. He, while directing the death throes of the Confederacy at Petersburg, sent two given to him recently by a lady and "one I found in my valise, dried up." He also recommended his beloved buttermilk, and it too is acid.

Basically the clipping says to squeeze a dozen lemons; boil their peels, pith and all, in a pint of water; strain water and juice together; and add 2 cups sugar to each pint of the combined liquid. Perhaps it is a plus that at the recommended strength of 1 to 2 teaspoons in a glass of water, the notebook's "lemonade" syrup can hardly be tasted at all. In larger amounts, the concentrate is bitter from so much lemon pith, reminiscent of tonic water, and almost passable with gin.

· COFFEE ·

Like olive oil, coffee was imported and therefore expensive; consequently, Americans in the 1850s drank four times more tea than coffee. Most southerners during the war and some even before it

Drinks

brewed coffee substitutes from such ingredients as parched acorns, rye, wheat, corn, peanuts, persimmons, cotton seed, and watermelon seeds. One man ranked browned okra seeds first and parched sweet potatoes next in order of palatability.

Until 1894, coffee beans came by the sack and were roasted and ground at home. Roasting degrees ranged from light to a chestnut brown, except in Louisiana, where the dark beans astounded visitors. Mrs. Tyree suggested blends of Mocha, Java, Lagaurya, and Rio; nowadays, say coffee roasters Terry and Melissa Schall, mild, freshly roasted and ground Colombian beans probably come closest to the coffee of the Lees' time.

Of the notebook's two receipts, the one from a newspaper describes brewing coffee as we still do over a campfire. Made, as the receipt directs, with scrupulously clean equipment and served immediately, the coffee is, as claimed, "delicious—fragrant and flavorful"—strong, too, considering the mild roast. To follow this method, pour 7 cups of unchlorinated boiling water over 1 cup of fresh grounds "not [to] exceed in size the head of a pin" (i.e., drip grind), boil "three minutes, not longer." Add 1 tablespoon of cold water to "force the grounds to the bottom" and "render the liquid clear as wine." This works. Goodbye to messy eggshells, the only way I used to know to clear the brew.

The newspaper method may be more useful to more people—reenactors camping out, for instance—but the notebook has another that is also good, and much more unusual. Basically a receipt for early instant coffee par excellence, it was written in by Mary Custis, I suspect in New Orleans; a Louisiana friend tells me it still remains common there. I have also encountered bottles of a similar essence in Mexico City on the tables at Tacuba, which claims to be the oldest restaurant in the western hemisphere. There may be no connection, but judging from the way other receipts in the notebook have migrated, perhaps there is.

Unlike my Louisiana friend and probably like most other people, I do not have a gadget like the "dripper" called for in the receipt, so producing a similar concentration has meant taking liberties with the receipt; those who own a dripper should proceed from the original. Refrigerated, the coffee lasts almost indefinitely, and it tastes amazingly fresh when hot or cold water is added. (With seltzer, a touch of sugar syrup, and ice cream, it makes a luscious grown-up soda, but that is my own discovery.)

Recipe for Making Strong Coffee

Wet a half pound of ground coffee which has been parched a light brown, with six spoonsful of boiling water — put in dripper — the coffee before putting in dripper must not be too wet but well dampened — when in the dripper put ten table spoonsful of boiling water; one hour afterwards, ten more spoonsful — then, one has essence of coffee which can be diluted to taste — be careful to save the essence of coffee in a bottle with a glass stopper — if there should be too much coffee in the dripper to allow putting all ten table spoonsful of water at once, put in gradually.

½ lb. high-quality, finely ground, lightly roasted coffee
   (I prefer dark roast)
3 c. boiling water, divided

Improvised equipment (to substitute for a dripper): Use a Chemex or Krups size 4 drip pot and filter holder, or a paper cone filter with a narrow-necked carafe, such as ones made by Chemex or Melitta.

Put coffee into filter, positioned over pot. Pour ⅔ cup boiling water slowly over grounds, stirring to wet them thoroughly. Pour over this 1 cup boiling water, slowly and evenly. Allow to stand until all dripping stops, about an hour. Repeat with 1⅓ cups boiling water. When second dripping stops entirely, cool, bottle in glass, close tightly, and refrigerate. Yields about 1½ cups concentrate. To reconstitute, add boiling or cold water to 1 tablespoon of concentrate to make a delicious 6-ounce cup.

Drinks

Home Remedies & Housekeeping

Medicinal Treatments

In Lexington, the Lees were attended by Dr. Barton, a widower whom the general described in sympathetic irony as Mildred's "last rose of summer," or last chance at matrimony. Therefore they had little need of the medical remedies so prominent in many earlier receipt books. A few cures for minor complaints appear sprinkled among the housekeeping uses for common substances. Otherwise the notebook lists only two medicines. Both are in the same unknown hand and purport to treat the rheumatoid arthritis that plagued Mrs. Lee for so many years.

A cure for Rheumatism
Get 12 & 1/2 cents worth sassaparil
1 handful lignum vita saw
dust, 1 stick of ~~beorts~~ licorice, put
these in one gal of water let
it boil to 1/2 a gal, strain it
& take three wineglassful
a day, when this is taken
no spirit should be drunk.

Another cure
Pour brandy on Pokeberries
let it stand, shake it up w
& take a wineglass full thre
times as day.

Cures for Rheumatism

Opposite:
Do not *try these*
notebook cures
for rheumatism.
(Courtesy of Vir-
ginia Historical
Society)

A Cure for Rheumatism

*Get 12 & ½ c worth of sarsparilla 1 handful lignum vitae sawdust
1 stick of licorice, put these in one gal of water let it boil to ½ a gal,
strain it & take three wineglassfuls a day. When it is taken
no spirits should be drunk.*

Another Cure

*Pour brandy on Porkberries let it stand, shake it up well &
take a wineglass full three times a day.*

Harry Sinclaire, a friend and physician, can see no reason why either
of these two remedies would do any good, and we deemed them too
dangerous and unpleasant to try. The first may only taste bad, but
the second would cause acute discomfort at the very least. No one
was plotting against Mrs. Lee; rather, the danger can be explained
by the obscure subject of folk etymology: the meaning of one word
migrated to another that sounds much like it.

The lignum vitae in the first cure, an extremely hard wood, means
"wood of life" in Latin, and the *Oxford English Dictionary* (*OED*)
quotes a source from 1616 that confirms the curative powers implicit
in its name. Resin from the wood was then "much used as a physicke
against the French disease," or syphilis. Also according to the *OED*,
the common name for lignum vitae was "Pockeweed." This seems to
have transmogrified over time into "pokeweed," a plant whose juicy,
purple berries were commonly used for dye. Pokeweed is also an
emetic and diarrhetic so powerful that it is commonly considered
poison, and its name is still sometimes pronounced "porkweed," an
ingredient listed in the second medication. And so the wood of the
first remedy seems to have turned into the weed of the second, and
in the process an intended remedy became a poison. If Mrs. Lee actually swallowed pokeberry juice three times a day, she must have

Home Remedies & Housekeeping

been desperate and, I hope, had a cast-iron stomach. But Mary Lee was well supplied with common sense as well as determination and fortitude. I like to think she took it only once, if that.

Household Hints

Cooking was not the only laborious and time-consuming chore the Lee daughters faced in Lexington. Through the housekeeping ideas they collected we can glimpse the drudgery mandated by gentility when women battled dirt, stains, insects, and disease with little more than common household substances and the occasional hazardous ingredient. Although a few ideas may be forgotten finds, most of them did little good, if little harm. Still others attracted the very pests that people worked so hard to keep at bay. And some were downright dangerous.

But reading these unromantic underpinnings of Victoriana made the rusty shutters on my own past creak open. When it rained during my childhood, we used to set out pots to catch rainwater to wash our hair. The faintly fragrant castile soap we used would not lather in our "hard" well water, loaded with minerals. And when I had a cold or no rain fell, my mother gave me dry shampoos by combing powdered orris root through my hair. That combing brought to mind another kind: during World War II, my friends and I combed the stores in search of scarce nylon stockings; when the color was impossible, we dyed them with tea.

I do not long to do those things again. Detergent shampoos do not need "soft" water, and acid rain may not be worth collecting anyway. Since pantyhose come in endless colors, I have no reason to dye them. Few of the housekeeping hints here tempt me either, but they do illuminate domestic life then, in unsentimental detail.

Many of the ideas in the notebook have become difficult or impossible to test; others, happily, are now irrelevant. And so I turned to

Home Remedies & Housekeeping

Harry Sinclaire and to a "chosen cousin," the kind of kin so distant that you claim them only if you want to. Like many Virginians, she prefers anonymity, but I can reveal that she is a nurse and spent her childhood summers with a grandmother born in 1865, whose housekeeping had hardly changed since Victoria was queen.

To Oil Floors

This, one of the few handwritten formulas, may be what Mrs. Lee meant Mildred to have applied to the floors "before your Papa returns" in 1869. While visiting Rooney at the White House, Mrs. Lee directed that "Mr. Charlton the painter" should first read the directions she was sending separately. I hope and expect these were detailed, for the receipt involves boiling highly flammable linseed oil ("be careful that it does not take fire") and adding red lead, a poison, plus lamp black and burnt umber "if the color is wished dark." Two coats were to be applied, with several days of drying in between.

To Clean Marble

The process recommended in this clear, flowing, unidentified hand is safe, and at least on white marble, it works. It ought to; it combines washing, bleaching, bluing, and a tremendous amount of time and elbow grease. Here, in paraphrase, is what had to be done: First cook up and put on a paste of water, soap, chalk, and bluing. Let it set, wash it off, and then apply "a stew of lemons separately" (presumably lemons boiled in water and also meant to be rinsed off).

To Remove Mildew

The same lady who may have liked her poultry bloody (see "Poultry," page 210) recommended this method of taking mildew out of white linen: "rub on soap, wet the place & rub on chalk." The soap would

Home Remedies & Housekeeping

help, and the chalk would cover it temporarily, but mildew is a fungus and would have returned.

The same person recommended removing spilt ink from floors by washing them with a teaspoon of oxalic acid (very dangerous) in a cup of hot water, then rinsing thoroughly with warm water. Without this last important step, the remaining acid would eat away the floor. Another way, this one a published hint, was to dampen sand with "oil of vitriol" (sulphuric acid) and scrub. Either recommended acid ought to take off ink, all right—and if not handled carefully, maybe fingers too.

Mildred's Miscellany of Clippings

Many of the other housekeeping tips were cut from periodicals such as *The Baltimorean*, probably by Mildred, who cheerfully confessed to her friend Mrs. Hay an "unfortunate mania for cleanliness." Some were pasted over earlier inventories, and the few that have dates range from 1870, the year the general died, to 1876, a period when Mary Custis, the only other living Lee daughter, spent most of her time traveling.

Sometimes Marvelous Salt

A long newspaper column titled "The Value of Salt" mixes household and medical uses ranging from common sense to wishful thinking to pathos. Salt, like countless other nostrums, will not keep hair from falling out or cure indigestion. Months of sniffing it warm twice a day might clear nasal passages and thus "completely cure... severe chronic cases of catarrh . . . when the best efforts of the best physicians failed to do any good," but it could also damage nasal membranes.

Home Remedies & Housekeeping

Recommending saltwater baths as "the next best thing to an ocean dip" was not as bathetic as it sounds; people at fashionable New Jersey beach resorts indulged in them, too. Salt will indeed harden gums and clean teeth. We still gargle with warm salt water for a sore throat, with reason. And "severe pains in the bowels and stomach" would indeed be relieved by bags of hot salt, since salt holds heat.

Salt was indispensable for Victorian-era housekeeping, too. Salt-water painted on beds and mattresses probably did not keep away bedbugs, as advised, but since it is a preservative, it may have safeguarded wood from dry rot. Though no more effective than plain water in its recommended use for cleaning summer matting (which customarily went down when the carpets came up in spring), it may have had the unintended benefit of prolonging the fiber's life. Repeated applications of salt will indeed soak up ink from table linen, as the list directs, but adding pepper to the salt, as recommended in another cutting, probably did not help, nor would applying the two together work "effortlessly," as promised.

I hope a teaspoon of salt made the wicks of kerosene lamps burn brighter; I miss their cozy glow. (And I hope even more that soaking the wicks in vinegar for 24 hours and then drying them kept the lamps from smoking. I do not miss cleaning soot-blackened chimneys at all.) Damp salt, a mild abrasive, should in fact remove tea stains from china cups, and sprinkling salt on heavy brown paper and covering it with muslin should smooth sadirons. I am glad I do not need to know that, though, or whether salt keeps hot and cold starch from sticking to those pre-electric instruments.

"When broiling steaks," says one hint, "throw a little salt on the coals and the blazes from the dripping fat will not annoy." That's good to know for cookouts: easier than the lettuce suggested in a modern book of handy hints, and it lets the kids keep their water pistols, a widely used standby today. This hint works well, too, for putting out small oven fires.

Home Remedies & Housekeeping

Soaking "calicoes" in strong saltwater for an hour before washing them may make them "less likely" to fade, one list says, but another clipping has an even better method, which I still use.

TO MAKE CLOTHES WASH WELL.—*Infuse three gills of salt in four quarts of boiling water; put the calicoes in while hot, and leave them till cold; in this way the colors are rendered permanent, and will not fade by subsequent washing. So says a lady who has frequently made the experiment herself.*

And so say I. I first tried this method on a bright raspberry-colored Indian handloom, with dye so fugitive the fabric would be useless if my experiment failed. The hot water took on only a faint, yellow tinge, and to my astonishment, even in later washings the color did not fade and the loosely woven cloth did not shrink. Results were equally successful with dark blue manufactured goods known to fade, including a cheap T-shirt, the kind almost guaranteed to shrink.

To make sure the fabric will be saturated, first crumple it into a large pot and mark how high it reaches. Then remove the cloth and fill the pot with water to a bit above that depth, measuring how many gallons you use. Add 12 ounces (¾ cup) salt for each gallon of water. Bring water to a boil, add the fabric, bring to a boil again, turn off the heat, leave overnight, and hold your breath. Then rinse in cold water. (Note: This method has worked for me so far on cotton fabrics, but dye is an intricate, chemical subject. Always test a sample first, and measure it before washing and after it has dried to check for shrinkage.)

All-purpose Ammonia

This favorite in the notebook gets short shrift from Mrs. Tyree and later household hint books, but Chosen Cousin gives it high, though selective, marks. One clipping calls it "a powerful alkali [that] dissolves grease and dirt with great ease." That sums up how and why ammonia works but ignores its pungent, unpleasant smell and dangerous drawback: when too strong, it can eat holes in fabric.

Few would argue now that a teaspoon of ammonia "adds much to the refreshing effects" of a bath, but it does cut grease, suggesting indirectly that Victorians did not bathe often—understandably, perhaps, when water had to be first pumped, heated on a wood stove, lugged to the tub, and poured in for each ablution. The advice to add ammonia to shampoo implies that the ladies' long, crowning glory was also washed infrequently, no doubt for the same reason. However, too much ammonia could irritate the scalp and harm the eyes.

As for the other recommended uses of this powerful base, I wouldn't brush my teeth with it on a bet nor would I clean silver using two teaspoons to a quart of hot, soapy water, but the latter may be personal prejudice: I grew up believing that the microscopic scratches made by good paste polish build the patina that makes old silver glow, and I still frown on short cuts.

Chosen Cousin says a few drops of ammonia on a wet rag will indeed remove fingerprints from windows and drinking glasses. She still cleans hairbrushes instantly by swishing them through ammonia in sudsy water; the clipping in the notebook prescribes a teaspoon to a pint. She agrees, too, that adding ammonia to hot, soapy water—the cutting says a teaspoon to a pint—washes lace well, because it "gets in all the nooks and crannies." It's also good, she says, for washing gold jewelry and chandeliers, information the youngest Lee daughter may not have needed in the family's reduced circumstances after the war.

My cousin calls a dab of ammonia on flannel "the best" way to clean woodwork and confirms that grease spots will come out of fabric doused with nearly full-strength ammonia, covered with a white blotter, and pressed lightly with a warm iron—but just the iron and blotter should do as well. Mixed with alcohol, ammonia does remove spots from fabric; alone, it takes out "the red stains produced by strong acids in blue and black clothes," because it neutralizes them.

The Benefits of Borax

We can see from the notebook's uses for borax that the Lees' well water was "hard," that is, loaded with minerals that reduce soap to ineffective curds. Borax "softens" water, so it may well have effected "a saving of fifty per cent in soap," as one cutting claims. It also disinfects, another advantage to soaking blankets overnight in "two large tablespoons of borax and a pint of soft soap" dissolved in cold water. (Then, according to this item, the blankets had to be "rubbed out," rinsed twice, and hung up to dry without wringing.)

A short list of other uses for the powder includes some that were new to me. "One half pound will drive the cockroaches out of any house," it begins. Had I but known that during my early New York days. Brushing teeth with borax, also recommended, could damage tooth enamel, but while it may not be, as claimed, "the best material for cleansing the scalp," I found it useful myself in India when only "hard" water and soap were available for shampooing.

The Benign, the Backward, & the Obsolete

Some of the notebook's housekeeping hints, while not much of an improvement over doing nothing, did little harm. Tepid tea does not clean grained wood better than plain water, but it probably does not bleach and might deepen the grain in some woods. Kerosene may not have been "the best possible furniture oil" even then, but it does polish, and since it is poisonous, it might indeed save wood "from the ravages of insects," as another clipping claims. On the other hand,

Home Remedies & Housekeeping

while knives coated with mutton fat will not rust, they would have drawn the very creatures women worked so hard to banish, as would oil cloth shined with skim milk (which Mrs. Tyree's book also recommends) and silk dresses "restored" with skim milk and glue. Not to mention the smell of sour milk.

Some hints have vanished beyond the reach of modern-day testing. Maybe "the fumes of a lighted sulphur match" erased fruit stains from fingers and "grass, grapejuice, and the like" from white cloth, but that kind of match is now extinct. Paint has changed, too. Rubbing grease into paint-stained cloth then washing it with "benzine or turpentine" may have removed paint and tar, but grease would loosen the fibers of the cloth, and benzene and turpentine are poisonous and flammable.

A stiff paste of gum arabic, plaster of Paris, and water will mend china, says a hint that I am glad not to depend on. Another recommends raising the pile on velvet by stretching it above a hot flatiron covered with wet muslin—a primitive steam iron, in effect. Rubbing whiting (powdered chalk or limestone) over walls before washing them was, like many of these procedures, laborious, but it did fill in the pits that plaster walls are prone to and would have been beneficial, so long as the walls were white.

Wondering at the need to paint picture frames with onion water to keep away flies, I asked my aunt. She did not remember that (nor did Chosen Cousin) but recalled, "Sometimes we had hundreds of flies. There weren't any screens, you know."

The Improbable

It's tempting to dismiss some tips, such as "half a cranberry bound on a corn will kill it," but a friend insists it works; maybe some enzyme does the trick. Just as unlikely is the idea of removing fruit stains from cotton cloth like this: "Before wetting them with any-

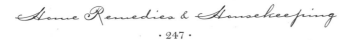

Recipe for Pleasant Evening.

Take two nice (not too nice) young ladies — one just going to Recitn — and the other jest whackey. Oh so much!!!; — that she was just going to — Then take too young gents — one ~~rale~~ over-done — & the other cut-drunk. — Let the ladies talk together rapidly — both at some time — for an hour or two — let the gentlemen slowly simmer — then put one of them out in the cold — and set the other down by Miss Liggu Kirkpatricks' stove — with one Moore already there. — Stir them all well — sweeten to your taste — & serve them up well-dressed if possible then put thing else, pour boiling water through the stains and they will disappear." But they do disappear. Stretch cotton fabric over a large bowl in the sink, pour boiling water over it from about two feet above, and watch the stain dim and vanish before your eyes. Occasionally you may need another kettleful.

The Irreplaceable

Opposite: This "Rect. for Pleasant Evng." ends abruptly, probably when General Lee decided it was time for the writer to go home. (Courtesy of Virginia Historical Society)

The Lee daughters, like other Victorian women, except perhaps the very rich, worked long and hard at both cooking and keeping house, but they had some gentle amusements that we lack. Among so many entries that speak of toil, the notebook has one that I would like to end with. It stops abruptly, probably at ten in the evening, when, if callers were still there, the general came into the parlor where his daughters entertained, closed the blinds, and said pointedly, "Good night, young gentlemen." For all our modern technological advances, we have lost something, too.

Rect. for Pleasant Evng.
_Take two nice (not _too_ nice) young ladies—one just going to Richmond—and the other just wishing—Oh so much!!!—that she was just going too—then take two _young_ gents—one [illegible] handsome—& the other courteous—Let the ladies talk together rapidly—both at same time—for an hour or two—let the gentlemen slowly simmer—then put one of them out in the cold and set the other down by Miss Lizzy Kirkpatrick's stove—with one Moore always there—Stir them all well—Sweeten to your taste & serve them up well-dressed—if possible then put [end of page]_

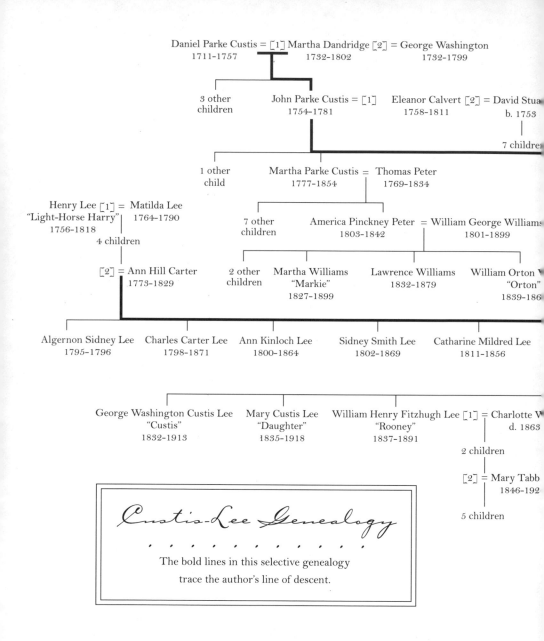

Daniel Parke Custis = [1] Martha Dandridge [2] = George Washington
1711-1757   1732-1802   1732-1799

3 other children

John Parke Custis = [1]   Eleanor Calvert [2] = David Stua
1754-1781   1758-1811   b. 1753

7 childre

1 other child

Martha Parke Custis = Thomas Peter
1777-1854   1769-1834

Henry Lee [1] = Matilda Lee
"Light-Horse Harry" | 1764-1790
1756-1818
4 children

7 other children   America Pinckney Peter = William George Williams
1803-1842   1801-1899

[2] = Ann Hill Carter
1773-1829

2 other children   Martha Williams "Markie" 1827-1899   Lawrence Williams 1832-1879   William Orton "Orton" 1839-186

Algernon Sidney Lee 1795-1796   Charles Carter Lee 1798-1871   Ann Kinloch Lee 1800-1864   Sidney Smith Lee 1802-1869   Catharine Mildred Lee 1811-1856

George Washington Custis Lee "Custis" 1832-1913   Mary Custis Lee "Daughter" 1835-1918   William Henry Fitzhugh Lee [1] = Charlotte W "Rooney" 1837-1891   d. 1863

2 children

[2] = Mary Tabb 1846-192

5 children

Custis-Lee Genealogy

· · · · · · · · · · · ·

The bold lines in this selective genealogy
trace the author's line of descent.

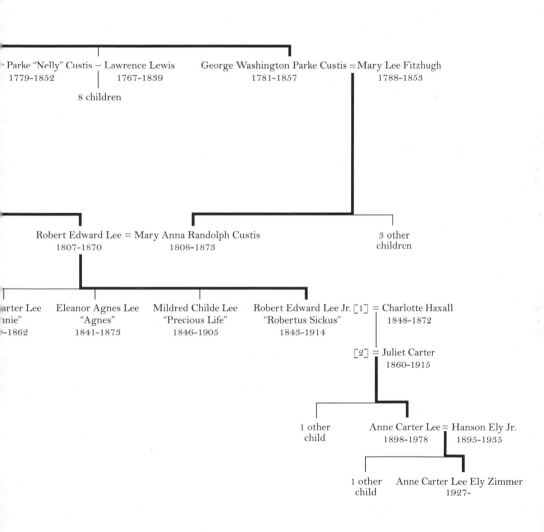

Parke "Nelly" Custis — Lawrence Lewis   George Washington Parke Custis = Mary Lee Fitzhugh
1779-1852   1767-1839   1781-1857   1788-1853

8 children

Robert Edward Lee = Mary Anna Randolph Custis   3 other
1807-1870   1808-1873   children

arter Lee   Eleanor Agnes Lee   Mildred Childe Lee   Robert Edward Lee Jr. [1] = Charlotte Haxall
nnie"   "Agnes"   "Precious Life"   "Robertus Sickus"   1848-1872
-1862   1841-1873   1846-1905   1843-1914

[2] = Juliet Carter
1860-1915

1 other   Anne Carter Lee = Hanson Ely Jr.
child   1898-1978   1895-1935

1 other   Anne Carter Lee Ely Zimmer
child   1927-

At a time when most people stayed put most of the time, the Lee family was extraordinarily peripatetic. Before the war, Robert's career accounted for many moves, as did Mary's homing instinct for Arlington—six of their seven children were born there, and the family tried to return to spend Christmas there together. The Lees lived with Mary's parents at Arlington on and off for thirty years, between military postings and when Lee was stationed in Washington. During the war, Mary and her daughters moved many times. Forced to leave Arlington in 1861, they continued to relocate as battle lines shifted in Virginia. After the war, they spent six months at Derwent, fifty miles west of Richmond, before settling in Lexington. After leaving Lexington, Mildred continued to add entries to the notebook, until her death in New Orleans in 1905.

1831   June 30: Marriage at Arlington, Va.
          August: Move to Fort Monroe, Va.
1834   Arlington
1838   St. Louis, Mo.
1839   Arlington
1841   Fort Hamilton, N.Y.
1843   Arlington
1849   Baltimore, Md.
1852   West Point, N.Y.

1855	Arlington
1861	May 8 or 10: Leave Arlington
1862	June 10: Arrive in Richmond, Va.; stay with Caskie family
1863	Rent small house on Leigh Street in Richmond
1864	January 1: Move to "The Mess" on Franklin Street in Richmond
1865	June–November: Derwent, Va.
	December 1: Move to Washington College, Lexington, Va.
1867	Move to new president's house in Lexington
1870	October 12: General Lee dies
1873	June: Mary's last visit to Arlington
	November 5: Mary Lee dies
1897	Custis and Mildred leave Lexington, Custis to live at Ravensworth, Mildred to spend winter and spring at Romancoke and summers traveling

Lee Household Chronology

SELECTED BIBLIOGRAPHY

The Lee family notebook on which this book is based is part of the George Bolling Lee Papers (1813–1924) at the Virginia Historical Society in Richmond. Unless otherwise noted here or in the text, other Lee family letters and papers cited are also part of the collection of the Virginia Historical Society. References to the Lee ladies in Lexington and their correspondence with Lexingtonians are at the Leyburn Library, Washington and Lee University, unless otherwise indicated.

Anderson, Maza Blair. Letter re Mrs. Lee's quilt. Virginia Military Institute Museum, Lexington, Va.

Andrews, Marietta Minnegerode. *Memoirs of a Poor Relation: Being the Story of a Post-War Southern Girl and Her Battle with Destiny.* New York: E. P. Dutton, 1930.

Andriot, John L., comp. and ed. *Population Abstract of the United States.* Vol. 1, *Tables.* McLean, Va.: Andriot Associates, 1983.

Anonymous. "The Burwell Genealogy." Mimeograph, n.d. Personal collection of Mary Randolph Burwell Nesbit, Upperville, Va.

———. "Randolph" [a genealogy]. Mimeograph, n.d. Personal collection of Mary Randolph Burwell Nesbit, Upperville, Va.

Barnard, Henry. "The South Atlantic States in 1833, As Seen by a New Englander, Being a Narration of a Tour Taken by Henry Barnard." *Maryland Historical Magazine* 13 (December 1918): 319–20.

Bass, Thomas E., III. "'Light Horse Harry' Lee: An American Patriot." *Northumberland County Historical Society* 25 (1983): 81–86.

Beeton, Isabella. *Mrs. Beeton's Book of Household Management.* New ed. London: Ward, Lock & Co., 1906.

Belden, Louise Conway. *The Festive Tradition: Table Decoration and Desserts in America, 1650–1900.* New York: W. W. Norton, 1983.

Belk, Sarah. *Around the Southern Table: Innovative Recipes Celebrating 300 Years of Eating and Drinking.* New York: Simon and Schuster, 1991.

Berard, Augusta Blanche. "Arlington and Mount Vernon 1856: As Described in a Letter of Augusta Blanche Berard." Introduction and notes by Clayton Torrence. *Virginia Magazine of History and Biography* 57, no. 2 (April 1, 1949): 140–62.

Berry, B. H. "An Inventory of the Slaves at Arlington belonging to the Estate of G. W. P. Custis, taken January 1st 1858." Alexandria County Court record, September 11, 1858. Alexandria, Va.

Bond, Christiana. *Memories of General Robert E. Lee*. Baltimore, Md.: Norman Remington, 1926.

Brock, R. A., ed. *General Robert Edward Lee*. Richmond, Va.: Royal Publishing Co., 1897.

Brooke, George M., Jr. *General Lee's Church: The History of the Protestant Episcopal Church in Lexington, Virginia, 1840–1975*. Lexington, Va.: News-Gazette, 1984.

Bruch, Virginia I. Genealogical charts of the Lee and Carter families. Mimeograph, n.d. Docent training material, The Boyhood Home of Robert E. Lee, Alexandria, Va.

———. "The Lee Children of Oronoco Street, Alexandria, Virginia." Mimeograph, 1990. Docent training material, The Boyhood Home of Robert E. Lee, Alexandria, Va.

Bryan, Mrs. Lettice. *The Kentucky Housewife*. Cincinnati, Ohio, 1839. Reprint (facsimile, with introduction by Bill Neal), Columbia: South Carolina Press, 1991.

Byrd, William. *William Byrd's Natural History of Virginia or the Newly Discovered Eden*. (Originally published in German.) Bern, 1737. Reprint (including an English translation by Richard Croom Beatty and William J. Malloy), Richmond, Va.: Dietz Press, 1940.

Calvert, Elizabeth Gibbon Randolph (1833–1911). "Childhood Days at Arlington Mixed with after Memories." Manuscript, Arlington House, Arlington, Va.

Carson, Jane. *Colonial Virginia Cookery: Procedures, Equipment and Ingredients in Colonial Cooking*. 1968. Reprint, Williamsburg, Va.: Colonial Williamsburg Foundation, 1985.

Carter, Charles Hill, III. "Hill-Carter Family Tree." Mimeograph, n.d. Shirley Plantation, Charles City, Va.

———. "Shirley Plantation—Built on a Tradition of Heritage and Hierarchy." *Colonial Williamsburg* 13, no. 3 (Spring 1991): 24–30.

Chesnut, Mary. *Mary Chesnut's Civil War*. Edited with an introduction by C. Vann Woodward. New Haven: Yale University Press, 1981.

Chester, Samuel H. "At College under General Lee." Manuscript, ca. 1920, Leyburn Library, Washington and Lee University, Lexington, Va.

Selected Bibliography.

Coulling, Mary P. "A Chronology of the Lee Ladies, 1865–1918." Manuscript, n.d. Private collection of Mary Coulling, Lexington, Va.

———. *The Lee Girls*. Winston-Salem, N.C.: John F. Blair, 1987.

———. "Marse Robert's Humor." Manuscript, n.d. Private collection of Mary Coulling, Lexington, Va.

———. "Nicknames, Cats, and Catsup Bottles." *W & L: The Alumni Magazine of Washington and Lee* 64, no. 1 (Winter 1989): 10–14.

Crump, Nancy Carter. *Hearthside Cooking: An Introduction to Virginia Plantation Cuisine*. McLean, Va.: EPM Publications, 1986.

Custis, Martha. "To make a great Cake." Manuscript, n.d. Mount Vernon Ladies' Association, Mount Vernon, Va.

David, Elizabeth. *English Bread and Yeast Cookery*. Newton Highlands, Mass.: Biscuit Books, 1994.

Davis, J. C. Letter to "Gen. R. E. Lee," January 20, 1866 [a list of gift supplies]. Virginia Historical Society, Richmond.

deButts, Mary Custis Lee, ed. *Growing Up in the 1850s: The Journal of Agnes Lee*. Chapel Hill: University of North Carolina Press, 1984.

Dowdy, Clifford. "Lee's Boyhood Home." Mimeograph, n.d. Docent training material, The Boyhood Home of Robert E. Lee, Alexandria, Va.

Dutton, Joan Parry. *The Good Fare and Cheer of Old England*. New York: Reynal, 1960.

Du Vall, Nell. *Domestic Technology: A Chronology of Developments*. Boston: G. K. Hall, 1988.

Egerton, John. *Southern Food: At Home, On the Road, In History*. New York: Alfred A. Knopf, and Toronto: Random House of Canada, 1987.

Fischer, David Hackett. *Albion's Seed: Four British Folkways in America*. New York: Oxford University Press, 1989.

Fishwick, Marshall. *General Lee's Photographer: The Life and Work of Michael Miley*. Chapel Hill: University of North Carolina Press, 1954.

———. "Southern Cooking." In *American Heritage Cookbook and Illustrated History of American Eating and Drinking*, edited by the editors of *American Heritage: The Magazine of History*. New York: American Heritage, 1964.

Fithian, Philip Vickers. *The Journal of Philip Vickers Fithian, 1773–1774*. Edited by Hunter Dickinson Farish. Williamsburg, Va.: Colonial Williamsburg, 1957.

Flood, Charles B. *Lee, the Last Years*. Boston: Houghton Mifflin, 1987.

Florman, Monte. *How to Clean Practically Anything*. Mount Vernon, N.Y.: Consumers Union, 1986.

Selected Bibliography

Fox-Genovese, Elizabeth. *Within the Plantation Household.* Chapel Hill: University of North Carolina Press, 1988.

Franklin, Linda Campbell. *300 Years of Kitchen Collectibles: Identification and Value Guide.* Florence, Ala.: Books Americana, 1981.

Freeman, Douglas Southall. *R. E. Lee.* 4 vols. New York: Charles Scribner's Sons, 1934–35.

Garrett. Elisabeth Donaghy. *At Home: The American Family, 1750–1870.* New York: Harry N. Abrams, 1989.

Gerard, John. *The Herball or General Historie of Plantes. Gathered by John Gerarde of London, Master in Chirugerie, London, 1597.* Facsimile reprint, Norwood, N.J.: Walter Johnson, 1974 (cited in Hess, *Martha Washington's Booke of Cookery and Booke of Sweetmeats*).

Gibbs, Patricia A. "Recreating Hominy: The One-Pot Breakfast Food of the Gentry and Staple of Blacks and Poor Whites in the Early Chesapeake." In *The Cooking Pot: Proceedings of the Oxford Symposium on Food and Cookery, 1988,* edited by Tom Jaine. London: Prospect, 1989.

Glasse, Hannah. *The Art of Cookery Made Plain and Easy.* Arlington, Va.: Cottom and Stewart, 1805 (cited in Women's Auxiliary of Olivet Episcopal Church, *Virginia Cookery–Past and Present*).

Hess, Karen, ed. *Martha Washington's Booke of Cookery and Booke of Sweetmeats.* New York: Columbia University Press, 1981.

Hilliard, Sam Bowers. *Hog Meat and Hoecake.* Carbondale: Southern Illinois University Press, and London: Feffer and Simons, 1972.

Hines, Mary Anne, Gordon Marshall, and William Woys Weaver. "The Larder Invaded: A Joint Exhibition Held 17 November 1986 to 25 April 1987." Philadelphia: The Library Company of Philadelphia and the Historical Society of Philadelphia, 1987.

Horry, Harriot Pinckney. *A Colonial Plantation Cookbook: The Receipt Book of Harriot Pinckney Horry, 1770.* Edited with an introduction by Richard J. Hooker. Columbia: University of South Carolina Press, 1984.

Houghton, Walter R., James K. Beck, James A Woodburn, Horace R. Hoffman, A. B. Philputt, A. E. Davis, and Mrs. W. R. Houghton. *Rules of Etiquette and Home Culture; or, What to Do and How to Do It.* 11th ed. New York: Rand, McNally, 1894.

Howard, Mrs. B. C. *Fifty Years in a Maryland Kitchen.* Revised by Florence Brobeck. New York: M. Barrows, 1944.

Johnston, Caroline. Letter to Mrs. William Preston Johnston, July 22 [no year]. Private collection of Mrs. Forest Fletcher, Staunton, Va.

Selected Bibliography

Kent, Emily. "Reminicence [*sic*] of a Virginia Lady: A Visit to the Home of
    General Robert E. Lee and Family." Manuscript, n.d. Private collection of
    Virginia Broun Lawson.

Lang, Jenifer Harvey. *Tastings: The Best from Ketchup to Caviar.* New York: Crown,
    1986.

Lattimore, Ralston B., ed. *The Story of Robert E. Lee: As Told in His Own Words and
    Those of His Contemporaries.* Source Book Series, No. 1. Philadelphia: Eastern
    National Park and Monument Association, 1964.

Lebsock, Suzanne. *Virginia Women, 1600–1945: A Share of Honour.* Richmond:
    Virginia State Library, 1987.

Lee, Agnes. Letter to Mrs. McDonald [n.d.]. Leyburn Library, Washington and
    Lee University, Lexington, Va.

Lee, Edmund Jennings. *Lee of Virginia 1642–1892: Biographical and Genealogical
    Sketches of The Descendants of Colonel Richard Lee.* 1895. Reprinted with additions
    and corrections, Baltimore, Md.: Genealogical Publishing, 1983.

Lee, George Washington Parke Custis. Letter to James T. Earle, January 14, 1867.
    Virginia Military Institute, Lexington, Va.

Lee, Fitzhugh. *General Lee.* New York: University Society, 1894.

Lee, Lucinda. *Journal of a Young Lady of Virginia, 1797.* Illustrated by Mary Custis
    Lee deButts. Richmond, Va.: Whittet and Shepperson, 1976.

Lee, Mary Custis. Letter to Anne Carter Lee, June 10, 1860. Arlington House,
    Arlington, Va.

———. Letter to Esther Coxe Lewis, January 7, 1853. Arlington House,
    Arlington, Va.

———. Letter to Mildred Lee, May 13, 1870. Virginia Historical Society,
    Richmond.

———. *Memoir of George Washington Parke Custis, by His Daughter: With the
    Epistolary Correspondence between Washington and Custis.* New York, 1859.

Lee, Mary Custis [daughter]. Will of Mary Custis Lee, February, 1918. Leyburn
    Library, Washington and Lee University, Lexington, Va.

Lee, Mildred. Letter to Lella Pendleton [n.d.]. Leyburn Library, Washington and
    Lee University, Lexington, Va.

Lee, Robert E., Jr. *Recollections and Letters of General Robert E. Lee: By His Son.*
    New York: Doubleday, Page, 1904.

Lenman, Bruce. "Alexander Spotswood and the Business of Empire." *Colonial
    Williamsburg* 13, no. 1 (August 1990): 44–55.

Lossing, Benson J. "Arlington House, the Seat of G. W. P. Custis, esq." *Harper's
    New Monthly Magazine* 7, no. 40 (September 1853): 432–48.

Lyle, Royster, Jr., and Pamela Hemenway Simpson. *The Architecture of Historic Lexington.* Photographs by Sally Munger Mann. Charlottesville: University Press of Virginia, 1977.

McDonald, Marshall. Letter to his fiancé, November 28, 1866. The Robert Edward Lee Papers, Duke University, Durham, N.C.

MacDonald [née McDonald], Rose Mortimer Ellzey. *Mrs. Robert E. Lee.* Boston: Ginn, 1939.

McPherson, James M. *Battle Cry of Freedom: The Civil War Era.* New York: Oxford University Press, 1988.

Matthews, Mary Lou. *American Kitchen Collectibles: Identification and Price Guide.* Vol. 2. Gas City, Ind.: L–W Promotions, 1971.

Miller, T. Michael. "The Formative Years of Robert E. Lee: A Speech Given Before the Sons of Confederate Veterans, 1990." Lloyd House collection, Alexandria Library of History and Genealogy, Alexandria, Va.

———. "The Lee Family and Their Attitudes toward Slavery." In *Annual Report of the Society of Lees of Virginia,* 15–27. Philadelphia, Pa.: Society of Lees of Virginia, 1992.

Montagné, Prosper. *New Larousse Gastronomique: The World's Greatest Cookery Reference Book.* Preface by Robert J. Courtine. Text translated from the French by Nina Froud, Patience Gray, Maud Murdoch, and Barbara Macrae Taylor. Additional material translated by Marion Hunter. Edited by Janet Dunbar. London: Hamlyn, 1977.

Moss, Roger W. *The American Country House.* New York: Henry Holt, 1990.

Mullins, Agnes Downey. "Arlington House and Its Occupants." In *Annual Report of the Society of Lees of Virginia,* Appendix K. Arlington, Va.: Society of Lees of Virginia, 1993.

———. "Christmas at Arlington: A Resource Paper." Unpublished manuscript, 1981. Arlington House, Arlington, Va.

Nagel, Paul C. *The Lees of Virginia: Seven Generations of an American Family.* New York: Oxford University Press, 1990.

———. "The Long Line of Lees." *Colonial Williamsburg* 13, no. 1 (Autumn 1990): 34–43.

Neal, Bill. *Bill Neal's Southern Cooking.* Rev. & enl. ed. Chapel Hill: University of North Carolina Press, 1989.

Nelligan, Murray H. "'Old Arlington': The Story of the Lee Mansion National Memorial." Unpublished manuscript, 1953. National Park Service National Capitol Parks, Arlington House, Arlington, Va.

Oxford English Dictionary. Compact ed. Oxford: Oxford University Press, 1987.

Selected Bibliography

Parks, Edward. "George Mason: The Squire of Gunston Hall." *Colonial Williamsburg* 13, no. 3 (Spring 1991): 12–22.

Parloa, Maria. *Miss Parloa's Kitchen Companion*. Boston: Estes and Lauriat, 1887.

Peterson, Harold L. *American Interiors: From Colonial Times to the Late Victorian*. New York: Charles Scribner's Sons, 1971.

Powell, Marietta Fauntleroy Turner. "Personal Recollections of General Robert E. Lee by His Cousin." In *Scraps of Paper*, by Marietta Turner Powell. New York: E. P. Dutton, n.d. (excerpted in docent training material, The Boyhood Home of Robert E. Lee, Alexandria, Va.).

Randolph, Mary. *The Virginia House-wife*. Historical notes and commentaries by Karen Hess; includes facsimile of 1824 1st ed. and materials from 1825 and 1828 eds. Columbia: University of South Carolina Press, 1984.

Riley, Franklin L., ed. *General Robert E. Lee after Appomattox*. New York: Macmillan, 1922.

Ripley, Eliza. *Social Life in Old New Orleans: Being Recollections of My Girlhood*. New York: D. Appleton & Co., 1912. (Excerpted in Garrett, *At Home*.) Reprint, Columbia: University of South Carolina Press, 1979.

Robert E. Lee Memorial Association. *Stratford Hall Annual Report*. Stratford, Va., 1991.

Robins, Sally Nelson. "Mrs. Lee during the War–Something about 'The Mess' and Its Occupants." In *General Robert Edward Lee*, edited by R. A. Brock, 330–34.

Rombauer, Irma S., and Marion Rombauer Becker. *The Joy of Cooking*. Indianapolis: Bobbs-Merrill, 1963.

Root, Waverley. *Food: An Authoritative and Visual History and Dictionary of the Foods of the World*. New York: Simon and Schuster, 1980.

Rouse, John E. *World Cattle*. 3 vols. Norman: University of Oklahoma Press, 1970.

[Rutledge, Sarah]. *The Carolina Housewife, or House and Home: By a Lady of Charleston*. Charleston: W. R. Babcock & Co., 1847.

Schmit, Patricia Brady, ed. *Nelly Custis Lewis's Housekeeping Book*. New Orleans, La.: The Historic New Orleans Collection, 1982.

Scott, Anne Firor. *The Southern Lady: From Pedestal to Politics, 1830–1930*. Chicago: University of Chicago Press, 1970.

Serow, William J. *The Population of Virginia: Past, Present and Future*. Charlottesville: University Press of Virginia, 1978.

Simmons, Amelia. *American Cookery*. Hartford, Conn.: Hudson & Goodwin, 1796. Reprint (facsimile, with introduction by Mary Tolford Wilson), New York: Oxford University Press, 1958.

Selected Bibliography

Smith, Mary Stuart. *Virginia Cookery-Book*. New York: Harper & Brothers, 1885.

Stark, Norman H. *The Formula Manual*. Cedarburg, Wisc.: Stark Research Corporation, 1973.

Stern, Philip Van Doren. *Robert E. Lee, the Man and the Soldier: A Pictorial Biography*. New York: Crown, by arrangement with McGraw-Hill, 1963.

Stewart, Robert G. "Auguste Hervieu, A Portrait Painter in Cincinnati." *Queen City Heritage: Journal of the Cincinnati Historical Society* 47, no. 1 (Spring 1989): 23–31.

Stonewall Jackson House Cookbook Committee, comp. *Historic Lexington Cooks: Rockbridge Regional Recipes*. Lexington, Va.: Historic Lexington Foundation, 1989.

Sugarman, Carole. "What We Found Out about Flour." *Washington Post*, December 6, 1995.

Tannenhill, Ray. *Food in History*. New York: Stein and Day, 1973.

Taylor, Joe Gray. *Eating, Drinking and Visiting in the South: An Informal History*. Baton Rouge: Louisiana State University Press, 1982.

Taylor, Walter. *General Lee: His Campaigns in Virginia 1861–1865 with Personal Reminiscences*. Brooklyn, N.Y.: Braunworth & Co., 1906.

Templeman, Eleanor Lee. "The Lees of Leesylvania." From *Northern Virginia Heritage*, October 1985 (excerpted in docent training material, The Boyhood Home of Robert E. Lee, Alexandria, Va.).

Trollope, Frances. *Domestic Manners of the Americans*. Edited, with a history of Mrs. Trollope's adventures in America, by Donald Smalley. New York: Alfred A. Knopf, 1949. (Original work published 1832)

Turner, Charles. *Old Zeus*. Verona, Va.: McClure Printing, 1983.

Tyree, Marion Cabell. *Housekeeping in Old Virginia*. John P. Morton & Co., 1879. Reprint, Louisville, Ky.: Favorite Recipes Press, 1965.

Webster, Thomas F. G. S. &c., assisted by The Late Mrs. Parkes. *An Encyclopedia of Domestic Economy: Comprising Such Subjects as Are Most Immediately Connected with Housekeeping*. New ed. London: Longmans, Brown, Green, and Longmans, and Boston: Little, Brown, 1852.

Wickham, Henry Taylor. "Address Delivered before the Joint Session of the General Assembly of Virginia." Virginia State Document No. 10. Richmond, 1940.

Wigginton, Eliot, ed. *The Foxfire Book*. New York: Anchor, 1972.

Wilson, Charles Reagan, and William Ferris, eds. *Encyclopedia of Southern Culture*. Chapel Hill: University of North Carolina Press, 1989.

Women's Auxiliary of Olivet Episcopal Church, Franconia, Va. *Virginia Cookery–*

Selected Bibliography

Past and Present: Including a Manuscript Cook Book of the Lee and Washington Families Published for the First Time. Franconia, Va.: Cooper-Trent of Va., 1957.

Young, Joanne. "Odyssey of Peale's Portrait of Washington." *Colonial Williamsburg* 12, no. 4 (Summer 1990): 36–42.

Zimmer, Fred A., Jr. A Robert E. Lee family chronology. Manuscript, n.d. Private collection of the author.

Selected Bibliography

GENERAL INDEX

Page numbers shown in italics refer to illustrations.

Beverley, Robert, 96

Bond, Christiana, 117; sketch of Lee's cottage, *118*

Book of Household Management (Beeton): sugar in, 98; cookies in, 158; jellies in, 180; Apple Snow of, 188; caramels in, 194

Borax, household uses of, 246

Boston Cooking School Cookbook (Farmer), 5, 211

Boude, Mrs., 80

Bouillon, commercial, 200

Bourbon, 228

Brady, Mathew, photo of Lee, 26

Brandy, 100, 226, 228, 229

Branham, Caroline, 17

Breads, 108–9; stale, 92–93, 121; oven-baked, 101–2; leavening of, 105; soft, 126–28

Brockenbrough, Judge John, 40, *53*

Brockenbrough, Mrs., 80

Brooke, Ralston, *4*

Bruce, William Cabell, 21

Buford, Captain, 58, 79, 84, 99

Burwell: family, 58, 77, 109, 151; Agnes Atkinson, 150; George, 150; Nathaniel, 150; Charles, 151; Edward, *152*

Butter: purchases of, 84; preservation of, 92; absorption into flour, 95, 96

Buttermilk, 232, 233

Butter Sponge Cake, 134

Byrd, William, 200, 217, 223

Cakes: heirloom, 130; sponge, 130, 134–36; great, 136–37, 145; layer, 136–37; gingerbread, 150–53; "small," 153. *See also* Cookies

Calories, 100–101, 128

Calvert, Elizabeth, *33*, 218

Campbell: Lucy, 79, 164; John Lyle, 164

Candies, 190–91, 194–97

Canning, 103

Card games, 119

The Carolina Housewife (Rutledge), 127, 216

"Caromels," 47, 190, 191

Carter, Charles (grandfather of Robert E. Lee), 184–85

Carter, Charles Hill, III, 184

Carter, Robert ("King"): slaves of, 2; descendants of, 21, 65, 150

Carter, Robert (son of "King"), 197; emancipation of slaves, 2

Carter family, 39, 150–51

Carter Hall, 150

Carters, Anne, 124

Caskie: family, 35–36, 140; Norvell, 140, *141*

Cats, 17, *58–59*

Caviar, 207

Cedar Grove, 77; Annie and Agnes at, *54*; Mary Custis Lee (daughter) at, 56, 178

Celery, 211

Chatham (Fitzhugh family home), 12

Chesnut, Mary, 109; on Mrs. Lee, 25; on wartime food scarcity, 38; on knitting enterprise, 74

Chester, Rev. S. H., 228–29

Chicken: fried, 206; cooking methods for, 210,; 212; à la king, 214

Childe, Blanche, 168, 176; receipt from, *187*

China: breakage lists of, 71, *72*, 73; repairing, 247

General Index

General Index

243–44; for ammonia, 244–46; for
borax, 246
Household manuals, 64; vagueness in,
5, 103; published, 66
Housekeeping in Old Virginia (Tyree),
69; butter in, 92; sugar in, 98; batters
in, 105; Sally Lunn in, 116; Robert E.
Lee cake in, 131; layer and jelly cakes
in, 136; gingerbread in, 151; Mildred's contributions to, 156, 173;
piecrusts in, 161; cream custards in,
176; jellies in, 180; apple desserts in,
188; candies in, 194; meats in, 206;
mock terrapin in, 214; salad dressing
of, 225; wine in, 227; tonics in, 233;
coffee in, 234; ammonia in, 244
"Housewives" (sewing kits), 47, *192*
Hygeia Hotel (Fort Monroe, Va.), 25

Ice cream, 71; Caramel, 168
Ices, Water, 184–85
Icing, nineteenth-century, 132, 145–46
Ingredients: in notebook receipts,
90–94; combining of, 104–5

Jackson, Stonewall, 43, 79, 80; house-
hold inventory of, 93, 127
Jamestown, cookery of, 114
Jefferson, Thomas, 65; and ice cream,
178; garden of, 223
Jellies (gelatin), 179–83
Jello, 180
Jelly, jam, and marmalade, 100
Jelly Cake, 134
Johnston, Margaret Avery, 151, *153*
Johnston, Mrs. Thomas Henry, 158
Johnston, Col. William Preston, 151
Jones, J. H. B., 77

Jones Spring, N.C., 36
Juleps, 228; mint, 128
Jumbles, 155, 158–59

Kerosene, 246
Kitchener, Lord: and invitation to
Mary Custis Lee, 56
Knitting: of socks for the Confederacy,
38, 74, 76, *78*
Krumbacher, Evelyn: waffles receipt of,
120, 214

Ladyfingers, 175
Lamb, boiled, 9
Lapland cakes, 123–24
"Larder Invaded," 213
Lauderdale (plantation), 158
Leavening: types of, 93–94; tempera-
tures for, 104; of bread, 105; for
cookies, 153
Lebsock, Suzanne, 86
Lee, Agnes (daughter of Robert E.), *38*,
54; beauty of, 8; birth of, 31; romance
with Orton Williams, 37–38, 51,
124, typhoid of, 39, 58, at Lexington,
49, 140; contributions to notebook,
52; death of, 60; on Lee's namesakes,
73; on ice cream, 178; at West Point,
233
Lee, Anna Maria "Nannie" Mason, 109,
110; yeast receipt of, 111–12
Lee, Anne (sister of Robert E.), 33
Lee, Ann Hill Carter (mother of
Robert E.), 23, *29*, 151, 169; hosts
Lafayette, 23
Lee, Annie (daughter of Robert E.), 27,
54; birth of, 30, 31; death of, 36, 51
Lee, "Black-Horse Harry," 27

General Index

hol, 226–29. *See also* Notebook, Lee
family
Lee of Virginia (Lee), 21
Lee residence (Lexington, Va.), 8, *48,
49*
Leftovers, 90; of Sally Lunn, 116; of
meat, 205
Lemonade, 232–33
Lemon juice, 100
Lemon trees, cultivation of, *233*
Letcher: Lizzie, 191, 230; "Honest
John," 230; Mrs. John, *231*
Lewis, Eleanor Parke "Nelly" Custis,
65; adoption by Washington, 14;
relationship to Mary Lee, 66; St.
Memin portrait of, *66.* See also *Nelly
Custis Lewis's Housekeeping Book*
Lexington, Va.: social life of, 48–50;
Lee family at, 42–50, 79–82, 197–98,
249; food shortages at, 43–44; Pres-
byterians of, 77
Liberia: settlement of slaves in, 15;
Custis servants in, 19
Lignum vitae, 239
Lloyd, Minnie, *122,* 122
Lloyd family, 122
Loughborough, Norvell Caskie Sharp,
141

McClellan, General George, 35
McCormick, Cyrus, 118
McDonald, Marshall, 49
McDonald, Mrs. Marshall, 166, *167*
MacDonald, Rose, *32,* 45, 49; biogra-
phy of Mrs. Lee, 167; and doll made
by Mary Lee, *168*
Madeira, 100, 214
Marriage prospects: of Lee daughters,

50–51; of white women in postbel-
lum South, 51, 134
*Martha Washington's Booke of Cookery
and Booke of Sweetmeats. See* Wash-
ington manuscript
Mason, George, 109
Maury, Matthew Fontaine, 108–9
Maury, Mrs. Dabney, 108, 109; receipts
of, 122, 165–66
Maximilian (Emperor of Mexico): offer
to Lee of Mexican army command,
40
Mayonnaise, 224–25
Mealtimes, 90, 198
Measurements: determination of, 5;
equivalents for, 106, 107; standard-
ized, 211, 225
Meats: purchases of, 84; roasting of,
102, 206; as main course, 205–6;
larding of, 207
Memories of General Robert E. Lee
(Bond), 117
Mérangue Pudding, 170
Meredith (cook), 74
Meringues, 156; bacteria in, 100
"The Mess" (Richmond, Va.), 38, *40,* 82
Mexican War, 28
Microwaving, 160, 162, 163–64
Miley, Michael, 48, 80
Milk: home-skimmed, 99; whole, 101;
new, 113, 173; household uses of, 247
Miller, Michael, 20
Mills, grain, 127; water-powered, 95
Mock turtle, 213
Molasses, 98, 147, 152; sauce, 189, 196
Morgan, Charly, 34
Morris, Robert, 23
Mount Vernon, slaves of, 15

General Index

directions for killing and cleaning of, 69

Powell, Marietta Turner, 12

Presbyterians: of Lexington, Va., 77

Preston: Margaret Junkin, 43, 80; Colonel J. T. L., 80, 138

Puddings, 160–64; boiled, 5, 160; Mérangue, 170

Pudding Sauce, 162

Punches, 228–29

Quilt, Mrs. Lee's, 191, *192*, 230

Randolph, David, 65

Randolph, Mary, 64, 65–66. See also *The Virginia House-wife*

Randolph, T. J., 77

Ravensworth (home of the Fitzhughs and Lees), 61

Rawlings, Marjorie Kinnan, 108

Reading Club (Lexington), 49, 52

Receipts: testing of, 4–5, 9; repeated in notebook, 64; modifications to, 69–70, 100–101, 131–33; flavorings in, 93, 100; interpretation of, 94, 103–7, 131–33; calories in, 100–101; time required for, 101; size of, 104; oral, 126–27; heirloom, 130, 133

Recipes. *See* Receipts

Red pepper, 100, 221

Refrigerator, 65–66

Richmond, Va.: Lee family in, 35–36, 38–39; fall of, 39, *41*

Ripley, Eliza Chinn, 97

Roasting, 206–7; in fireplaces, 102

Robert E. Lee cake, 98, 130–34

Robert E. Lee Memorial Church (Lexington), 9, 191, *192*, 231

Robins, Sally Nelson, 36, 74

Rolls, "pulled" and Parker House, 113–14

Romancoke (home of Robert E. Lee Jr.), 42, *208*; Mary Custis Lee's visits to, *52–53*; Robert Jr. at, 60, 208; Custis Lee at, 61; baking at, 96; shad fishing at, 207

Roosevelt, Theodore: visit to Romancoke, 52–53

Root, Waverly, 111

Rose water, 9, 93, 159; sources for, 100; in icing, 145

Rum, 100

"Running" (social custom), 45, 47

Rutledge, Sarah, 127, 216

Sago, 169

St. Louis, Mo.: Lee family in, 30

Salads, 222–23; dressing for, 223–26

Saleratus, 93, 94

Sally (Lee servant), 27, 82

Sally Lunn, 114, 116, 146

Salmonella, 99–100, 225–26

Salt: household uses of, 6, 243–44; medicinal uses of, 242–43

Sam (Lee servant), 47

Sassafras leaves, 216

Schall, Terry and Melissa, 234

Schmit, Patricia Brady, 65, 66

Sea turtle soup, 213

Seeds, colonists' importation of, 217

Self-help organizations, women's, 86

Shad bakes, 208, *209*

Shampoo, 240; ammonia in, 245

Sherbets, 184

Sheridan, Philip, 44

Sherry, 100, 214

General Index

General Index

General Index

INDEX OF RECEIPTS

Page numbers shown in italics refer to illustrations.

Index of Receipts